John Reed for *The Masses*

John Reed for
The Masses

Edited by
James C. Wilson

McFarland & Company, Inc., Publishers
Jefferson, North Carolina, and London

Frontispiece: John Reed's passport photograph (no date),
by permission of the Houghton Library,
Harvard University.

Library of Congress Cataloguing-in-Publication Data

Reed, John, 1887–1920.
John Reed for *The Masses*.

Articles appearing in The Masses, 1913–1917.
I. Wilson, James C. 1948–   . II. Masses. III. Title.
PS3535.E2786A6   1987   082   85-43598

ISBN 0-89950-214-8 (acid-free natural paper)

Printed in the United States of America.

McFarland   Box 611   Jefferson NC 28640

To Almon G. Wilson
(1920–1983)

To Alan and Linda
Roger and Jane
Sam, Amy, and Kathy

And most of all to
Cindy

Table of Contents

Table of Contents

I can almost see troubadour Reed
seeking his lofty princess all over the
world, in Mexico, Serbia, Russia . . .
the lady of his sonnets, the Revolution.

— Waldo Frank

Introduction

JOHN REED'S reputation as a writer rests primarily on *Insurgent Mexico* and especially *Ten Days That Shook the World,* his brilliant account of the Russian Revolution of November 1917. In contrast, the early work that Reed published in *The Masses* between January 1913 and November 1917 has been all but forgotten by scholars and historians alike, and until now has not been reprinted (with one or two notable exceptions such as "War in Paterson"). This is unfortunate because, even though he was never paid for it, Reed saved much of his best work for *The Masses,* which was and has remained historically one of America's most famous radical magazines. Altogether Reed contributed fifty-one pieces to *The Masses,* including thirty major signed articles and one play.[1]

During the five years that he wrote for *The Masses,* Reed became a prominent and highly paid journalist. Lincoln Steffens praised his work, and Walter Lippmann (whom Reed had met at Harvard) called him a "genius." "It's kind of embarrassing to tell a fellow ... he's a genius," Lippmann wrote when Reed's articles on the Mexican Revolution began appearing in *The Masses* in April 1914. "If all history had been reported as you are doing this, Lord—I say that with Jack Reed reporting begins."[2] Later the two friends quarreled as Reed's politics became more radical and Lippmann's more conservative, but Lippmann could still write that "whenever his sympathies marched with the facts, Reed was superb."[3] Even before he went to Mexico, Reed was recognized as a hero of the American Left, the "wonder boy of Greenwich Village," as Van Wyck Brooks wrote. But his dispatches from Mexico, published in *Metropolitan Magazine* and in Joseph Pulitzer's *New York World,* as well as in *The Masses,* consolidated Reed's reputation as a writer. The editors of *Metropolitan Magazine* advertised the installments as "word pictures of war by an American Kipling.... What Stephen Crane and Richard Harding Davis did for the Spanish War in 1898, John Reed, 26 years old, has done for Mexico."[4]

Reed's association with *The Masses* began one morning in early December 1912. Reed had just read the December issue of *The Masses,* the

1

first number published under the editorship of Max Eastman. Reed was so impressed that he telephoned Eastman at home and insisted on bringing over an article that he wanted to submit. Initially Eastman was not favorably impressed by Reed, whom he found "distracted" and a bit frantic. In his autobiography, *Enjoyment of Living,* Eastman remembered that Reed "stood up or moved about the room all through his visit and kept looking in every direction except that in which he was addressing his words."[5]

Eastman was rather irritated by the young intruder, and he decided, after Reed had gone, to bring out one more issue and then resign as editor. But Reed's manuscript changed his mind. Reading "Where the Heart Is," which told the story of a New York prostitute who takes a trip abroad but enjoys returning to Manhattan even more than the trip, Eastman realized that *The Masses* could provide an outlet for "creative literature stifled by commercial journalism," for "here was a man writing about a significant phase of American life that no other magazine would dare to mention unless sanctimoniously."[6] Eastman accepted the article for publication and asked Reed to become a regular contributor to *The Masses.*

That Reed sought out *The Masses* was no accident; he shared many of the artistic and political assumptions advocated by America's leading journal of art, satire, and socialism. Born in Portland, Oregon, on October 22, 1887, Reed was influenced at an early age by his father's progressive politics. C. J. Reed had been active in Portland politics, an ardent supporter of Teddy Roosevelt, and a friend of Lincoln Steffens. From 1906 to 1910 Reed attended Harvard, where he contributed to and served on the editorial boards of the *Lampoon* and the *Harvard Monthly,* and where he associated with the Socialist Club (founded by Walter Lippmann and several other students). After graduation Reed traveled to Europe, but by March 1911 he had settled in Manhattan, determined to make a career as a writer. To help him get started, Lincoln Steffens found Reed a half-time position working for *American Magazine,* which had been taken over six years earlier by the journalists who had won fame as muckrakers for *McClure's Magazine* — Ida Tarbell, Ray Stannard Baker, John Siddall, and Steffens himself. Though Reed's work for the magazine was often rudimentary, he had at least broken into the highly competitive world of New York journalism, and soon he was selling short stories to *Century* and the *Smart Set* and articles to *Collier's* and *Trend.* By 1912 Reed's circle of friends had widened to include a number of influential writers and editors. His career was solidly launched.

When Reed walked into Max Eastman's apartment in December 1912, *The Masses* was in a state of transition. The magazine had been founded as a socialist organ by Piet Vlag, the manager of a restaurant in the Rand School of Social Science, a meeting place for bohemians and radicals, artists and intellectuals. Vlag managed to enlist the financial support of Rufus W. Weeks, Vice President of the New York Life Insurance Company, who agreed to subsidize the printing and engraving costs of the magazine. The assistance from Weeks proved essential, since *The Masses* was never self-supporting and could never afford to pay its contributors. To edit the magazine Vlag found Thomas Seltzer, a translator of Russian and German books who was familiar with European socialism. However, Seltzer's interest soon faded, and he resigned at the end of four months. His replacement, Horatio Winslow, a friend of Vlag's and a former contributor, lasted only nine months, after which Vlag himself assumed the editorship. Shortly thereafter a major crisis occurred when Weeks announced that he was withdrawing his subsidy, and Vlag desperately tried to save *The Masses* by merging it with *Progressive Women,* a feminist and socialist magazine based in Chicago and edited by Josephine Conger-Kaneko. But the writers and artists of *The Masses* rebelled; they insisted that the magazine remain in New York and were determined somehow to raise the necessary funds. In response Vlag terminated his association with *The Masses.*

A way out of this impasse was suggested by cartoonist Art Young, who had recently met Max Eastman at a dinner given in honor of Jack London. Young nominated Eastman as the next editor and, when his colleagues agreed, sent Eastman a brief note: "You are elected editor of *The Masses,* no pay."[7] Eastman was initially skeptical of the offer, but nevertheless agreed to edit the December 1912 issue. Finally he was persuaded to become the fourth — and last — editor of *The Masses.*

Eastman quickly transformed *The Masses,* changing to a more attractive format and encouraging a livelier writing style. With a genius for raising money from wealthy New York socialites and socialist sympathizers, he managed to keep the magazine solvent until the government declared it "unmailable" at the end of 1917. Among the writers who contributed to *The Masses* were Carl Sandburg, Sherwood Anderson, Vachel Lindsay, Randolph Bourne, Amy Lowell, Witter Bynner, Djuna Barnes, Mabel Dodge, William Carlos Williams, and Upton Sinclair.

Of course, *The Masses* was primarily a political magazine. It supported labor, socialism, pacifism, and a host of other causes considered radical by mainstream America, including birth control. Critical of organized religion, as well as the rising militarism and patriotism of World War I America, it was often censored and banned, from New York to proverbial Boston. Eastman and his staff repeatedly found themselves in legal difficulties; for example, Eastman and Art Young were indicted and charged with criminal libel for claiming that the Associated Press distorted news of labor strikes (the charge was later dismissed). After Congress passed the Espionage Act on June 15, 1917, several of *The*

Masses editors and contributors were indicted for violating that act, specifically for conspiring to promote insubordination and mutiny in the military and naval forces of the United States. Two trials and two hung juries later, the defendants were acquitted, but the damage had already been done — *The Masses* had been effectively suppressed by the government.[8]

Such was the magazine that John Reed joined in December 1912. His first contribution, "Where the Heart Is," was published in the January 1913 issue and was followed by fifty more over a period of five years — an average of nearly one per month. Reed's work for *The Masses* can be classified according to five rather distinct periods and subject matters: Greenwich Village (1913), The Mexican Revolution (1914), World War I: Europe at the Abyss (1915–1917), World War I: Opposition and Repression at Home (1917), and The Russian Revolution (1917). Each period of Reed's writing career for *The Masses* demonstrates both a thematic consistency and his overall development as a writer.

I. Greenwich Village

IN THE SUMMER of 1911, John Reed moved into an apartment at 42 Washington Square South. His arrival in the Village, the new Mecca for artists and intellectuals fleeing bourgeois American society, very nearly coincides with the beginning of what critics have referred to as the "little renaissance" in American literature (1910-1919). From all parts of the nation, bohemians and radicals flocked to the Village, where new magazines, art exhibitions, manifestos and political movements seemed to occur daily. Contributing to the frenzy of creative activity were the famous "evenings" at Mabel Dodge's salon at 23 Fifth Avenue — events that attracted such artists as Andrew Dasburg, writers as Max Eastman, intellectuals as Walter Lippmann, wobblies as Big Bill Haywood, anarchists as Emma Goldman, and other celebrities of various artistic and political persuasions. Indeed, anyone of any renown would appear sooner or later at Dodge's salon, and the conversation would range over all the topics then current in the Village: birth control and free love, the I.W.W. and industrial unionism, Freudianism and cubism, anarchism and socialism.

By 1913 Reed was at the center of Village life. He had been elected to the editorial board of *The Masses,* and he had become not only one of Mabel Dodge's most celebrated and frequent guests, but her lover as well. His long poem, *The Day in Bohemia,* had been published in February and been warmly received by friends and acquaintances in the Village, many of whom had been included in his day in the life of "bohemia." More importantly, Reed organized the Paterson Pageant at Madison Square Garden in order to publicize the grievances of the striking mill workers of Paterson, New Jersey. The reaction to the pageant and to the other major event of the year, the Armory Show of February 17 (introducing modern art to America), demonstrated the prevailing if incorrect assumption that revolution in art and society were one and the same. In 1913 Reed shared the belief that economic exploitation was connected to puritanism in art and society, and that the liberation of the working class would accompany the downfall of traditional bourgeois morality.

Reed's writing for *The Masses* during this period reflects his immersion in the life of the city. The work has a Dickensian quality, both in terms of its energy and the richness and eccentricity of its cityscapes and city-dwellers. Significantly, these eight articles (and one play) do not dwell on the artists and intellectuals among whom Reed moved personally. Instead, he writes about the dark underside of Manhattan life, the prostitutes and the working class women who are forever tempted to turn to prostitution, the alcoholics and vagrants who stalk the streets by day and litter the park benches by night—all of them outcasts, victims of a capitalist society that grants and denies privileges and social standing on the basis of wealth.

Fact and fiction blend in these early articles. Though Reed based them on his experience in the Village, he took occasional liberties with the facts in order to enhance the artistic integrity of his creations. Rather obviously, Reed shaped dialogue, reorganized chronologies, and constructed plots that read more like fiction than nonfiction, especially in "Where the Heart Is" and "Seeing Is Believing," where long narratives are made more interesting by novelistic techniques such as extended dialogue, scene-by-scene construction, plot reversal, and other methods of creating and maintaining suspense.

Another important point needs to be made here. Aside from the straight "analysis" columns that Reed wrote from time to time, his journalism is always personal—a blend of journalism and fiction. Like the New Journalists of a half century later, Reed did his best work when he wrote himself into a story, when he became actor as well as narrator. In most of his articles on the Village, and in his reports on the Mexican Revolution, Reed participates in the events being described. In fact, in articles such as "A Taste of Justice" and "Another Case of Ingratitude" Reed actually *provokes* the event, thus creating the story. One example of Reed's ability to provoke a story—"the central passion of his life . . . an inordinate desire to be arrested," as Walter Lippmann humorously wrote in 1914—can be seen in articles as different as "A Taste of Justice" and "War in Paterson." His arrests, and the purpose they serve, bear unmistakable resemblance to Norman Mailer's altercations in *The Armies of the Night* and *Miami and the Siege of Chicago,* just to mention two prominent examples of New Journalism.

Multiple turn-of-the-century literary influences also can be found in these early articles. Some of Reed's precise and vivid descriptions of New York nightlife are reminiscent of the work of Stephen Crane. For example, "The Capitalist" begins, "You know how Washington Square looks in a wet mist on November nights—that gray, luminous pastel atmosphere, softening incredibly the hard outlines of bare trees and iron railings, obliterating the sharp edges of shadows and casting a silver halo about each high electric globe. All the straight concrete walks are black onyx, jeweled in every little unevenness with pools of steely rain-water." Or the description of the dancer in "Broadway Night"—one of Reed's many portraits of the liberated women of the time—who "blew into the soft warmth, gold mirrors, hysterical ragtime of the place like a lawless wind."

Moreover, as Daniel Aaron points out in *Writers on the Left,* "a touch of O. Henry" can be detected in many of these tales, with their unexpected and ironic plot twists at the end.[9] "The Capitalist" (April 1916) tells the story of William Booth Wrenn, who finds himself accused of being a "capitalist" by an old alcoholic woman because she sees him fondling what turns out to be his last 65 cents. The old woman manages to talk him out of the money, and when a policeman comes along and orders him out of the park we learn that William Booth Wrenn is, like the old woman, a transient. What is interesting about this tale, and what distinguishes it from the simple machination of an O. Henry story, is Wrenn's psychological need to patronize the old woman and lecture her on the "extravagance" of working people. That need—or compulsion— leads him to give away his last few pennies in order to appear "successful." "A Taste of Justice," "Another Case of Ingratitude," and "Seeing Is Believing" all have similar plot reversals.

These early works reflect the dominant literary movement of their time: naturalism. They are naturalistic in technique—that is, they employ realistic descriptions and dialogue; they are naturalistic in subject matter—that is, they focus on society's victims, from vagrants to working class women, many of whom recall Stephen Crane's Maggie or Theodore Dreiser's Sister Carrie; and they are naturalistic in their sociological interest in the downtrodden and the class system that isolates and victimizes them. On close examination, Reed's Village proves as mechanistic as Crane's Bowery or Dreiser's Chicago, and his characters equally determined by social and physical forces beyond their control.

"Another Case of Ingratitude" (July 1913) provides a good example of Reed's naturalism. In it Reed tells the story of his dubious attempt to help a cold, hungry vagrant whom he discovers walking along Fifth Avenue late one night. Reed takes the man to a restaurant, buys him a meal, and gives him money for a bed that night. Early in the article Reed describes the vagrant as "bestial" and "canine," but once fed and warmed, the man—who turns out to be an unemployed bricklayer—goes through a remarkable metamorphosis that Reed finds gratifying. "Where there had been a beast, a spirit lived; he was a man!" Reed writes. Docile and obedient before, the bricklayer becomes assertive and refuses to talk, refuses to indulge in a hard-luck story for Reed's further gratification. "You t'ought that just because you give me a hand-out, I'd do a sob-story all over you. Wot right have you got to ask me all them questions? I know you fellers. Just because you got money you t'ink you can buy me with a meal," the bricklayer says. When Reed protests that he had acted unselfishly and stood to gain nothing from his beneficence, the bricklayer retorts: "You get all you want.... Come on now, don't it make you feel good all over to save a poor starvin' bum's life? God! you're pure and holy for a week." The tale, whose title is ironic, contains an explicit material-istic view of life—all that separates man from beast, Reed from the brick-layer, are food and shelter, both distributed unequally according to class.

In "Broadway Night" (May 1916) Reed's naturalism is equally apparent. The article describes the circuslike consumerism of Broadway after hours, including an old man hawking copies of the "Matrimonial News." The old man speaks mechanically, without any expression whatever: "Buy the 'Matrimonial News.' If you want a wife or husband. Five cents a copy. Only a nickel for wedded bliss." Reed asks, humor-ously of course, for a "guarantee," and then:

> He turned upon me his calm and kindly gaze and took my nickel before answering.
> "Turn to page two," he bade me. "See that photo? Read. 'Beautiful young woman, twenty-eight years old, in perfect health, heiress to five hundred thousand dollars, desires correspondence with bachelor; object, matrimony, if right party can be found.' Thousands have achieved felicity through these pages. If you are disappointed, we give your nickel back."
> "Have you tried it yourself?"
> "No," he answered thoughtfully. "I will be frank with you. I have not."

The humor comes to an abrupt end when the old man tells Reed his life story. Now fifty-two years old, he has survived his wife and two chil-dren, his wife having died in childbirth and his children of typhoid and scarlet fever respectively. He tells of their deaths, and of the financial losses that have forced him to become a paperboy for the "Matrimonial News," and he does so without a trace of emotion or sentiment. In fact, the total absence of passion in the old man's tale makes it extremely powerful, implying as it does both a deterministic universe and a preda-tory society. "I'm past blaming anyone for anything," the old man says and then begins to chant, this time with unmistakable irony, "Only a nickel for wedded bliss. Half a dime for a lifetime of felicity."

Next Reed encounters three prostitutes. The first remarks that "business" isn't what it used to be on Broadway. "Pikers and charity boys nowadays—that's what it is," she says. The article ends when Reed goes off with one of the prostitutes, followed by a final throwaway comment about life's "mad inconsequentiality, its magnificent lack of purpose." However, Reed's last line does not disguise his portrait of America as an open market where everything—including sex and happiness, love and marriage, life and death—has become a commodity to be bought and sold.

Even "Moondown," the one play that Reed published in *The Masses* (September 1913), has a hard naturalistic core under its apparent romantic or sentimental facade. The simple one-act play, first performed by the Washington Square Players in 1916, consists of a dramatic dialogue between two working class women: Mame, a cynical and sharp-witted prostitute; and Sylvia, her young, romantic, and unemployed roommate. As the play opens, Sylvia has returned to their apartment after meeting a young man—a "poet" from the Village—who has promised to come that night before the moon goes down and take her away. Mame remains skeptical and advises Sylvia to be more realistic, namely to give up her pipe dreams and become a prostitute. Much of the ensuing dialogue is extremely humorous, as cynical experience comments on romantic youth:

> S. Then he put his hand on my shoulder so gentle that I didn't take it away, and he pointed up through the trees to the moon. He says, "The moon is a woman—a little woman with silver feet—"
> M. *(Sarcastically.)* O my God.
> S. O it was beautiful! Then he told me the most wonderful things about the stars. He told me about a wind that comes up from the sea at night and sweeps away the dust from the stars—
> M. Say, what's a matter with you? That'd give me the willies.
> S. He asked me what I did and I told him. He's a poet—
> M. A poet! They get a dollar seventy-five a week. Go on.
> S. Then he says, "You're the most beautiful of all the beautiful things of the night—"
> M. Help! Help!

Needless to say, Sylvia's poet does not come for her. The moon symbolically goes down, and Sylvia's hopes and dreams expire with it, as does her belief that a "girl can keep straight" and still survive in New York. "Moondown" rather obviously makes fun of romantics and dreamers, but more importantly it presents a disturbing portrait of working class women caught in the grips of a sexist, exploitative society. It is not simply that Sylvia (and by implication all other young working class women) faces an either-or choice between innocence and experience, naiveté and prostitution. The problem is much more complex than this, for as Mame explains: "Well, suppose he *does* come. You'll live in a dirty little flat up on 126th Street, scrubbing and cooking and washing. You'll have some puking little kids, and they'll grow up into panhandlers and street-corner bums." And the poets, the "charity boys" as Mame calls them, do nothing to help the situation. "You're nothing to him but material for a poem. He'll sell you to a magazine for seven dollars," Mame tells Sylvia. Ironically, the poet in the play goes by the name of

Jack—as if Reed were indicting himself for using, and exploiting, people like Sylvia in his own writing.

Inherent in the naturalism of Reed's early work is a Marxist class analysis that hints at his later embracing of socialism and the Russian Revolution. For example, in "A Taste of Justice" (April 1913), Reed illustrates the inequities of the American legal system—the fact that justice, too, is dispensed according to class. The article describes the late-night activities at the "corner," a notorious rendezvous for prostitutes and their customers. The prostitutes are worn and cheaply dressed, and their dispositions reflect whether or not they have eaten that night. By way of contrast, Reed describes the policeman who patrols the beat as having "the satisfied arrogance of an absolute monarch." The policeman appears from time to time, for it is his job to keep both the women and the men moving so that the business conducted at the "corner" will not *appear* to be prostitution. "Society allows vice no rest. If women stood still, what would become of us all?" Reed asks sarcastically.

On the night described here, Reed makes the mistake of standing still, and for his breach of decorum he finds himself arrested and taken before the Night Court. Waiting his turn, Reed notices the prisoner ahead of him, a "slight girlish figure that did not reach the shoulder of the policeman who held her arm. Her skirt was wrinkled and indiscriminate, and hung too closely about her hips; her shoes were cracked and too large; an enormous limp willow plume topped her off." For "soliciting," as she is politely charged with, the judge sentences the young woman to ten days in jail. However, when Reed comes before the bench, the judge recognizes him as a friend and dismisses the case with a few words of warning to the bewildered policeman. "A Taste of Justice" illustrates that, unlike Reed and his colleagues, the lower classes "stood before judges unprotected by reputations or powerful friends," as Robert A. Rosenstone writes in his biography of Reed.[10]

So, too, do the striking mill workers described in "War in Paterson" (June 1913) stand unprotected before the law. In this article, the most famous of his Village material, Reed makes it clear that his sympathies lie with the workers. Reed became interested in the Paterson strike after hearing about it from I.W.W. leader Big Bill Haywood, whom he had met at one of Mabel Dodge's "evenings." Haywood invited Reed to come to Paterson and see the situation firsthand, and Reed accepted the invitation. Shortly after his arrival in Paterson, Reed was arrested for standing on a porch and refusing a policeman's order to move on, and the result was four days in jail. Out of this experience came "War in Paterson," which has been praised as a milestone of radical journalism in America.

From the very first paragraph Reed strikes a note of anger—an anger that sets the piece apart from his other writing during this period. "There's war in Paterson," he writes. "But it's a curious kind of war. All the violence is the work of one side—the Mill Owners. Their servants, the Police, club unresisting men and women and ride down law-abiding crowds on horse-back. Their paid mercenaries, the armed Detectives, shoot and kill innocent people. Their newspapers, the Paterson *Press* and the Paterson *Call,* publish incendiary and crime-inciting appeals to mob-violence against the strike leaders. Their tool, Recorder Carroll, deals out heavy sentences to peaceful pickets that the police-net gather up. They control absolutely the Police, the Press, the Courts." *They control absolutely*—that was what influenced Reed the most about what he found in Paterson. He saw the strike in terms of a class struggle between the mill owners and the workers, and more generally between those who owned the means of production and those who actually produced. On the side of the mill owners were aligned all the powers of the state: the police, the courts, the government itself. The press and even the clergy sided with the owners, as they traditionally had done in labor disputes. On the other side were 25,000 mill workers determined to win an eight-hour day, their cause inspired by leaders like Elizabeth Gurley Flynn and Big Bill Haywood. Though Flynn and Haywood inspired enormous confidence (and sacrifice) on the part of the workers, they were no match for the combined power of the mill owners and the state. Reed understood this implicitly. It was the intractable nature of American capitalism, as much as his own developing political consciousness, that led him to the radical politics of his later years.

In Paterson Reed committed himself to the cause of the striking workers. His article was not meant to be objective in any modern sense of the word; it was meant to offset the news blackout executed by the conventional press and to publicize the grievances of the workers. He had begun to realize that writing could be a political tool when he wrote, "*They* were the strike—not Bill Haywood, not Gurley Flynn, not any other individual. And if they should lose all their leaders other leaders would arise from the ranks, even as *they* rose, and the strike would go on! Think of it! Twelve years they have been losing strikes—twelve solid years of disappointments and incalculable suffering. They must not lose again! They can not lose!"

Reed continued his efforts to help the strikers by organizing the Paterson Pageant. Reed wrote the script and directed the staging, and in order to make the dramatization as immediate and powerful as possible he utilized hundreds of the striking workers in the cast. Unfortunately, the project was not a financial success; in fact it was counterproductive in that it diverted attention and resources from the strike itself. Eventually the strike failed, but by that time Reed, exhausted from his efforts, had gone on an extended vacation in Europe with Mabel Dodge. At the end of

the third week in June, only two weeks after the pageant, Reed and Dodge
boarded the steamship *Amerika* for France. Reed's Greenwich Village
period had come to an end.

Where the Heart Is

JANUARY 1913

"TWO!" barks the giant in the aged dinnercoat, over your shoulders to the ticket window. He is grizzled and massive, with a face like a Roman senator; his hand closes belligerently over your tickets as he surveys you keenly to see if you're drunk. Then you push open the always-swinging, colored-glass doors, — and the lights and movement, the blatant dance-rhythms of the Haymarket hits you like a physical blow.

Bill the Bouncer, also informally dressed, leans against the brass rail that fences you off from the main floor, and grins at you like a prize fighter, if you know him; otherwise he takes your measure with a surly nod. Bill stands for the proprieties. Woe to the youthful collegian who bursts into song. Woe to the elderly rake whose manners are anything but conventional. Woe also to the dancer who frolics, or to the girl who dares to outrage decency by smoking cigarettes in public. The Haymarket is the most respectable place in town.

It is all too brightly lighted, reflections from mirrors along the wall; there is utterly unlimited crash from the brazen orchestra, metallic tones of conversations curiously off-key from the ordinary human voice, female figures in impossible caricatures of the extreme mode, men and women waltzing slowly on the crowded floor in every unnatural posture ... round wooden tables everywhere, and the continuous stream of derby hats moving in and out of the place ... As you stop and try to reduce these varied impressions to some sort of order, you will suddenly feel Eyes upon you, — notice that all over the hall, from tables right near the rail, from seats in the gallery, girls are watching steadily each new arrival: girls pretty, hideous, badly-dressed, gorgeously-dressed, but never poorly-dressed. They do not invite, those eyes, nor challenge, nor say evil things. They simply watch you steadily, hungrily, as a cat watches a mouse; and the effect is all the more startling because the atmosphere of the place speaks stridently of careless freedom, — fun. There is no freedom in most of the eyes. But as soon as you begin to sentimentalize about it, some devil-may-care, reckless-mouthed woman will sweep across the floor,

15

insolently swinging her hips, or some little fiend with a demon blazing out
of her eyes will laugh out, — and you'll realize life-force indomitable.

So I came into the Haymarket after many months. It was the same
that it always had been. "Bill," I said, "it's good to see you." And it was.
"Is Martha here?"

Bill nodded, — he is a man of few words, — and jerked a thumb
toward the rear room. But even there, — a place of yellow play-bills and
photographs of dead-and-gone burlesquers, and the inevitable tables,
each with its girl, — I failed to find her. Of course she might have changed
... I didn't go upstairs to the balcony, however, but went through one of
the doors that give onto the dancing-floor, and sat at a table. A waiter
came and I whispered to him. And a few moments later I saw a woman
rise and move across the hall toward me. It was Martha, slender, dressed
in a dark blue suit, with a dull yellow plume on her hat.

"Hello, dear," she said. That's the manner of greeting in the Haymarket. Then she gave me a small hand, smiled decorously, and sat down.
I noticed that her hair was still soft and dark, her face oval and delicately
colored, her eyes honest and unclouded.

We ordered beer.

"Why," she said suddenly, "I've seen you before — I know you . . ."

"Not for four years," I told her. "I knew you . . ."

"Oh, yes," her eyes lit up like an old friend's. "In the old days. May
Munroe was here then, and Laura Chevalier and Babe Taylor. . . . All the
old crowd. I guess I'm the only one left of the bunch."

"Tell me what you've been doing with yourself all this time."

She shrugged her shoulders. "Nothing much. Same . . . O, now wait!
I guess I've been to Europe since I saw you last . . ."

"Europe!" I said wondering. She nodded, smiling, because she
understood my circumscribed ideas. Why shouldn't she go to Europe? I
couldn't have answered, but it came to me as a shock that a Haymarket
girl should have rational human desires. The dancing had ended for the
moment, and on the tawdry stage two men and a woman sang a song
about the "Turkey Trot," yelling at the top of their voices and beating a
drum and cymbals. The obvious, sordid chords of the music jarred fearfully with the mangled voices. The noise was deafening. The singers'
bodies moved from the hips in nervous, grotesque rhythm. There was
something brutally abandoned and not unpleasant about it, — something
that chimed in with hard-eyed artificial women and mirrors. They sang
"It's a bear! It's a bear! It's a bear!" . . .

"That certainly is a good song," murmured Martha, dreamy-eyed.
"Well, about Europe — 'D you ever go there?"

"Yes" I smiled, because I thought I knew what she would tell me of.
"I suppose you saw the Moulin Rouge and the Abbaye . . . and the Globe
in London . . ."

Martha leaned over, intensely interested. "You remember Windsor Castle? And Shakespeare's House at Stratford-on-Avon? An' the Tooleries Gardens in Paris? ..."

"Do you?" I asked, rather sarcastically.

"You bet I do. And I won't get over it soon. You ought to 'a seen me trotting around with my little Baydicker—that's the guide-book, you know—you'd 'a laughed.... No, I didn't go around to many of the sporting places ... Seen enough of that."

"Martha," said I, curious, "what made you go abroad?"

She frowned, thinking. "Well, I wanted to learn something. You know—or p'raps you don't—how you've got a lot of things in your head that you got out of school books when you was a kid; like the Tower of London, and the King of Germany. Well, p'raps you believe they're *there* all right, but you have to *see* 'em to know for sure. I guess that's why so many rich bugs go there ..."

That wasn't why I had gone.

She went on, "I always saved my money. Don't know why, unless it was to buy a little cottage out in the country some day, and keep chickens ... I'm going to do that when I get all in. Last spring I got to thinking ... An' so one day I drew my money out of the bank an' bought a new suit an' took the *Lusitania*—first cabin. No, you can bet I'm no cheap skate...."

"But surely you didn't have enough money—"

Martha laughed. "Only enough to get to London and stay there like a real tourist for a week. No, of course I didn't know what would happen to me after that. Just trusted to Gawd.... On the boat I met a nice couple of old boneheads ... Preacher and his wife, I guess ... and went down to London with 'em. Say, they were certainly good people ... thought I was a college girl. I always dress quiet, you know. I like it. A girl who dresses loud is in bad from the start. We put up at the Waldorf in London—quiet an' respectable as hell—an' the three of us certainly did that town. London Bridge, Westminster, Crystal Palace; we laid out the burg in sections ... Some tourists, believe me! ... O, sure I went to the Alhambra and the Globe, when the Chaperonies were pounding their ear ... but English girls are awful snobs."

She mused reminiscently. "I'll never forget that week ... Good time? Say, I acted like a kid about two years old ... Seein' all the things you'd heard about ..."

Beyond us the band crashed into the braying "Gabby Glide." Bill the Bouncer leaned threateningly on the rail. I had once seen him drag a girl, who had stabbed a waiter with her hat-pin, across the floor and throw her bodily through the outer door. Right near us was a table at which sat a young, fresh girl timidly talking to a derby hat,—flushing and paling ... A new one ... The astounding grandeur of Martha's adventure struck me. Alone in London,—with money enough for a week,—*learning*.

"But what did you do — "

"I'm coming to that. One morning I woke up with seven shillings . . . An' that day a young American spoke to me when I was killing time in Hyde Park . . . I was getting sort of doped with London . . . So that night I kissed the old lady good night, went up to my room an' packed . . . We lit out at two in the morning . . . I've often wondered what she thought in the morning. So that's how I went to Paris. We certainly lived like two kings in the Grand Hotel. Say, did you ever sit on the sidewalk in front of one of those cafés about five o'clock, an' see the birds parade up and down? That for mine. You feel kind o' lazy . . . I bet I wore out three pair of shoes tramping through the Louvre, with a catalogue in my mitt. The fellow? O, he was all right. Bought me some nifty dresses — you've seen the black silk. Nothing flashy, though. Lots of American girls in Paris. . . . But it's not worth it, the life they have to live. I was in Paris two weeks, an' one day my friend beat it . . . I would 'a been on the street in another day if I hadn't run into the Englishman . . .

"He was about sixty years old an' had a stomach . . . His face looked like a walrus . . . But he certainly treated me white. We travelled up through Belgium and Holland; Brussels, the Hague, Ostend, then took a trip through Germany . . . I never missed a trick. Up at Waterloo I spent a whole day reading a history book. It seemed to me as if I was itching until I'd seen everything in the Baydicker — that's the guide-book. But after a while, when we got around to Strassburg, he began to get sore. 'Look here,' he says to me, 'chop the Cook's Towrist stuff, can't you?' So I simply cleared out one night and left him. I wasn't going to be anybody's dog, you bet. Just had money enough to get to Paris. . . . But I knew nothing could happen to me, with *my* luck. The very first night I went up on Monmarter an' ran into an American girl who let me sleep in her bed . . . All us American girls stick by each other, you know. Sure, I went into all of the joints. Monmarter is just like New York, except it isn't so *honest,* if you know what I mean. Well, say, of all the luck! The very next night in Pigalle's I danced with a man that looked like a half-coon, only he wasn't. Nobody is, over there. An' he gave me his card an' asked me to go to Brazil with him. The card had a little crown on it, an' 'Count Manuel da Portales.'

"I'd heard a lot about bogus counts and so forth putting one over on poor girls; so when I saw Mabel I showed her the card, and asked her if he was a fake. 'Go to it,' she says. 'Take a chance.' But even then I wasn't satisfied. I didn't get any sleep that night, you can believe *me.* Suppose he'd take me somewhere where I didn't know the language and nobody talked American, and leave me? But I trusted to Gawd and went. . . . It took us two weeks on the boat, — then Rio. I guess Rio's the most beautiful place in the world. I had a great time there. Every Friday night we'd go to the High-Life Club for dinner, an' Saturday after supper the whole town would put on costumes — fancy dress, you know, — an' ride up an' down in hacks . . . I stayed there four months.

"No, I wasn't very happy . . . You see, you get tired of wondering at things . . . Everything in foreign countries is so much finer than you ever thought it would be . . . Then you get excited when you see something that you've always heard about. It kind of gets on your nerves, and takes it out of you. I was going to stick around Rio for a year . . . but I didn't.

"I can remember just as plain . . . One night we came in rather tight after a big party at the club. Manuel dropped off to sleep, but I couldn't seem to close my eyes. It was in April, and the window was open, an' I could see straight up about a million miles in the sky. The stars are bearcats down there. I don't know what got me to thinkin' about Broadway, but right off the bar I seemed to see it, wrigglin' and squirmin' with electric signs; with all the low-brows coming out of the moving pitcher shows, an' the shirt fronts comin' out of the theayter — the hurdy-gurdies playing that 'Irish Rag' — at that moment I was sick as a hound for old, honest, low-brow New York. You see, in foreign countries everybody is a high-brow. Then I saw the old Market, with all the girls sitting around, an' the beer-stains on the table, an' the Sweet Caporal cigarette smoke. About then all the college boys would be down for their vacation, an' of course come roaming into the Market. I began to feel real tender about Big Bill there. So I gave Manuel a poke. 'What's a matter,' says he. 'I've got a cable-gram from New York,' says I. 'It's very important. Coney Island will open on the first. When's the next boat?' I says. 'I'm going to breeze.'

"I will say the Count was O. K. He bought me a first cabin on the steamer, an' told me to come again next year. That trip up the coast was the best time I ever had in my life. I lived strictly alone, an' didn't allow a man on board to get fresh. Just read books; didn't talk to anyone; did a lot of thinking. I never was so happy.

"Well, from the first minute we began to see the old town loom up the bay I was so excited I couldn't talk. It hurt. I didn't wait for anything. When we landed I checked my stuff in the Erie Station and took a ferry. Then I took the El to Twenty-eighth Street and blew in here. The old gink outside says, 'Here, you can't walk in here without a ticket' — An' then he looked closer. 'Well, what the — ! Say, where have you been?' I couldn't answer him. I stood there like a deaf and dumb and blind bonehead — I was absolutely off my nut. An' then he held the door open an' I sort of *fell* inside. There was Bill, and behind him all the crowd was dancing, and the little tables * * * Home! That's what it was! Home! I heard the Big Fellow rumbling 'Martha! By God! The Female White Hope has come back!' O Gawd! You couldn't understand . . . I just fell on a table and bawled . . . Come on, let's dance."

A Taste of Justice

APRIL 1913

As soon as the dark sets in, young girls begin to pass that Corner — squat-figured, hard-faced "cheap" girls, like dusty little birds wrapped too tightly in their feathers. They come up Irving Place from Fourteenth Street, turn back toward Union Square on Sixteenth, stroll down Fifteenth (passing the Corner again) to Third Avenue, and so around — always drawn back to the Corner. By some mysterious magnetism, the Corner of Fifteenth Street and Irving Place fascinates them. Perhaps that particular spot means Adventure, or Fortune, or even Love. How did it come to have such significance? The men know that this is so; at night each shadow in the vicinity contains its derby hat, and a few bold spirits even stand in the full glare of the arc-light. Brushing against them, luring with their swaying hips, whispering from immovable lips the shocking little intimacies that Business has borrowed from Love, the girls pass.

The place has its inevitable Cop. He follows the same general beat as the girls do, but at a slower, more majestic pace. It is his job to pretend that no such thing exists. This he does by keeping the girls perpetually walking — to create the illusion that they're going somewhere. Society allows vice no rest. If women stood still, what would become of us all? When the Cop appears on the Corner, the women who are lingering there scatter like a shoal of fish; and until he moves on, they wait in the dark side streets. Suppose he caught one? "The Island for her's! That's the place they cut off girls' hair!" But the policeman is a good sport. He employs no treachery, *simply stands a moment,* proudly twirling his club, and then moves down toward Fourteenth Street. It gives him an immense satisfaction to see the girls scatter.

His broad back retreats in the gloom, and the girls return — crossing and recrossing, passing and repassing with tireless feet.

Standing on that Corner, watching the little comedy, my ears were full of low whisperings and the soft scuff of their feet. They cursed at me, or guyed me, according to whether or not they had had any dinner. And then came the Cop.

His ponderous shoulders came rolling out of the gloom of Fifteenth Street, with the satisfied arrogance of an absolute monarch. Soundlessly the girls vanished, and the Corner contained but three living things: the hissing arc-light, the Cop, and myself.

He stood for a moment, juggling his club, and peering sullenly around. He seemed discontented about something; perhaps his conscience was troubling him. Then his eye fell on me, and he frowned.

"Move on!" he ordered, with an imperial jerk of the head.

"Why?" I asked.

"Never mind why. Because I say so. Come on now." He moved slowly in my direction.

"I'm doing nothing," said I. "I know of no law that prevents a citizen from standing on the corner, so long as he doesn't hold up traffic."

"Chop it!" rumbled the Cop, waving his club suggestively at me, "Now git along, or I'll fan ye!"

I perceived a middle-aged man hurrying along with a bundle under his arm.

"Hold on," I said; and then to the stranger, "I beg your pardon, but would you mind witnessing this business?"

"Sure," he remarked cheerfully. "What's the row?"

"I was standing inoffensively on this corner, when this officer ordered me to move on. I don't see why I should move on. He says he'll beat me with his club if I don't. Now, I want you to witness that I am making no resistance. If I've been doing anything wrong, I demand that I be arrested and taken to the Night Court." The Cop removed his helmet and scratched his head dubiously.

"That sounds reasonable." The stranger grinned. "Want my name?"

But the Cop saw the grin. "Come on then," he growled, taking me roughly by the arm. The stranger bade us good-night and departed, still grinning. The Cop and I went up Fifteenth Street, neither of us saying anything. I could see that he was troubled and considered letting me go. But he gritted his teeth and stubbornly proceeded.

We entered the dingy respectability of the Night Court, passed through a side corridor, and came to the door that gives onto the railed space where criminals stand before the Bench. The door was open, and I could see beyond the bar a thin scattering of people on the benches — sightseers, the morbidly curious, an old Jewess with a brown wig, waiting, waiting, with her eyes fixed upon the door through which prisoners appear. There was the usual few lights high in the lofty ceiling, the ugly, dark panelling of imitation mahogany, that is meant to impress, and only succeeds in casting a gloom. It seems that Justice must always shun the light.

There was another prisoner before me, a slight, girlish figure that did not reach the shoulder of the policeman who held her arm. Her skirt was wrinkled and indiscriminate, and hung too closely about her hips; her shoes were cracked and too large; an enormous limp willow plume topped her off. The Judge lifted a black-robed arm — I could not hear what he said.

"Soliciting," said the hoarse voice of the policeman, "Sixth Av'nue near Twenty-third — "

"Ten days on the Island — next case!"

The girl threw back her head and laughed insolently.

"You — " she shrilled, and laughed again. But the Cop thrust her violently before him, and they passed out at the other door.

And I went forward with her laughter still sounding in my ears.

The Judge was writing something on a piece of paper. Without looking up he snapped:

"What's the charge, officer?"

"Resisting an officer," said the Cop surlily. "I told him to move on an' he says he wouldn't — "

"Hum," murmured the Judge abstractedly, still writing. "Wouldn't, eh? Well, what have you got to say for yourself?"

I did not answer.

"Won't talk, eh? Well, I guess you get — "

Then he looked up, nodded, and smiled.

"Hello, Reed!" he said. He venomously regarded the Cop. "Next time you pull a friend of mine — " suggestively, he left the threat unfinished. Then to me, "Want to sit up on the Bench for a while?"

A Matter of Principle

MAY 1913

MRS. SHUGRUE deigns to launder my weekly shirt and two collars. Withal, she is my philosopher and friend. Every Saturday night she gets drunk; each Sunday morning she repents. And from continual change and upheaval, her soul is always healthy and youthful. Mrs. Shugrue's personality is plump, unkempt and aggressive. When she brings back my shirt and collars of a Friday morning, she will stop and converse with me, as I lie in bed.

One Friday she toiled up my stairs, and instead of the usual "God walk with you," she greeted me with a short "Mornin'," and wiped her face sullenly with her petticoat. I said nothing. So she finally began.

"Glory be to God," said Mrs. Shugrue sadly. "The ongratitude of childer is a turrible thing, surely. It's about my son Tim, he that do be working for a fine piece of money on the New York Cintral. Ye know I told ye how he was going to marry himself with a daughter of a dirty Protestant out of Ulster?" I nodded.

"It's a good straight Catholic I am, Mister, communicating and confessing and putting my nickel in the poor-box every couple of Sundays. Poison it is for a religious woman like meself to see her son, — and him with a fine job on the New York Cintral, — caught by the tricks of a Belfast wench, at all. But I'm broadminded too, I am, and that's no lie; so when himself come to me, telling me about it, I says to him, 'Young blood will be young blood, and I can see it's love entirely in yer bright blue eye, Timmy, me boy; an' a hard thing it is on mothers, the way their sons do be leaving them for other women, and they after suffering the pains of birth and all. It's a bitter thing, surely, for any mother to see her son marrying himself out of the Church into some small religion where the Virgin herself ain't treated with the respect owing to a lady. But I'll not complain, God help me,' I says. 'Though never yet did I know of a wife being suitable to her mother-in-law,' I says. 'I'm not acquent with yer Mary.' 'Ye will be,' says Timmy. 'We'll be after making a social visit with her next Sunday afternoon.'

23

"It come a Sunday after mass. Mind ye now, I'm that broadminded the like of me ye'll not find in the whole town at all. Straight from mass I come, with the blessed words of the priest a-ringing in my ear, and me wearing my decent black suit with the jet buttons, the way there's no woman on the street can make a better showing on Saints Days and the Sabbath; and we went walking down to make a visit with his Mary.

"'What does she work at?' says I. 'She's a stenographer,' says Timmy. 'God help her,' says I, and right away we come to one of them iligant marble hallways that looks like the Pope's tomb. 'It is here she lives with her mother,' says Timmy, and a young felly with a uniform of a Gineral in the Queen's Guards runs us up in the elevator. 'I do be thinking,' says I, 'ye're making a mistake and courting Mr. Vanderbilt's daughter,' I says. 'I'm not crazy about this place,' I says, going up in the elevator.

"Well, Mister, it would disgust you entirely to look at the parlor where we went in; what with a bit of a chair here, and a slim tiny table ye couldn't eat off of, and not even a coal stove for to warm your legs at, and never a sight or light of a sofy where a tired woman could rest her back-side. And when Mary come in, God love me, I says to myself, 'A fine wife she won't be making my boy Tim,' I says. 'The way she teeters around on them little heels, with her thin stockings and her high hair up for all the world like a fleecy cloud. Them soft hands,' I says, 'will do small washing and cooking I'll be bound.' 'Pleased to meet you, ma'am,' she says, holding out two fingers up high in the air, like she was afraid I'd dirty 'em on me own. 'Come down,' says I, 'I got a twinge under me right arm,' I says. 'Anyhow no one 'll see ye. We're alone,' says I. I could see she didn't like that a little bit. A spiteful look she give me, God help her.

"'Will ye have something, Mrs. Shugrue? she asks of me a-setting there on the naked edge of the little chair.

"'I will then, and thank you kindly,' I says. 'So much praying at mass dries up me throat the way that a drop of beer —'

"'Beer!' says me fine lady, hoisting up her eyebrows like they was going to crawl into her hair. 'There is no beer in this place,' she says. 'Perhaps you'll take a cup of tea?' she says.

" 'And perhaps I won't,' says I. 'Faith, it's a simple matter to send down a can to the corner,' I says.

"'No intoxicating liquors shall ever come into my house,' says she, short and haughty. 'Will you take a drop of tea, once and for all?'

"'I will not,' says I. 'Be damned to your tea. And what's further,' says I, 'you'll marry no son of mine, you Protestant whelp, and keep the beer away from him, the time he comes home of the evening, all weary with working himself to the bone for you,' says I, 'and your childer, if you have any, which I doubt,' says I. And with that I up and took my leave.

"I'm a broad-minded woman, I'm telling you, Mister. Bitter it was for me to see my Timmy marrying himself to a Protestant woman out of Ulster, surely, but God help me, I would not destroy the holy passion of love for what the priests do be saying. But I call it wicked, bad hospitality and no kindness at all to refuse an old woman her drop of beer that the good Lord put on the world, the way people can be praising Him with the drinking of it."

Mrs. Shugrue fetched a gusty sigh. "The ongratitude of childer is a turrible thing, surely," she said. "He will be marrying the girl this day."

War in Paterson

JUNE 1913

THERE'S war in Paterson. But it's a curious kind of war. All the violence is the work of one side—the Mill Owners. Their servants, the Police, club unresisting men and women and ride down law-abiding crowds on horse-back. Their paid mercenaries, the armed Detectives, shoot and kill innocent people. Their newspapers, the Paterson *Press* and the Paterson *Call,* publish incendiary and crime-inciting appeals to mob-violence against the strike leaders. Their tool, Recorder Carroll, deals out heavy sentences to peaceful pickets that the police-net gathers up. They control absolutely the Police, the Press, the Courts.

Opposing them are about twenty-five thousand striking silk-workers, of whom perhaps ten thousand are active, and their weapon is the picket-line. Let me tell you what I saw in Paterson and then you will say which side of this struggle is "anarchistic" and "contrary to American ideals."

At six o'clock in the morning a light rain was falling. Slate-grey and cold, the streets of Paterson were deserted. But soon came the Cops— twenty of them—strolling along with their night-sticks under their arms. We went ahead of them toward the mill district. Now we began to see workmen going in the same direction, coat collars turned up, hands in their pockets. We came into a long street, one side of which was lined with silk mills, the other side with the wooden tenement houses. In every door-way, at every window of the houses clustered foreign-faced men and women, laughing and chatting as if after breakfast on a holiday. There seemed no sense of expectancy, no strain or feeling of fear. The side-walks were almost empty, only over in front of the mills a few couples— there couldn't have been more than fifty—marched slowly up and down, dripping with the rain. Some were men, with here and there a man and woman together, or two young boys. As the warmer light of full day came the people drifted out of their houses and began to pace back and forth, gathering in little knots on the corners. They were quick with gesticulating hands, and low-voiced conversation. They looked often toward the corners of side streets.

Suddenly appeared a policeman, swinging his club. "Ah-h-h!" said the crowd softly.

Six men had taken shelter from the rain under the canopy of a saloon. "Come on! Get out of that!" yelled the policeman, advancing. The men quietly obeyed. "Get off this street! Go on home, now! Don't be standing here!" They gave way before him in silence, drifting back again when he turned away. Other policemen materialized, hustling, cursing, brutal, ineffectual. No one answered back. Nervous, bleary-eyed, unshaven, these officers were worn out with nine weeks incessant strike duty.

On the mill side of the street the picket-line had grown to about four hundred. Several policemen shouldered roughly among them, looking for trouble. A workman appeared, with a tin pail, escorted by two detectives. "Boo! Boo!" shouted a few scattered voices. Two Italian boys leaned against the mill fence and shouted a merry Irish threat, "Scab! Come outa here I knocka you' head off!" A policeman grabbed the boys roughly by the shoulder. "Get to hell out of here!" he cried, jerking and pushing them violently to the corner, where he kicked them. Not a voice, not a movement from the crowd.

A little further along the street we saw a young woman with an umbrella, who had been picketing, suddenly confronted by a big policeman.

"What the hell are *you* doing here?" he roared. "God damn you, you go home!" and he jammed his club against her mouth. "I *no* go home!" she shrilled passionately, with blazing eyes. "You bigga stiff!"

Silently, steadfastly, solidly the picket-line grew. In groups or in couples the strikers patrolled the sidewalk. There was no more laughing. They looked on with eyes full of hate. These were fiery-blooded Italians, and the police were the same brutal thugs that had beaten them and insulted them for nine weeks. I wondered how long they could stand it.

It began to rain heavily. I asked a man's permission to stand on the porch of his house. There was a policeman standing in front of it. His name, I afterwards discovered, was McCormack. I had to walk around him to mount the steps.

Suddenly he turned round, and shot at the owner: "Do all them fellows live in that house?" The man indicated the three other strikers and himself, and shook his head at me.

"Then you get to hell off of there!" said the cop, pointing his club at me.

"I have the permission of this gentleman to stand here," I said. "He owns this house."

"Never mind! Do what I tell you! Come off of there, and come off damn quick!"

"I'll do nothing of the sort."

With that he leaped up the steps, seized my arm, and violently jerked me to the sidewalk. Another cop took my arm and they gave me a shove.

"Now you get to hell off this street!" said Officer McCormack.

"I won't get off this street or any other street. If I'm breaking any law, you arrest me!"

Officer McCormack, who is doubtless a good, stupid Irishman in time of peace, is almost helpless in a situation that requires thinking. He was dreadfully troubled by my request. He didn't want to arrest me, and said so with a great deal of profanity.

"I've *got* your number," said I sweetly. "Now will you tell me your name?"

"Yes," he bellowed, "an' I got *your* number! I'll arrest you." He took me by the arm and marched me up the street.

He was sorry he *had* arrested me. There was no charge he could lodge against me. I hadn't been doing anything. He felt he must make me say something that could be construed as a violation of the Law. To which end he God damned me harshly, loading me with abuse and obscenity, and threatened me with his night-stick, saying, "You big —— —— lug, I'd like to beat the hell out of you with this club."

I returned airy persiflage to his threats.

Other officers came to the rescue, two of them, and supplied fresh epithets. I soon found them repeating themselves, however, and told them so. "I had to come all the way to Paterson to put one over on a cop!" I said. Eureka! They had at last found a crime! When I was arraigned in the Recorder's Court that remark of mine was the charge against me!

Ushered into the patrol-wagon, I was driven with much clanging of gongs along the picket-line. Our passage was greeted with "Boos" and ironical cheers, and enthusiastic waving. At Headquarters I was interrogated and lodged in the lockup. My cell was about four feet wide by seven feet long, at least a foot higher than a standing man's head, and it contained an iron bunk hung from the side-wall with chains, and an open toilet of disgusting dirtiness in the corner. A crowd of pickets had been jammed into the same lockup only three days before, *eight or nine in a cell,* and kept there without food or water for *twenty-two hours!* Among them a young girl of seventeen, who had led a procession right up to the Police Sergeant's nose and defied him to arrest them. In spite of the horrible discomfort, fatigue and thirst, these prisoners had *never let up cheering and singing* for a day and a night!

In about an hour the outside door clanged open, and in came about forty pickets in charge of the police, joking and laughing among themselves. They were hustled into the cells, two in each. Then pandemonium broke loose! With one accord the heavy iron beds were lifted and slammed thunderingly against the metal walls. It was like a cannon battery in action.

"Hooray for I. W. W.!" screamed a voice. And unanimously answered all the voices as one, "Hooray!"

"Hooray for Chief Bums!" (Chief of Police Bimson).

"Boo-o-o-o!" roared forty pairs of lungs—a great boom of echoing sound that had more of hate in it than anything I ever heard.

"To hell wit' Mayor McBride!"

"Boo-o-o-o!" It was an awful voice in that reverberant iron room, full of menace.

"Hooray for Haywood! One bigga da Union! Hooray for da Strike! To hell wit' da police! Boo-o-o-o! Boo-o-o-o! Hooray! Killa da A. F. of L.! A. F. of *Hell,* you mean! Boo-o-o-o!"

"Musica! Musica!" cried the Italians, like children. Whereupon one voice went "Plunk-plunk! Plunk-plunk!" like a guitar, and another, a rich tenor, burst into the first verse of the Italian-English song, written and composed by one of the strikers to be sung at the strike meetings. He came to the chorus:

"Do you lika Miss Flynn?"

(Chorus) "Yes! Yes! Yes! Yes!"

"Do you like Carlo Tresca?"

(Chorus) "Yes! Yes! Yes! Yes!"

"Do you like Major McBride?"

(Chorus) "No! *No!* NO! *NO!!!*"

"Hooray for I. W. W.!"

"Hooray! Hooray!! Hooray!!!"

"Bis! Bis!" shouted everybody, clapping hands, banging the beds up and down. An officer came in and attempted to quell the noise. He was met with "Boos" and jeers. Some one called for water. The policeman filled a tin cup and brought it to the cell door. A hand reached out swiftly and slapped it out of his fingers on the floor. "Scab! Thug!" they yelled. The policeman retreated. The noise continued.

The time approached for the opening of the Recorder's Court, but word had evidently been brought that there was no more room in the County Jail, for suddenly the police appeared and began to open the cell doors. And so the strikers passed out, cheering wildly. I could hear them outside, marching back to the picket-line with the mob who had waited for them at the jail gates.

And then I was taken before the Court of Recorder Carroll. Mr. Carroll has the intelligent, cruel, merciless face of the ordinary police court magistrate. But he is worse than most police court magistrates. He sentences beggars to *six months' imprisonment* in the County Jail without a chance to answer back. He also sends little children there, where they mingle with dope-fiends, and tramps, and men with running sores upon their bodies — to the County Jail, where the air is foul and insufficient to breathe, and the food is full of dead vermin, and grown men become insane.

Mr. Carroll read the charge against me. I was permitted to tell my story. Officer McCormack recited a clever *mélange* of lies that I am sure he himself could never have concocted. "John Reed," said the Recorder. "Twenty days." That was all.

And so it was that I went up to the County Jail. In the outer office I was questioned again, searched for concealed weapons, and my money and valuables taken away. Then the great barred door swung open and I went down some steps into a vast room lined with three tiers of cells. About eighty prisoners strolled around, talked, smoked, and ate the food sent in to them by those outside. Of this eighty almost half were strikers. They were in their street clothes, held in prison under $500 bail to await the action of the Grand Jury. Surrounded by a dense crowd of short, dark-faced men, Big Bill Haywood towered in the center of the room. His big hand made simple gestures as he explained something to them. His massive, rugged face, seamed and scarred like a mountain, and as calm, radiated strength. These slight, foreign-faced strikers, one of many desperate little armies in the vanguard of the battle-line of Labor, quickened and strengthened by Bill Haywood's face and voice, looked up at him lovingly, eloquently. Faces deadened and dulled with grinding routine in the sunless mills glowed with hope and understanding. Faces scarred and bruised from policemen's clubs grinned eagerly at the thought of going back on the picket-line. And there were other faces, too — lined and sunken with the slow starvation of a nine weeks' poverty — shadowed with the sight of so much suffering, or the hopeless brutality of the police — and there were those who had seen Modestino Valentino shot to death by a private detective. But not one showed discouragement; not one a sign of faltering or of fear. As one little Italian said to me, with blazing eyes: "We all one bigga da Union. I. W. W. — dat word is pierced de heart of de people!"

"Yes! Yes! Dass righ'! I. W. W.! One bigga da Union" — they murmured with soft, eager voices, crowding around.

I shook hands with Haywood, who introduced me to Pat Quinlan, the thin-faced, fiery Irishman now under indictment for speeches inciting to riot.

"Boys," said Haywood, indicating me, "this man wants to *know* things. You tell him everything" —

They crowded around me, shaking my hand, smiling, welcoming me. "Too bad you get in jail," they said, sympathetically. "We tell you ever't'ing. You ask. We tell you. Yes. Yes. You good feller."

And they did. Most of them were still weak and exhausted from their terrible night before in the lockup. Some had been lined up against a wall, as they marched to and fro in front of the mills, and herded to jail on the charge of "unlawful assemblage!" Others had been clubbed into the patrol-wagon on the charge of "rioting," as they stood at the track, on their way home from picketing, waiting for a train to pass! They were being held for the Grand Jury that indicted Haywood and Gurley Flynn. *Four of these jurymen were silk manufacturers, another the head of the local Edison company — which Haywood tried to organize for a strike — and not one a workingman!*

"We not take bail," said another, shaking his head. "We stay here. Fill up de damn jail. Pretty soon no more room. Pretty soon can't arrest no more picket!"

It was visitors' day. I went to the door to speak with a friend. Outside the reception room was full of women and children, carrying packages, and pasteboard boxes, and pails full of dainties and little comforts lovingly prepared, which meant hungry and ragged wives and babies, so that the men might be comfortable in jail. The place was full of the sound of moaning; tears ran down their work-roughened faces; the children looked up at their fathers' unshaven faces through the bars and tried to reach them with their hands.

"What nationalities are all the people?" I asked. There were Dutchmen, Italians, Belgians, Jews, Slovaks, Germans, Poles —

"What nationalities stick together on the picket-line?"

A young Jew, pallid and sick-looking from insufficient food, spoke up proudly. "T'ree great nations stick togedder like dis." He made a fist. "T'ree great nations — *I*talians, Hebrews an' Germans" —

"But how about the Americans?"

They all shrugged their shoulders and grinned with humorous scorn. "English peoples not go on picket-line," said one, softly. "'Mericans no lika fight!" An Italian boy thought my feelings might be hurt, and broke in quickly: "Not all lika dat. Beeg Beell, *he* 'Merican. *You* 'Merican. Quinl', Miss Flynn, 'Merican. *Good! Good!* 'Merican workman, he lika talk too much."

This sad fact appears to be true. It was the English-speaking group that held back during the Lawrence strike. It is the English-speaking contingent that remains passive at Paterson, while the "wops," the "kikes," the "hunkies" — the "degraded and ignorant races from Southern Europe" — go out and get clubbed on the picket-line and gaily take their medicine in Paterson jail.

But just as they were telling me these things the keeper ordered me to the "convicted room," where I was pushed into a bath and compelled to put on regulation prison clothes. I shan't attempt to describe the horrors I saw in that room. Suffice it to say that forty-odd men lounged about a long corridor lined on one side with cells; that the only ventilation and light came from one small skylight up a funnel-shaped air-shaft; that one man had syphilitic sores on his legs and was treated by the prison doctor with sugar-pills for "nervousness"; that a seventeen-year-old boy *who had never been sentenced* had remained in that corridor without ever seeing the sun for over *nine months;* that a cocaine-fiend was getting his "dope" regularly from the inside, and that the background of this and much more was the monotonous and terrible shouting of a man who had lost his mind in that hell-hole and who walked among us.

There were about fourteen strikers in the "convicted" room — Italians, Lithuanians, Poles, Jews, one Frenchman and one "free-born" Englishman! That Englishman was a peach. He was the only Anglo-Saxon striker in prison except the leaders — and perhaps the only one who *had been* there for picketing. He had been sentenced for insulting a mill-owner who came out of his mill and ordered him off the sidewalk. "Wait till I get out!" he said to me. "If them damned English-speaking workers don't go on picket *I'll* put the curse o' Cromwell on 'em!"

Then there was a Pole — an aristocratic, sensitive chap, a member of the local Strike Committee, a born fighter. He was reading Bob Ingersoll's lectures, translating them to the others. Patting the book, he said with a slow smile: "Now I don' care if I stay in here one year." One thing I noticed was the utter and reasonable irreligion of the strikers — the Italians, the Frenchman — the strong Catholic races, in short — and the Jews, too.

"Priests, it is a profesh'. De priest, he gotta work same as any workin' man. If we ain't gotta no damn Church we been strikin' t'ree hund'd years ago. Priest, he iss all a time keeping working-man down!"

And then, with laughter, they told me how the combined clergy of the city of Paterson had attempted from their pulpits to persuade them back to work — back to wage-slavery and the tender mercies of the mill-owners on grounds of religion! They told me of that disgraceful and ridiculous conference between the Clergy and the Strike Committee, with the Clergy in the part of Judas. It was hard to believe that until I saw in the paper the sermon delivered the previous day at the Presbyterian Church by the Reverend William A. Littell. He had the impudence to flay the strike leaders and advise workmen to be respectful and obedient to their employers — to tell them that the saloons were the cause of their unhappiness — to proclaim the horrible depravity of Sabbath-breaking workmen, and more rot of the same sort. And this while living men were fighting for their very existence and singing gloriously of the Brotherhood of Man!

The lone Frenchman was a lineal descendant of the Republican doctrinaires of the French Revolution. He had been a Democrat for thirteen years, then suddenly had become converted to Socialism. Blazing with excitement, he went round bubbling with arguments. He had the same blind faith in Institutions that characterized his ancestors, the same intense fanaticism, the same willingness to die for an idea. Most of the strikers were Socialists already — but the Frenchman was bound to convert every man in that prison. All day long his voice could be heard, words rushing forth in a torrent, tones rising to a shout, until the Keeper would shut him up with a curse. When the fat Deputy-Sheriff from the outer office came into the room the Frenchman made a dive for him, too.

"You're not producing anything," he'd say, eyes snapping, finger waving violently up and down, long nose and dark, excited face within an inch of the Deputy's. "You're an unproductive worker — under Socialism we'll get what we're working for — we'll get all we make. Capital's not necessary. Of course it ain't! Look at the Post Office — is there any private capital in that? Look at the Panama Canal. That's Socialism. The American Revolution was a smuggler's war. Do you know what is the Economic Determinism?" This getting swifter and swifter, louder and louder, more and more fragmentary, while a close little circle of strikers massed round the Deputy, watching his face like hounds on a trail, waiting till he opened his mouth to riddle his bewildered arguments with a dozen swift retorts. Trained debaters, all these, in their Locals. For a few minutes the Deputy would try to answer them, and then, driven into a corner, he'd suddenly sweep his arm furiously around, and bellow:

"Shut up, you damned dagos, or I'll clap you in the dungeon!" And the discussion would be closed.

Then there was the strike-breaker. He was a fat man, with sunken, flabby cheeks, jailed by some mistake of the Recorder. So completely did the strikers ostracize him — rising and moving away when he sat by them, refusing to speak to him, absolutely ignoring his presence — that he was in a pitiable condition of loneliness.

"I've learned my lesson," he moaned. "I ain't never goin' to scab on working-men no more!"

One young Italian came up to me with a newspaper and pointed to three items in turn. One was "American Federation of Labor hopes to break the Strike next week"; another, "Victor Berger says 'I am a member of the A. F. of L., and I have no love for the I. W. W. in Paterson' "; and the third, "Newark Socialists refuse to help the Paterson Strikers."

"I no un'erstand," he told me, looking up at me appealingly. "You tell me. I Socialis' — I belong Union — I strike wit' I. W. W. Socialis', he say, 'Worke'men of de worl'. Unite!' A.F. of L., he say, 'All workmen join togedder.' Bot' dese or-gan-i-zashe, he say, 'I am for de Working Class.' Awri', I say, I am de Working Class. I unite, I strike. Den he say, 'No! You *cannot* strike!' Why dat? I no un'erstan'. You explain me."

But I could not explain. All I could say was that a good share of the Socialist Party and the American Federation of Labor have forgotten all about the Class Struggle, and seem to be playing a little game with Capitalistic rules, called "Button, button, who's got the Vote!"

When it came time for me to go out I said good-bye to all those gentle, alert, brave men, ennobled by something greater than themselves. *They* were the strike—not Bill Haywood, not Gurley Flynn, not any other individual. And if they should lose all their leaders other leaders would arise from the ranks, even as *they* rose, and the strike would go on! Think of it! Twelve years they have been losing strikes—twelve solid years of disappointments and incalculable suffering. They must not lose again! They can not lose!

And as I passed out through the front room they crowded around me again, patting my sleeve and my hand, friendly, warm-hearted, trusting, eloquent. Haywood and Quinlan had gone out on bail.

"You go out," they said softly. "Thass nice. Glad you go out. Pretty soon we go out. Then we go back on picket-line"—

Another Case of Ingratitude

JULY 1913

WALKING late down Fifth avenue, I saw him ahead of me, on the dim stretch of sidewalk between two arc-lights. It was biting cold. Head sunk between hunched-up shoulders, hands in his pockets, he shuffled along, never lifting his feet from the ground. Even as I watched him, he turned, as if in a daze, and leaned against the wall of a building, where it made an angle out of the wind. At first I thought it was shelter he sought, but as I drew nearer I discerned the unnatural stiffness of his legs, the way his cheek leaned against the cold stone, and the glimmer of light that played on his sunken, closed eyes. The man was asleep! Asleep — the bitter wind searching his flimsy clothes and the holes in his shapeless shoes; upright against the hard wall, with his legs stiff as those of an epileptic. There was something bestial in such gluttony of sleep.

I went to him and shook him by the shoulder. He slowly opened an eye, cringing as though he were often disturbed by rougher hands than mine, and gazed at me with hardly a trace of intelligence.

"What's the matter — sick?" I asked.

Faintly and dully he mumbled something, and at the same time stepped out as if to move away. I asked him what he had said, bending close to hear.

"No sleep for two nights," came the thick voice. "Nothing to eat for three days." He stood there obediently under the touch of my hand, swaying a little, staring vacantly at me with eyes that hung listlessly between opening and shutting.

"Well, come on," I said, "we'll go get something to eat and then I'll fix you up with a bed." Docilely he followed me, stumbling along like a man in a dream, falling forward and then balancing himself with a step. From time to time his thick lips gave utterance to husky, irrelevant words and phrases. "Got to sleep walking around," he said again and again, and "They kept moving me on."

I took his arm and guided him into the white door of an all-night lunch-room. I sat him at a table, where he dropped into a dead sleep. I set

35

before him roast beef and mashed potatoes, and two ham sandwiches, and a cup of coffee, and bread and butter, and a big piece of pie. And then I woke him up. He looked up at me with a dawning meaning in his expression. The look of humble gratitude, love, devotion was almost canine in its intensity. I felt a warm thrill of Christian brotherhood all through my veins. I sat back and watched him eat.

At first he went at it awkwardly, as if he had lost the habit. Mechanically he employed little tricks of table manners — perhaps his mother had taught them to him. He fumblingly changed knife and fork from right hand to left, and then put down his knife and took a dainty piece of bread in his left hand; removed the spoon from his coffee cup before he drank, and spread butter thinly and painstakingly on his bread. His motions were so somnambulistic that I had a strange feeling of looking on a previous incarnation of the man. These little niceties, so instinctive to him, and yet so unaccustomed — what did they mean? It flashed through me that they must belong to his youth.

As the dinner progressed, a marvelous change took place. The warmth and nourishment, heating and feeding his thin blood, flooded the nerve centers of that starving body; a quick flush mounted to his cheeks, every part of him started widely awake, his eyes flashed. The little niceties of manner dropped away as if they had never been. He slopped his bread roughly in the gravy, and thrust great knife-loads of food into his mouth. The coffee vanished in great gulps. He became an individual instead of a descendant; where there had been a beast, a spirit lived; he was a man!

The metamorphosis was so exciting, so gratifying, that I could hardly wait to learn more about him. I held in, however, until he should have finished his dinner.

As the last of the pie disappeared, I drew forth a box of cigarettes and placed them before him. He took one, nodded and accepted one of my matches. "T'anks," he said.

"How much will it cost you for a bed — a quarter?" I asked.

"Yeh," he said. "T'anks."

He sat looking rather nervously at the table, — inhaling great clouds of smoke. It was my opportunity.

"What's the matter — no work?"

He looked me in the eye, for the first time since dinner had begun, in a surprised manner. "Sure," said he briefly. I noticed, with somewhat of a shock, that his eyes were gray, whereas I had thought them brown.

"What's your job?"

He didn't answer for a moment. "Bricklayer," he grunted. What was the matter with the man?

"Where do you come from?"

Meme jeu. "Albany."

"Been here long?"

"Say," said my guest, leaning over. "Wot do you t'ink I am, a phony-graft?"

For a moment I was speechless with surprise. "Why, I was only asking to make conversation," I said feebly.

"Naw you wasn't. You t'ought that just because you give me a hand-out, I'd do a sob-story all over you. Wot right have you got to ask me all them questions? I know you fellers. Just because you got money, you t'ink you can buy me with a meal...."

"Nonsense," I cried, "I do this perfectly unselfishly. What do you think I get out of feeding you?"

He lit another of my cigarettes. "You get all you want," he smiled. "Come on now, don't it make you feel good all over to save a poor starvin' bum's life? God! You're pure and holy for a week!"

"Well, you're a strange specimen," said I angrily. "I don't believe you've got a bit of gratitude in you!"

"Gratitude Hell!" said he easily. "Wot for? I'm thankin' my luck, — not you, — see? It might as well 'a' been me as any other bum. But if you hadn't struck me, you'd 'a' hunted up another down-and-outer. You see," he leaned across the table, explaining. "You just had to save somebody to-night. I understand. I got a appetite like that too. Only mine's women."

Whereupon I left that ungrateful bricklayer and went to wake up Drusilla, who alone understands me.

Moondown

SEPTEMBER 1913

Place—New York. Time—the Present.
Persons:
MAME: *about twenty-three. Light.*
SYLVIA: *about eighteen. Dark.*
Scene—*A typical room in a typical New York boarding-house on West Thirteenth street. A double bed, bureau, and two chairs. A door left, and at the rear two windows opening on the street, of which one is ajar.*

(It is a warm spring night. MAME *sits in her nightgown, with a violently colored kimono over it, reading what is called a "French Novel," and smoking a cigarette. Her legs are crossed, and her feet bare, except for enormously high-heeled slippers. She wears an exaggerated quantity of puffs. Enter* SYLVIA. *She is dressed in a modest, careless, shabby blue suit and shirt-waist. She takes off her coat and hat, and hangs them behind the door. Her hair is dark, and piled on her head in careless waves. She sinks into a chair, with an air at once weary and quietly joyous. Mame watches her stealthily over the edge of her novel.)*

M.   You're lookin' happy. Got a job?

S.   Nope.

M.   How much money you got left?

S.   *(Producing them with a little laugh.)* One dime and a subway ticket.

M.   I s'pose you'll want me to lend you another half-dollar in the morning.

S.   *(Independently.)* No thanks.

M.   Well, I won't, so there. You was a fool to quit your job just because the manager wanted to give you a good time.

S.   But I hate him. He's like a big white worm. Ugh!

M.   But he spends money like a cop off duty. I'd like to see him offer to buy *me* a hat. Would I fall? *(She shakes her head in mock disgust.)*

S.   I been beating the pavement all day long. Guess I must 'a been in fifty places. There don't seem to be no work for a girl.

38

M.   Sure there is. For a good-looker like you. Ain't I got a steady job? And didn't I offer you one at my place? I got a pull with the floor-walker.

S.   No, thanks, Mame. I believe that a girl can keep straight and get work if she wants to.

M.   Well, she can't. I know this town. *You're* a kid yet, and you've always been a little fool. I used to be that kind too; but I got over it. Take it from me, it's money that counts in little old Manhattan.

S.   No, it ain't. *It can't be. (With confidence.)* I *know* it ain't.

M.   Why, what's happened to you?

S.   I'm quit with this rotten game. I got somebody to look after me.

M.   *(Surprised.)* Who?

S.   Jack.

M.   Jack who?

S.   I don't know his last name; I —

M.   Steer clear of the boys that don't give their names.

S.   I only met him to-night —

M.   *(Interested.)* What is it, a flat for yours in the White-hot District, or an apartment at the Plaza?

S.   He said we'd live up in Harlem until he —

M.   Has he got money?

S.   No.

M.   My God, you ain't goin' to get married and have a lot of dirty kids?

S.   *(Spiritedly.)* They won't be dirty.

M.   Say, you got me going. Only met him to-night, — don't know his last name, — going to get married —

S.   *(Swiftly.)* I was comin' across Madison Square about six o'clock, and along came a fellow behind me. He says "Good evening." I thought he was one of them loafers that hunt girls down the side streets at night. They often speak to me. So I says "Go along and mind your business." Then he says, very soft, "I'm not trying to insult you. Won't you speak to me?"

M.   I know the kind. They ain't got a nickel in their pants.

S.   I turned around and looked at him. I guess he had the finest face I ever saw. Slim, and dark and young; and big eyes like a coal fire. He says very quiet, "Sit down." ... We sat on a bench in the park.

M.   Never sit down with a man. When a girl sits down with a man she's giving him something for nothing.

S.   Then he put his hand on my shoulder so gentle that I didn't take it away, and he pointed up through the trees to the moon. He says, "The moon is a woman — a little woman with silver feet — "

M.   *(Sarcastically.)* O my God.

S.   O it was beautiful! The he told me the most wonderful things about the stars. He told me about a wind that comes up from the sea at night and sweeps away the dust from the stars —

M. Say, what's a matter with you? That'd give me the willies.

S. He asked me what I did and I told him. He's a poet —

M. A poet! They get a dollar seventy-five a week. Go on.

S. Then he says, "You're the most beautiful of all the beautiful things of the night — "

M. Help! Help!

S. And he says, "Will you marry me?" . . . And then he took me in his arms so tenderly, so tenderly, like my mother . . . a long time ago —

M. And then you got a taxicab and went up to the Fifth Avenue Baptist Church, and they all lived happily ever after —

S. No, I says, "I got to go to one place more," I says. And he says, "I'll try and wait for you here, dear. What's your name, dear?" "Sylvia," says I. "What's yours, dear?" "Jack," he says. Then he kissed me, and it seemed like all the stars was falling through the trees —

M. Go on, go on.

S. He says, "If you're not back in half an hour, I'll go home and fix up for you. Where do you live?" I told him. "All right, dear," he says. "I'll call for you to-night when the moon goes down. You be sitting at the window — "

M. So you finished your business quick, and when you come back, he was gone.

S. Why, yes. How did you know?

M. I know them fellows that talk about moons and make dates. Take it from me, your Pegasus is a kidder. He'll never come.

S. *(Serenely.)* O yes, he will. . . . Is the moon going down? *(She crosses to the window, right.)* Hurry, moon, and go down. I feel like I was on fire. *(She stands looking out the window.)*

M. Well, *I'm* going to hit the hay. *(She grinds the cigarette under her [h]eel, takes off her puffs, and lays them on the bureau, kicks off her slippers, throws off her kimono, turns the gas low, and gets into bed.)*

S. Where's the cigarettes?

M. On the bureau. One's all you get. You've smoked up a whole box since you lost your job.

S. *(Takes cigarette and lights it. Laughing happily.)* Never mind. I'll pay you back. Jack'll pay you back.

M. *(From the bed.)* He'll never come. I know them charity boys. They live down on Washington Square.

S. I never saw the stars so beautiful as to-night. They look so calm way up there in the quiet sky. . . . And the moon *is* like a woman, too. Funny, I never noticed it before. . . . Like a woman with silver hair. It goes down so slow, the moon —

M.   That "silver hair" you're talkin' about means rain to-morrow. Freddy promised to take me for an auto ride. You see what you're missing.

S.   You *don't know* what you're missing.

M.   I'm old enough to know better. Now look a' here, Sylvia, you got to make up your mind. This Jack won't come—

S.   *(Serenely.)* O yes, he will. When the moon goes down.

M.   You're moony all right. Well, suppose he *does* come. You'll live in a dirty little flat up on 126th street, scrubbing and cooking and washing. You'll have some puking little kids, and they'll grow up into panhandlers and street-corner bums. Why, you might as well live in Jersey City as New York—

S.   It will be so wonderful to have a baby of my own—like my mother had me and your mother had you—

M.   I don't want to have no children like me.

S.   O don't you see, Mame! It don't make no difference what they're goin' to be. Just to have 'em, to have 'em, to have 'em—

M.   Well, you'd better be sensible and take that job in my place. I've got a pull. You'll have a good time. There's several nice gentlemen up at the store just looking for somebody to spend money on. You'll have nothing but lunches at Shanley's, and auto rides, and theatres, and good clothes, and champagne—I tell you that's *living*. You don't know this town.

S.   I don't want to know it—like that. The moon's going down fast now. It's almost to the house-tops. *(The moon appears through the open window.)*

M.   He'll never come. You're nothing to him but material for a poem. He'll sell you to a magazine for seven dollars. Come on now, Sylvia, do you want that job?

S.   *(Light-heartedly.)* I'd take it if he didn't come. But he will— *(Silence. Sylvia sits in the window.)*

S.   I'll let down my hair, so he can see it when he comes up the street. He said my hair was beautiful.... *(She lets it down out of the window.)* It *is* beautiful. It looks like the hair of the moon. *(She smokes.)* The old moon's nearly down. It's touching the roofs. He ought to be here soon.

M.   Come to bed, Sylvia. Don't be such a little fool. You'll catch cold.

S.   *(Joyfully.)* He's coming now! I hear footsteps! *(She leans out the window. Silence. Footsteps approach, pass, and die away.)*

S.   No, it's not him. *(A little frightened.)* He ought to be here by now. The moon's almost half gone. *(She smokes.)*

M.   *(Drowsily.)* He'll never come.

S.   *(To herself.)* O if he shouldn't come! *(She looks up the street.)* Nothing! I don't see him! *(Aloud.)* Mame, Mame!

M.   *(Drowsily.)* What d'you want?

S.   Mame! If he shouldn't come —

M.   Of course he won't come. He's back in his dinky studio chewing off a lyric about you.

S.   Mame! The moon is almost gone, and he hasn't come. There's nobody on the street —

M.   Haven't I been telling you that he's too busy writing up his Romance to remember a date?

S.   There's only a little tip left! I'm afraid!

M.   It'll go like this:
    "When the moon was going down,
    For she wears not Virtue's crown."

S.   Mame! If he doesn't come will you lend me just a little more money? Only a quarter? I'll get a job, honest to God I will. I won't eat any lunch, I'll —

M.   No. I told you once I wouldn't. It's for your own good. A girl's got to depend on herself in this burg. It's bad for you to begin borrowing. And you go[t] to learn to be less stuck-up.

S.   O, *please,* Mame! I'll never ask you another thing as long as I live. If I don't get a job to-morrow I'll —

M.   You'll do a high dive off Brooklyn Bridge with no charge for admission. I guess not. I ain't going to see you make a fool of yourself any more. Come on to bed.

S.   Mame! Have a little pity! I ask you like I was praying to God!

M.   You'd get just about as much if you did, I guess. There ain't anything in this God business. I tell you a girl's got to stand on her own feet. And money's the only thing that counts.

(Silence.)

M.   He'll never come. You'll take that job.

(Silence.)

M.   How's your moon now?

S.   The moon's gone down. *(She bows her head upon her knees and sobs.)*

Seeing Is Believing

DECEMBER 1913

Whether the girl was straight or not, George doesn't know yet. It's a thing you can usually detect in a five minutes' conversation—or anyway, George can. And this case is the more important because George has rather settled ideas about that sort of thing. He is an attractive, more than usually kind-hearted fellow, who has been known to yield to our common weakness for women, and yet who has strict ideas about the position of such creatures in the social scale. I may add that he is abnormally sensitive to attempts upon his money and sympathy, and knows all the tricks.

It seems that he came out of his club on Forty-fourth street just as a girl strolled past. She was a very small girl with fluffy hair, dressed in a cheap blue tailor suit and a round little hat with a feather sticking straight up. Now, it's usual for women to stroll down Forty-fourth street; but it certainly isn't the appropriate promenade for small, shabby girls dressed in mail-order clothes. I wonder the police didn't stop her.

Anyway, there she was; and as George came through the swinging door, she slowed her pace very obviously and grinned at him. Now comes the most amazing part of the story; George fell into step with her and walked along. That may not seem extraordinary to you—but then, you don't belong to a Forty-fourth street club. Why, we *never* pick up a girl in front of our club. It was the first time George had ever done it, either; and now that he looks back at it, he says that the girl must have hypnotized him from the first.

"Going anywhere in particular?" he asked, according to the formula.

She looked up at him frankly, and he noticed, all of a sudden, how extraordinarily innocent her eyes were.

"Yes," she answered, giggling a little. "I'm going with you." She caught her breath, and George wondered, for the first time, if any of his friends would see him. "I've been walking most all night, except I went into the ladies' room at Macy's and slept two hours before they saw me."

"What do you want?" asked George, putting his hand in his pocket,

43

and by this time pretty much ashamed of walking on the street with her. She didn't answer, and he raised his eyes to find hers filled with tears. She stopped right in the middle of the sidewalk, and turned to face him squarely, shaking her small head solemnly to and fro.

"No," she said. "No. I don't want you to pay me for letting you go. I want to talk to you."

Now, if George had been his rational self, he would have either hurled indignantly away, or taken her to one of those hotels in which the region abounds. They were within a few steps of Sixth avenue. But some entirely new feeling made him blush, (George blushing!) and instead he heard himself say: "Let's go over to the waiting-room of the Grand Central Station. We can talk there." So they faced around and walked back past the club toward Fifth avenue. Killing, isn't it?

I can imagine them as they went along rather silently — George uncomfortable at the thought of being seen with her, unaccountably angry with himself for being so, and perhaps wondering what kind she was; and she with chin lifted, seeming to drink in the air and the bustle around her, her gaze fixed on the tops of buildings. It had turned out one of those blue, steely days of early winter.

George kept stealing glances at her out of the corner of his eye. He was curious, and yet there were few things one could ask this girl.

"Live in New York?" he asked. It was perfectly evident that she didn't.

"We-e-ell," she hesitated. "Not just. I came here from Chillicothe, Ohio. But I like it here — awfully. The skyscrapers *do* tickle you so, don't they?"

"Tickle?"

"O, *you* know," she explained. "When you lean back and look up at 'em, with their high towers all gold up above the highest birds, something just pricks and bubbles in you, and you *laugh*," and she gave a sort of ecstatic little chirp, like a baby.

"I see," he murmured, more at sea than ever. Was the girl bluffing?

"You know that's all I came for," she went on. "That and the millions of people."

"You mean you came to New York to see the crowds and the sky-scrapers?" asked George, sarcastically. You see. George was too wise for that kind of talk.

She nodded. "It seems to me that all my life I heard about nothing but New York. Every time a drummer used to come into Simonds's — Simonds's is where I worked, you know — or when Mr. Petty went East for the fall stock, they used to talk about the Elevated, and the Subway, and the skyscrapers, and Broadway, and — oh, they used to talk so I couldn't sleep thinking of the towers and the roaring and the lights. And so here I am — "

"But how? — "

"O, I know it seems funny to you a girl like me would have enough money to come," she said, with bird-like nods of her little head. "But you see I'm seventeen now, and I began to save when I was eleven. I saved fifty dollars."

At this moment they passed through the eastern door to the great Concourse.

George shot at her rudely: "How much have you got now?"

"Nothing," she replied. And then the marble terrace, and the gracious flight of steps, and the mighty ceiling of starry sky, with the mystical golden procession of the Zodiac marching across it, burst upon her sight. "Oh," she cried, and gripped the marble balustrade hard with her stubby fingers. "This is the beautifullest thing I ever saw in my life!"

"Never mind that!" said George, taking her by the arm. "You come along. I want to talk to you." She could hardly be moved from the terrace. She seemed to have forgotten everything in her rapt wonder at the place. She wanted to know what it was. What were all the people doing, where were they going, why did they go around bumping into each other and never speaking? If it was a railway station, where were the trains, and why was it so beautiful? What was the Zodiac, and why didn't one see it in the sky outside? It suddenly struck George as particularly strange that a girl who professed to come from Chillicothe, Ohio, should know nothing about the Grand Central Station.

"By the way," he said. "Didn't your train from Ohio come to this station?"

"O, dear no," she threw off carelessly. "I crossed the river on a ferryboat." She had parried that exquisitely. George piloted her as quickly as possible toward the waiting-room. He was very angry; he said to himself that he had never been the victim of such flagrant fiction.

"Look here!" he said, as they sat side by side. "How long have you been in New York?"

"About two weeks — but I haven't seen half — "

"And I suppose you've tried to get a job everywhere," George sneered, "but there wasn't any work. And now you are turned out of your room, and they've seized your baggage?"

"O, yes," nodded the girl, a little troubled. "They did all that. But you're mistaken. It wasn't that I couldn't get a job. I didn't *try* to find a job. You see, I've been riding on the Seeing–New York automobiles all day long every day, and that costs a dollar a ride, and there are so many places they don't go."

George was mad. "O, come," he said. "You can't expect me to believe that. I live here, you know. (George is very proud of being a New-Yorker.) Perhaps if you'd tell me the truth, I could help you."

The girl gave a sudden surprised little chuckle, and bent her round eyes upon him.

"Why, mother always said I was a dreadful fibber. And maybe I made some things sound worse'n they really are. But I guess I know what you mean," she went on gently. "You think I've—that I—with men. But no, no, no," she shook her head. "I know all about things, but I'm a good girl."

George felt a sharp pain in his heart. He had hurt himself. As for the girl, she seemed to dismiss the incident from her mind. There was a pause.

"What are you going to do?" he asked finally, in a stiff voice.

"That's what I wanted to talk to you about," she turned to him a little excitedly. "You see, last night, when I went home to my room she wouldn't let me in; and she said through a crack in the door that she wouldn't give me my clothes. So I walked around thinking what to do. It was so much fun going down the quiet streets in the night and the grey morning that I forgot to think much what I was going to do. And then I slept a little while in Macy's—and—and, well, I'd just about made up my mind when I saw you."

"Well, what?" he asked impatiently.

"Well, I think I've got to see the rest of New York. Only I guess it'll cost money. You see, I've got to eat and sleep. Eat anyway." Here she puckered her brow in a delightful little frown. "And that's what I want to ask your advice about."

The simple-minded recklessness of this fairly took George off his feet. Always providing the story was not a deliberate lie. And, great Heavens, how he wanted to doubt that story!

"Look here!" he said. "You go home to Chillicothe. That's my advice. You go home. Why, you don't know the risks you run in this terrible city! (New Yorkers love their Sodom and Gomorrah.) You could starve to death as easily as not. And as for other things—well, it's lucky you didn't meet some of the men that live in this town. Ugh! (George shuddered to think of some of the monsters that infest Babylon.) Suppose it hadn't been *me*. Do you know what any man would have thought?"

"Yes," she said unsmilingly. "Just what you thought. And he'd do pretty much what you are doing, too. I'm not afraid of men. I always trusted everybody, and nobody ever did me any harm. O, I've lived through a good deal, and being hungry doesn't scare me much. Somebody always helps me—and that's because I've got faith."

"You go home!" said George roughly. "You don't know what you're talking about. I'll get you a ticket and give you money enough to buy your food. Go home to your mother quick, before you get caught in the whirl-pool. (George is pretty proud of his metaphors.) Now I know you don't want to go, and you're a very brave girl; but if you don't I swear I'll—" He was about to threaten her with the Gerry Society when he suddenly saw that her face was buried in her hands and her shoulders shaking. Was she laughing at him? He pulled her arm brutally away from her face. She seemed to be shaken with sobs, although there were no tears. Poor George didn't know what to think.

"O," she said brokenly. "You're right. I want to go home. I want to go home. I've been just going on my nerve. O, send me home."

George asked her how much the fare was, and in the end it came to about twenty dollars, according to her. It also developed that a train left in fifteen minutes which would take her on her way.

"Now," said George. "Come on. We'll go and buy your ticket."

The girl had stopped crying with unnatural suddenness, George says, and not the slightest trace of it remained. At this remark she stood still and laid her grimy little hand on his arm.

"No," she said. "Give me the money and let me buy it myself." George looked sardonic. "Let me buy it myself," she went on gently. "You didn't believe me, and you must, or else I'll have to find someone else. Let's say good-bye here."

George hesitated only a moment. Then he said to himself, "O, well, what if she is stinging me? What if she does take my money and go out the Forty-second street door? I'm a damn fool already, anyhow." And he gave her the money.

She must have seen what he was thinking. For she fixed her eyes steadily on his, shaking her head slowly in that quaint way of hers.

"You've got no faith," she said. "But never mind. Because you were good to me, I'll tell you where I lived in New York. And you can go there." ...

After she had gone, leaving him in the waiting-room, he came home and was indiscreet enough to tell us all about it. Of course we guyed him to death for a sentimental sucker, and he got pretty ashamed of his knight-errantry. The more so because he wasn't that kind of a fellow at all.

At dinner Burgess argued the matter out with him.

"I know the kind," said Burgess loftily. "I suppose she kissed you purely just before you parted?"

"No," answered George. "And that was funny, because I wanted to. You'd have thought gratitude—"

"Well, then, she took your name and address and promised some day to pay it back!"

"On the contrary. She gave me hers—where she said all her baggage was held up. And I, when the reaction came on me, went up there, knowing that I wouldn't find anything."

"And you didn't?"

George shrugged. "It's out in the hall now. That suitcase. All — all just as she said."

"I'll frankly admit," said Burgess, "that I never heard of anything like that before. But the girl doesn't exist, or the man either, with a drop of sporting blood in his veins, who would quit this town with twenty new dollars. No, sir. The explanation is that she strayed out of her district. Now that she's flush she'll go back there. I'll bet, if you hunted long enough, you could find her almost any night on Sixth avenue near Thirty-third street."

And they bet five on that, although I didn't see any sense in it.

One night about three weeks later, George came in late and marched straight up to Burgess, saying, "Here's your five!"

"What for?" asked Burgess, who had forgotten as completely as any of us.

"Saw the girl," muttered George, without looking anybody in the eye. "Sixth avenue and Thirty-third street."

"Tell us," said Burgess, who was a real sport after all. And so we heard the sequel.

George had spent the holiday out on Long Island with the Winslows, and had taken the eight–ten train. He got in to the Pennsy Station about a quarter past nine, and thought he'd walk down. And at the corner of Thirty-third and Sixth avenue, who should bump into him but the girl! George says that he was paying no attention to anything but his own thoughts, when the girl stopped and cried out to him:

"Going anywhere in particular?"

He looked up suddenly and recognized her. She had passed him a few feet, and now turned squarely in the middle of the sidewalk and rested her hands on her hips like a small washerwoman. A little flurry of anger swept him — but it was a long time since the incident, and he decided to feel cynically amused.

"I'm going with you," he mimicked calmly, and joined her. "Where do you want to go?"

For answer she stepped up to him, took him by both shoulders, and looked into his face, shaking her head slowly back and forth.

"I want something to eat," is all she said, simply. George shrugged his shoulders and mentioned Baber's. That searching look of hers had made him most uncomfortable, and as they walked along he covertly glanced at her. It seemed to him that she was thinner, less well-nourished, smaller, shabbier — but just as innocent. That was another proof of her guilt. For no one could run around the streets five weeks and remain undefiled. So she must have been always spotted. And her candid, untroubled expression as she walked beside him — when any ordinary girl would have been explaining how it was she stayed in the city. (George is a rare analyst of human nature.)

"You know," she said, "it's lucky I met you. I haven't had anything to eat to-day."

"Why me, particularly?" sneered George. "Won't the others stand for it?"

"O, yes," she said quietly. "Somebody always takes me to lunch or something. But I just didn't feel hungry all day. I've been down on the docks looking at the ships. It is like a picture of the world there. Every ship smells of somewhere else." George decided to revenge himself upon her by not mentioning the matter of their former visit. If she possessed a conscience, that would punish her. She should speak first. "And, oh," she remembered all at once. "You are my friend and I don't hesitate to ask — I need ten dollars to pay for a suit I ordered; you see, I'm still wearing my old clothes, and they're not warm enough."

"Well!" gasped George. Of all the nerve!"

"Well, perhaps it was pretty nervy to order it," assented the girl. "But I knew that somebody would help me — they always do."

Alas for George's good resolutions. When the suspicious head-waiter at Baber's had been reassured by the whiteness of George's linen, the poor fellow's impatient curiosity consumed him bodily. What would she say? How would she explain it? Or would she simply own up to the fraud? Or would she tell as marvelous and incredible a story as before? The object of his conjectures was calmly looking around the room, contented, sufficient, aloof. He couldn't stand it any longer.

"I thought you went back to Chillicothe." George was very ironic. She glanced at him, and he thought he detected a faint gleam of amusement in her eyes, and a faint shadow of sadness.

"I forgot that you'd want to hear about that first," she said. "Well, when I left you, I got on the train" — she paused, searching his face, and then repeated — "I got on the train — and went along as far as Albany. And after that a really nice man came and sat down beside me and we got to talking. He was a tall, red man, with a yellow mustache — lots older than you — and his name was Tom, he said. Now I was thinking to myself, 'Here you are going back home with only the clothes on your back, after your mother worked all winter to make you clothes enough for this one. You never ought to have left New York without getting your clothes out of that boarding-house.' And I was worrying about going back to Chillicothe without any clothes, so I told Tom about it. He said: 'Come on and get off at Utica, and I'll take you back to New York and get your clothes out of the boarding-house for you.'"

"This beats the other story," said George.

"You see?" she answered radiantly. "I told you before I just had to see

the rest of New York. And there was Tom when I needed him. Well, we got
back here and he did all he said he would. But when we got to the
boarding-house, the clothes were gone. They told me a young man had
come and taken them, and I knew right away it was you. But I didn't
know where to find you," she continued, smiling at him, "unless I went
and walked up and down in front of that place I saw you first. And Tom
didn't want me to do that. You see, Tom was awfully good to me. He got
me a room and paid the rent two weeks in advance; and he bought me
some nice dresses. We used to go to dinner together every night."

"What became of Tom?" asked George, with just the proper cynical
inflection.

Which, however, the girl didn't seem to notice, because she went on,
in a softer voice. "Poor Tom. He didn't understand. I don't know why,
but I don't think he *could* understand. I think he must have been sick.
Because, after he had been so good to me all that time, he suddenly began
to — O, well, you know what he wanted. Poor Tom."

"O, this is rich," cried George, rocking.

She gazed at him meditatively. "I wonder if even you understand?"
she asked. "It wasn't his fault — I know that. He was too nice to me to be
so mean. He just didn't understand. But of course I couldn't stay there;
and I couldn't go on wearing his dresses. So I walked out one night, and
that was a week ago."

"Where are you living now?"

"Well, I haven't any room just now — "

"What!" burst from him in spite of himself. "A whole week? But — "

The girl smiled mysteriously — or perhaps it was maliciously. "When
night comes," she said quietly, "I just pick out some nice-looking house
and ring the door bell. And I say to the people, 'I am tired and I have no
place to go, and I want to sleep here.'"

"And? — " asked George, playing the game.

"Well, it's only once in a while that they don't understand. Then I
just have to go to another house."

George poked a finger at her across the table. "I don't know why I
listen to your tales," he said, in a hard voice. "But I guess it's because I
think you must be all right at bottom. Come now, please tell me the
absolute truth. I know it's hard for a girl to get a job; but have you really
tried?"

"Tried to get a job? Me? Why, no!" she looked surprised. "I don't
want to *work* here. I want to *see* things. And, oh, there are so many
millions of things to see and feel! Yesterday I walked — a long distance I
walked, from early in the morning until almost noon. I went up a long
shining street that climbed the roofs of the houses, between enormous
quivering steel spider-webs, until at last I could look down on miles and

miles of smoky city spread flat—where all the streets boiled over with children. Think of it! All that to see—and I didn't know it was there at all!"

George says he had the strangest, most irrational sensation—for a moment he actually believed the girl. He seemed to look into a world whose existence he had never dreamed of—a world from which he was eternally excluded, because he knew too much! It hurt. The girl might have been a little white flame burning him. And in his pain he had to say all this. But the girl just wagged her little head solemnly.

"No," she said. "It's because you know too little."

But of course this curious mood only lasted a second. Then his common sense came back, and he told her just what he thought of her, and left her.

But one of the queerest things about the whole business was her parting from him. He says that she listened to all he said with her head bird-like on one side, and when he had finished she leaned over and took one of his hands in both of hers, and pressed it against her breast. Then her eyes filled with tears, and just when he thought she was going to cry, she burst out laughing.

"We'll meet again," she cried, shrilly. "I'll see you just when I need you most—"

And then the indignant George came home.

"Well," said Burgess, twisting the five-dollar bill over and over, when the story was done. "Well, it's such a good story that I'm willing to pay for hearing it. I'll stand five of that ten—"

"What ten?" snapped George.

"That ten you gave her to pay for her suit," and Burgess held out the bill.

George stood there, getting redder and redder, looking at all of us to see if we were laughing at him. Then he said "Thanks" in a stifled voice and took it.

The Capitalist

APRIL 1916

YOU know how Washington Square looks in a wet mist on November nights — that gray, luminous pastel atmosphere, softening incredibly the hard outlines of bare trees and iron railings, obliterating the sharp edges of shadows and casting a silver halo about each high electric globe. All the straight concrete walls are black onyx, jeweled in every unevenness with pools of steely rain-water. An imperceptible rain fills the air; your cheeks and the backs of your hands are damp and cool. And yet you can walk three times around the Square with your raincoat open, and not get wet at all.

It was on such a night that William Booth Wrenn, strolling from somewhere to nowhere in particular, stopped under the two arc lights near Washington Arch to count his wealth. It was almost midnight. William Booth Wrenn had just received his compensation for doing — no matter what. It amounted to sixty-five cents in all. This was the third time he had counted it.

A hasty glance at Mr. Wrenn, if you were not particularly observant, would have convinced you that he was an ordinary young man in ordinary circumstances, perhaps a clerk in some flourishing haberdashery shop. His tan shoes showed traces of a recent shine, his hat was of formless English cloth, and his raincoat was of the right length. There was an air about him as of a young man who knew how to wear his clothes. The indulgent mist aided this impression. One must appear so if one is hunting a job in New York. But if you had looked closer, you might have noticed that his high collar was frayed and smudgy-looking; if you could have peered beneath his coat, you would have seen that the collar was attached to a mere sleveless rag that was no shirt at all; if you could have examined the soles of his shoes, you would have discovered two gaping holes there, a pair of drenched socks coming through. How were you to know that the raincoat was "slightly damaged by fire" within? Or that the English hat was fast ungluing in the wet? After reckoning up his resources, William flipped a coin in the air. It came heads: he took the right-hand path across the Square, jingling the coins cheerfully in his pocket.

Between two arc lights on that path there is a dreary stretch of hard wooden benches. In the dim light, he made out two persons occupying opposite sides of the walk. One was a sodden bundle of a drunkard, uncomfortably draped across the iron arm rests which the city rivets there to prevent tired, homeless people from sleeping. His bloated face was turned blindly skyward, and he snored raspingly. Tiny drops of water thickly encrusted him, twinkling as his chest rose and fell. The other occupant was an old woman. A strong odor of whisky emanated from her. A green cheesecloth scarf, glistening with dew, traversed her scant gray hair and was knotted under her chin. She sang:

> "Oh, I know my love (hic) by his way o' walkin' (hic),
> And I (hic) know my love by his way o' (hic) talkin',
> And I know my (hic) love by his coat o' blu-u-ue,
> And if my love left me (hic) — "

At that, she seemed to hear the jingling of William's coins, and suddenly broke off, saying "C'mere!"

William stopped, turned, and lifted his hat with a courtly gesture.

"I beg your pardon, madam?"

"C'mere! I said." He sat beside her on the bench and peered curiously into her face. It was extraordinarily lined and drawn, withered like the faces of very old scrubwomen that one sometimes sees after hours in office buildings; the lower lip trembled senilely. She turned a pair of glazed, faded eyes upon him.

"Gawd damn your soul!" said she. "Ain't (hic), ain't you got better manners 'n to jingle yer money at that feller an' me?"

William smiled.

"But, my good woman — " he began in his best manner.

"Good woman (hic) be cursed to you!" said the old lady. "I know ye — you rich fellers. I bet ye never worked one minute fer yer money — yer father left it to ye — now didn't he? I thought so. I know ye — " she sought the right word — "ye *Capitalist!*" A pleasant glow of satisfaction pervaded William. He nodded complacently.

"How'd you guess?"

"Guess!" laughed the woman unpleasantly. "Guess! (hic). Don't ye think *I* worked in fine houses? Don't ye think *I* had rich young fellers — when I was a young gurrul? *Know* ye? Wid yer jinglin' money an' yer dainty manners? What one o' ye would take off yer hat (hic) to 'n old souse like me — if ye weren't jokin'?"

"Madam. I assure you — "

"My Gawd!" *Listen* to 'm! Aw, yes; many's the fine rich young lover (hic) I had when I was a young gurrul. They took off their hats *then* — "

William wondered if this hideous old ruin had ever been beautiful. It stimulated his imagination.

"When I was a young (hic) gurrul —

"Oh, I know my love —

"Say-y-y ... I was a-thinkin' when I heard that money jinglin' — Ain't it funny how ye jingle everything ye got? You do — I do — Everybody does. I say, I was a-thinkin' (hic), wouldn't you like to come along with me and have some fun?" She leaned over and leered at him, an awful burlesque of her youth; the smell of bad whisky fouled his nostrils. "C'mon! Give you a goo (hic) good time, kid. Wan' go somewhere, have some fun?"

"No, thank you. Not to-night," answered William gently.

"Sure," sneered the old lady. "*I* know ye, ye Cap'tal'sts! Give us work w'en we don't want it. But ye won't give 's work w'en we (hic) want it. Take yer hand out 'o yer pocket! *I* won't take yer dirty charity.... Had enough o' charity. I *work* fer what I get. See? (hic). No decent woman 'd take yer charity.... C'mon, give ye a good — "

"Why are you sitting out here? You'll catch cold — "

"Why you — Wot t'ell do ye think I'm sittin' out here for? I just can't stay 'n my boodwar these here fine summer evenin's! If I got paid fer wot I done, think I'd be sittin' out here? Jesus!" She blazed out at him furiously. "You b'long to the City?"

William shook his head. He drew from his pocket a cheap cigarette box, and opened it. There were two cigarettes.

"Do you mind if I smoke?" he asked politely. The old lady stared at him.

"Do I mind if you smoke! What t'ell you want, young feller? Why d'ye ask me w'ether you c'n smoke? W'at business is it o' mine w'ether you — sure, I'll take one — " He struck a match.

"Yer a Cap'tal'st," she went on, the cigarette trembling in her lips. "Ye wouldn't be so p'lite to *me* if you didn't want sumpin' ... *I* know ye ... You don't b'long to the City? If you did, *you'd* be gettin' paid. I don't get paid, an' I (hic) belong t' the City.... Look at this here." She fumbled in the bosom of her dress, and produced a brown card. Stooping so as to catch the rays of the arc light, he read:

"Pass Mrs. Sara Trimball for one month from date to Randall Island.... To visit Daughter."

"That's me," said Mrs. Trimball, with a kind of alcoholic pride. "Work up t' Ran'all's Island — sort o' git-along-there-do-this-do-that fer the nurses 'n' doctors (hic). We get paid to-day. I come all the way down to City Hall: Get there at fi' minutes past three, 'n' I don't get m' money.

Y'un'erstand? Don't get *any* money till next Friday (hic). Ain't that hell? The nurses an' doctors they get *their* money up t' five o'clock.... W'y can't I get my money? *They* know I ain't got no place t' sleep.... W'y — ? So I say (hic) 'aw-right,' an' go sleep in the park. Jus' b'fore you come, a big cop comes an' says, 'get out o' here.' City won' pay me w'at I work fer.... I go sleep in City Park.... City cop comes an' drives me 'way.... Where'll I go? Go t' the devil. *Ain't* that a round o' pleasure (hic)?"

"You have a daughter there?"

"Sure got a daughter.... Sixteen years old. Here's 'nother funny thing (hic). If I didn't work up there, I c'd keep 'er there fer nawthin'. But I work up there, an' it costs me two dollars a week to keep her there."

"Why do you work up there?" William protested loftily. "That's criminal extravagance for a poor person like you —"

"Hear 'm talk, the dirty loafer!" she responded with heat. "Don't ye think I wan' to *see* 'er sometimes? O Gawd, what *do* I do 't fer? She ought to be out on the streets, earnin' enough to take care o' me in my old age."
. . .

"Of course she ought. It's ridiculous —"

"*I* don' know w'y I keep her shut away like that.... It ain't (hic) got any sense to it. Will ye tell me w'y I don' want my kid to be like me? *I* always had a good time — *I* always lived happy.... W'y don't we want our kids to be like us? She ought to be workin' fer me — but I go on keepin' her there, so she won't be like me.... W'at difference does it make (hic)? W'en I'm gone she'll have to, anyhow." ... Mrs. Trimball began to cough, slightly at first and then more violently, until her whole body was wrenched. The mist came steadily down. William felt the subtle chill of it stealing through his body. The sleeper across the way suddenly swallowed a prodigious snore, sneezed, and slowly sat up.

"Why can't ye let a guy sleep?" he mumbled. "All that damn coughin' —"

"O Gawd," said Mrs. Trimball weakly, the paroxysm past. "I wisht I had a drink."

"How much does a room cost?" asked William suddenly.

"A quarter. You wan' a room? I know a good place right down Fourth Street.... Naw, w'at you giv'n' us? *You* don' want no room." ...

"No, but *you* do. Wait a minute, please! I'm not going to offer you charity." He held out a quarter. "You can borrow it from me; I'd do the same with you, you know — and you can pay me back sometime — when you get paid." He dropped it into her shaking hand. She clutched at it and missed. The coin clinked upon the pavement and rolled. Quick as light a long, ragged arm shot out from the opposite bench, and the sleeper was reeling away down the path with his precious find.

Mrs. Trimball half rose from her seat. "You drunken bum!" she screamed shrilly. "Come back with that, you dirty thief — "

"Never mind," said William, his arm on hers. "There's plenty more at home like that. Here's another." This time she clutched it. . . .

"I'm thankin' you very much," said Mrs. Trimball with dignity. "Between friends borrowin's all right (hic). I'll ask ye to give me your name an' address, an' I'll return it to you." She fumbled in her bag and produced a much-bitten pencil and a letter. "Perhaps ye might be able to put another dime on that, so 's I can get a drop to warm me stomach."

William hesitated only for an instant. "Certainly," he agreed. Then he set his wits to work, conjuring up all his remembrances of the Society Page in the Sunday papers. He wrote upon the letter:

"Courcy De Peyster Stuyvesant
Hotel Plaza"

"Didn't I tell ye?" cried the old lady as he orated this. "I know ye (hic). *I'll* have no truck wid ye. You gettin' yer money from yer pa, and me workin' on my knees seven days out o' the week. Ain't that a hell of a name to have wished on ye? Are ye ashamed to walk a few steps with an ol' souse like me, Mr. Cursey Dee Poyster Stuyvesant?"

"Not at all. A pleasure, I assure you." William rose stiffly to his feet, and took the old lady's arm. He shivered. It seemed as if standing up exposed to the chill other parts of his body that had been fairly warm while he remained seated. . . .

"Look at us!" remarked Mrs. Trimball. "Here we all elect a President of the United States . . . the very feller that promises to make everything all right (hic). I say, here we elect a Presid'nt, an' all we get is — Police."

William bluffed magnificently. "But, dear lady, we *must* safeguard society" . . .

Mrs. Trimball turned at her door. "You're a good enough young feller for a Cap'tal'st. You got the stuff in you. All you want is a little hard work."

"If you working people weren't so extravagant, you'd save enough to make you comfortable in your old age." . . .

William Booth Wrenn walked back into the Square. His feet were without feeling, but the dampness had worked through his thin clothing, and all his body was damp and chilled. He sought the bench he had just quitted, fingering the nickel in his pocket. In a dry corner underneath the seat, between the iron and the wood, he found the stump of his cigarette. After four trials, a damp match was induced to sputter into blue flame. He lighted the tobacco, drew a long breath of it into his lungs, and warmed his hands over the match.

Just then a well-nourished, cape-muffled policeman appeared, motioning with his club.

"Move on," he said briefly. "You can't sit here."

William took another puff at his snipe, and, without moving, drawled insolently, "My man, do you know who I am?"

The policeman took in the dirty collar, the cheap hat, the wet shoes. Policemen's eyes are sharper than old ladies'. Then he leaned forward and peered into William's face.

"Yes," he said, "I know who you are. You're the guy that I chased out of here twice already last night. Now git, or I'll fan you."

Broadway Night

MAY 1916

HE stood on the corner of Broadway and Forty-second Street, a neat man with greyish side-whiskers, a placid mouth, benevolent spectacles perched on the tip of his nose, and the general air of a clergyman opposed to preparedness on humane grounds. But on the front of his high-crowned Derby hat was affixed a sheet labelled "Matrimonial News"; another hung down his chest; a third from his outstretched right arm, and he carried a pile of them on his left hand. And every little while his mouth fell mechanically open, and he intoned, in ministerial accents:

"Buy the 'Matrimonial News.' If you want a wife or husband. Five cents a copy. Only a nickel for wedded bliss, Only a half a dime for a lifetime of happiness."

He said this without any expression whatever, beaming mildly on the passing throng.

Floods of light—white, green, brazen yellow, garish red—beat upon him. Over his head a nine-foot kitten played with a monstrous spool of red thread. A gigantic eagle slowly flapped its wings. Gargantuan toothbrushes appeared like solemn portents in the sky. A green and red and blue and yellow Scotchman, tall as a house, danced a silent hornpipe. Two giants in underclothes boxed with gloves a yard across. Sparkling beer poured from bottles into glasses, topped with incandescent foam. Invisible fingers traced Household Words across the inky sky in letters of fire. And all between was ripples and whorls of colored flame.

"If you want a wife or husband. Only a nickel for wedded bliss," came the brassy voice.

He stood immovable, like a rock in a torrent. The theaters were just letting out. As a dynamited logjam moves down the river, a double stream of smoking, screaming motors filled Broadway, Seventh Avenue, Forty-second Street, rushing, halting, breaking free again.... An illuminated serpent of streetcars, blocked, clang-clanged.

The sidewalks ran like Spring ice going out, grinding and hurried and packed close from bank to bank. Ferret-faced slim men, white-faced slim

58

women, gleam of white shirt-fronts, silk hats, nodding flowery broad
hats, silver veils over dark hair, hard little somber hats with a dab of
vermilion, satin slippers, petticoat-edges, patent-leathers, rouge and
enamel and patches. Voluptuous exciting perfumes. Whiffs of cigarette
smoke caught up to gold radiance, bluely. Cafe and restaurant music
scarcely heard, rhythmical. Lights, sound, swift feverish pleasure....
First the flood came slowly, then full tide—furs richer than in Russia,
silks than the Orient, jewels than Paris, faces and eyes and bodies the
desire of the world—then the rapid ebb, and the street-walkers.

"Five cents a copy. Only half a dime for a lifetime of happiness."

"Can you guarantee it?" said I.

He turned upon his calm and kindly gaze and took my nickel before
answering.

"Turn to page two," he bade me. "See that photo? Read. 'Beautiful
young woman, twenty-eight years old, in perfect health, heiress to five
hundred thousand dollars, desires correspondence with bachelor; object
matrimony, if right party can be found.' Thousands have achieved felicity
through these pages. If you are disappointed,"—he peered gravely over
his glasses—"if you are disappointed, we give your nickel back."

"Have you tried it yourself?"

"No," he answered thoughtfully. "I will be frank with you. I have
not." Here he interrupted himself to adjure the passing world: "Buy the
'Matrimonial News.' If you want a wife or husband. . . .

"I have not," he went on. "I am fifty-two years old, and my wife is
dead this day five years ago. I have known all of life; so why should I
try?"

"Nonsense!" I exclaimed. "Nowadays life is not finished at fifty-two.
Look at Walt Whitman and Susan B. Anthony."

"I am not acquainted with the parties you mention," responded the
Matrimonial Newsboy seriously. "But I tell you, young man, the time of
the end of living depends upon whether or not you have lived. Now I have
lived." Here he turned from me to bawl "Five cents a copy. Only a nickel
for wedded bliss. . . .

"My parents were working people. My father was killed by a fly-
wheel in the pump-house of the Central Park Reservoir. My mother died
of consumption brought on by doing piece-work at home. I was errand-
boy in a haberdashery-shop, bell-boy in a hotel, and then I drove a
delivery-wagon for the *Evening Journal* until I was thrashed in a fight—
my constitution was poorly—and so I went to Night School at the
Y. M. C. A. and became a clerk. I worked in several offices until finally I
entered the Smith-Tellfair Company, Bankers and Brokers, 6 Broad
Street. And there my life began." Methodical, unhurried, he again
shouted the virtues of the "Matrimonial News."

"At the age of twenty-seven, I fell in love, for the first time in my life; and in time we married. I shall not dwell upon our initial hardships, nor the birth of our first child, who soon after died—largely because our means did not permit us to dwell in a neighborhood where there was sufficient light and air for a sickly baby.

"Afterward, however, things became more easy. I rose to be Chief Clerk at Smith-Tellfair's. By the time the second child was born—a girl— we had taken a small house at White Plains, for which I was gradually paying by the strictest economy in our living." Here he paused. "I have often wondered, after my experience, if thrift is really worth while. We might have had more pleasures in our life, and it would have all come to the same in the end." He seemed lost in meditation. Above, the nervous chaos of lights leaped in glory. Two women with white, high-heeled shoes passed, looking back over their shoulders at the furtive men. My friend called his wares once more.

"However. My little girl grew up. We had decided that she should learn the piano, and some day be a great musician with her name on an electric sign here." He waved his arm at Broadway. "When she was five years old, a son was born to me. He was to be a soldier—a general in the Army. When she was six years old, she died. The trouble was in the Town sewer-pipes—the contractors who did the work were corrupt, and so there was an epidemic of typhoid.

"She died, I say—Myrtle did. After that my wife was never quite the same. Unfortunately soon afterward she was going to have another baby. We knew that her condition wouldn't permit it, and tried our best to find some means of prevention. I've heard there were things—but we did not know them, and the doctor would do nothing. The child was born dead. My wife did not survive it.

"That left me and little Herbert—who was to be a general, you remember. It was about this time that young Mr. Tellfair succeeded his father at the head of the business; he was just out of college, with ideas about efficiency and office reorganization. And he discharged me first, for my hair was already white.... I then persuaded the Building and Loan Association to suspend my payments on the house for six months, while I procured another situation. Herbert was fourteen. It was extremely important that he remain in school, in order to prepare for the West Point examinations—for there he was to go.

"It was impossible for me to find another place as clerk, though I searched the city everywhere. I finally became night watchman in a paint and leather house near the financial district. Of course the salary was less than half what I had been earning. My payments on the house resumed, but I was unable to meet them. So of course I lost it.

"I brought Herbert with me to the city. He went to the Public School.

And when he was sixteen, just twelve months ago, my little Herbert died of scarlet fever. Shortly afterward, I stumbled upon this employment, which yields a comfortable living."

He ceased, and turning again to the passersby, wildly called upon them to "Buy the 'Matrimonial News.' Only a nickel for wedded bliss. Half a dime for a lifetime of felicity." . . .

The glaring names, the vast excited conflagrations, the incandescent legs of kicking girls, — all the lights that bedeck the facades of theatres — went out one by one. The imitation jewelry shops switched off their show-window illuminations, for wives and fiancées had gone home, and kept women, actresses and great cocottes were tangoing to champagne in dazzling cabarets. Domestic Science and Personal Hygiene still rioted across the sky. But Broadway was dimmer, quieter, and the fantastic girls parading by ones, by twos, with alert, ranging eyes, moved alluringly from light to shadow. In the obscurity men lurked; and around corners. They went along the street, with coat-collars pulled up and hats pulled down, devouring the women with hard eyes; their mouths were dry, and they shivered with fever and the excitement of the chase.

"Here. Gimme one," said a voice like rusty iron. A fat woman in a wide, short skirt, high-heeled grey shoes laced up the back, a pink hat the size of a button, held out a nickel in pudgy fingers gloved in dirty white. From behind, at a distance of three blocks in a dark street, you might have thought her young. But close at hand her hair had silver threads among the bleached, and there were white dead lumps of flesh under all that artificial red, — hollows and wrinkles.

"Good evening, madam," said my friend, with a courtly lift of his hat. "I trust I find you well. How is business tonight?"

"It ain't what it used to be when I first done Broadway," responded the lady, shaking her head. "Pikers and charity boys nowadays — that's what it is. A couple of fresh guys got funny down by Shanley's — asked me to supper. God, what do you know about that? They was kidding me, it toined out. I been [at] as swell places in my time as any goil in town. The idea! I met a fella up on Forty-fifth Street, and he says, 'Where'll we go?' And I says, 'I know a place over on Seventh Avenoo.' 'Seventh!' says he. 'Seven's my unlucky number. Good night!' and he beat it. The idea!" Here she shook with good-natured mirth. Presently I entered her horizon. "Who's your young friend, Bill?" said she. "Interdooce us." She dropped her voice: "Say, honey, want some fun? No?" She yawned, revealing gold teeth. "O well, it's time for bed anyhow. I'll go home and pound my ear off."

"Looking for a husband?" I asked, pointing to the "Matrimonial News."

"The idea! Say, did you ever know a goil that wasn't? If you got any nice friend with a million dollars, you leave word with Bill here. He sees me every night."

"But you only buy the 'Matrimonial News' Saturday nights," said Bill.

"To read Sundays," she replied. "I get a real rest Sundays. I don't do no business on the Lord's day—never have." She proudly tossed her head. "Never have, no matter how broke I was. I was brought up strict, and I got religious scruples." . . . She was gone, swaying her enormous hips.

The "Matrimonial News" agent folded up his papers.

"It's bed for me too, young man," said he. "So good-night. As for you, I suppose you'll go helling about with drink and women." He nodded half-sadly. "Well, go your ways. I'm past blaming anyone for anything."

I wandered down the feverish street, checkered with light and shade, crowned with necklaces and pendants and lavallieres and sunbursts of light, littered with rags and papers, torn up for Subway construction, patrolled by the pickets of womankind. One tall, thin girl who walked ahead of me I watched. Her face was deadly pale, and her lips like blood. Three times I saw her speak to men—three times edge into their paths, and with a hawk-like tilt of her head, murmur to them from the corner of her mouth.

I quickened my pace and passed her, and as I drew abreast she looked at me, coldly, a fierce invitation.

"Hello!" said I, slowing down. But she stopped suddenly, looked at me hatefully, a stranger, and drew herself up.

"To whom do you think you're talking to!" she answered, in a harsh voice. . . .

"This," said I, "is what they call Natural Selection." . . .

The next one was not so difficult. Around the corner on Thirty-seventh Street she stood, and seemed to be waiting for me. We came together like magnet and steel, and clasped hands.

"Let's go somewheres and get a drink," said she.

She was robust and young, eager, red and black to look at. No one could dance like her, in the restaurant we went to. Everyone turned to watch her—the blank-faced, insolent waiters, the flat-chested men biting cigars, the gay and discontented women who sat there as if it had all been created to set them off. In her black straw hat with the blue feather, her slightly shabby brown tweed suit, she blew into the soft warmth, gold, mirrors, hysterical ragtime of the place like a lawless wind.

We sat against the wall, watching the flush of faces, the whiteness of slim shoulders, hearing the too loud laughter, smelling cigarette smoke and the odor that is like the taste of too much champagne. Two orchestras brayed, drummed and banged alternately. A dance for the guests — then professional dancers and singers, hitching spasmodically, bawling flatly meaningless words to swift rhythm. Then the lights went out, all except the spot on the performers, and in the drunken dark we kissed hotly. Flash! Lights on again, burst of hard hilarity, whirl of shouting words, words, words, rush of partners to the dance floor, orchestra crashing syncopated breathless idiocy, bodies swaying and jerking in wild unison. . . .

Her name was Mae; she wrote it with her address and telephone number on a card, and gave references to South African diplomats who had enjoyed her charms, if I wanted recommendations. . . . Mae never read the newspapers, and was only vaguely conscious that there was a war. Yet how she knew Broadway between Thirty-third and Fiftieth Streets! How perfectly she was mistress of her world!

She came from Galveston, Texas, she said — boasted that her mother was a Spaniard, and hesitatingly admitted that her father was a gypsy. She was ashamed of that, and hardly ever told anyone.

"But he wasn't one of these here kind of gypsies that go like tramps along the road and steal things," added Mae, asserting the respectability of her parentage. "No. He came of a very fine gypsy family." . . .

This mad inconsequentiality, this magnificent lack of purpose is what I love about the city. Why do you insist that there must be reason for life?

II. The Mexican Revolution

JOHN REED returned to America in September 1913; he was restless and eager to work again. Though he moved into the salon at 23 Fifth Avenue, his relationship with Mabel Dodge degenerated steadily. Reed was interested not only in art, but in politics and revolution as well, whereas Dodge seemed primarily concerned with collecting celebrities for her "evenings." "She suffocates me—I can't breathe," Reed explained to a mutual friend.[11] When in November Dodge took an overdose of Veronal, apparently because of his indifference, Reed had had enough. They were, he realized, simply incompatible. On November 21, Reed left for Boston, not knowing where he would end up or where his next writing assignment would take him.

Events south of the border made the decision for him. In Mexico, Francisco "Pancho" Villa and his famed Northern Division had just won decisive military victories over the Federalist army at Juarez and Chihuahua City, and his troops were massing for a final push to south Torreón and Mexico City. The Mexican Revolution, fought primarily for agrarian reform, had begun some three years earlier when Francisco I. Madero overthrew the thirty-five-year-old dictatorship of General Porfirio Díaz. Madero became a symbol and martyr of the revolution where he was imprisoned and executed by an ex-*porfirista* general by the name of Victoriano Huerta. With Madero's death on February 13, 1913, the true revolution began. Against Huerta and his Federalists stood a number of groups that represented a broad spectrum of Mexican society and that demanded serious social and political changes—all rallying under the Constitutionalist banner. Venustiano Carranza, later to become president, appointed himself Commander in Chief of the Constitutionalist army, his forces supported by Pancho Villa in the north and Emiliano Zapata in the south. By early December the revolution appeared to be coming to a dramatic conclusion, and American war correspondents rushed down to border towns such as El Paso and Presidio. Reed went with them, commissioned by *Metropolitan Magazine,* with assignments from Joseph Pulitzer's *New York World* and, of course, *The Masses.*

From El Paso, Reed traveled to Presidio, then waded across the Rio Grande to the town of Ojinaga, defying a Mexican general who threatened to shoot him if he did so. By Christmas Day Reed had made his way as far south as Chihuahua City, where he interviewed Villa in the governor's palace and managed to strike up a rather amiable friendship with the general. Villa issued Reed a pass, which asked that both civil and military authorities give Reed aid and protection, and which allowed Reed to use both railway and telegraph lines without charge. In Chihuahua City Reed also met a twenty-five-year-old "American in the raw" by the name of Mac, who had worked as a mechanic in a Durango mine. Mac provided a drinking companion and material for Reed's first Mexico article for *The Masses,* "Mac — American." On the first day of 1914, the two companions boarded a freight train crowded with soldiers and rode it to Jiménez, arriving late that evening. Jiménez, and the Station Hotel at which they stayed, became the material for another article for *The Masses,* "Jiménez and Beyond." From Jiménez, Reed traveled by buggy to Durango and Las Nieves, where he joined and rode with the troops, called *La Tropa,* of General Tomas Urbina. Two weeks later *La Tropa* engaged the Federalists at La Cadena and were routed. Reed and the few other survivors retreated into the hills, making their way on foot to the nearest village. After returning briefly to El Paso, Reed journeyed to Nogales to interview Carranza, then back to Chihuahua City to join Villa's army as it began the long-awaited advance on Torreón. Reed covered the initial fighting outside the city, filing the first report (to the *New York World*) on the fall of Torreón on March 25.[12] As what seemed then the final act of the revolution came to a close, Reed returned to El Paso on March 30 and began the long journey home.

Back in Manhattan in early April, Reed spent the next three months writing about his experience in Mexico. Both he and his editors knew the material was his best work to date. That summer he collected and published his articles on the Mexican Revolution — seven from *Metropolitan Magazine* and two from *The Masses* ("Happy Valley" and "Jiménez and Beyond") — as *Insurgent Mexico,* which secured his reputation as one of America's best war correspondents. Well received by his contemporaries, the book has been generously praised ever since its publication. For example, the Mexican journalist Renato Leduc prefers *Insurgent Mexico* to *Ten Days That Shook the World* because it was written with "more color, emotion, and — why not say it? — more poetry."[13] And Robert A. Rosenstone declares it "a book for the eye, a vast panorama like one of the great murals of the Mexican painters, full of color, motion and the life-and-death struggle of a people. Its power comes from the close identification of the author with his subject."[14]

Years later Reed wrote that the time he spent in Mexico was the "most satisfactory period" of his life. He loved the arid vegetation, the clear tones of the desert, and the colorful adobe villages sprawled on hillsides and dusty plains. He never forgot the sights and smells, or the striking images of Old Mexico. For example, Valle Allegre, "Happy Valley," he describes in terms of color, the way a painter might approach his subject:

> The color of the street was red—deep, rich red clay—and the open space where the burros stood olive drab; there were brown crumbling adobe walls and squat houses, their roofs heaped high with yellow cornstalks or hung with strings of red peppers. A gigantic green mesquite tree, with roots like a chicken's foot, thatched on every branch with dried hay and corn. Below, the town fell steeply down the arroyo, roofs tumbled together like blocks, with flowers and grass growing on them, blue feather of smoke waving from the chimneys, and occasional palms sticking up between. They fell away to the yellow plain where the horse-races are run, and beyond that the barren mountains crouched, tawny as lions, then faintly blue, then purple and wrinkled, notched and jagged across the fierce, bright sky.

Reed also loved the Mexican people, whom he found warm and earthy and generous in spite of their poverty. He found them brave, occasionally reckless, and generally idealistic in their commitment to the revolution. He greatly admired their passion for drinking, singing, dancing, loving, and fighting—the proper pursuits of *los hombres*. More than anything else, it was this passion, on the battlefield and at the fiesta, that animated the Mexican people and that Reed managed to capture in his writing.

Like his previous work, the Mexican articles incorporate elements of both fact and fiction in a dramatic structure, with Reed participating as a character in the action. Details, dialogue, even characters are occasionally altered for purposes of a higher reportage that transcribes an emotional, rather than literal truth. This artistic license enables Reed to offer more than a straight factual account, and thus to render the more intangible qualities of Mexico and its people. "Jiménez and Beyond" (August 1914) provides a good example of Reed's artistic license. Briefly, the article concerns Reed's journey by train to Jiménez, his short stay at Dona Louisa's Station Hotel, and his journey by buggy to Magistral. In actuality Mac (of "Mac—American") had accompanied him to Magistral, but Reed introduces a new character, Lieutenant Antonio Montoya, to make the journey with him here. The reasons for this are obvious: Montoya personifies both the revolution and the Mexican people. By traveling with Montoya, Reed can introduce his readers, just as he had been introduced by such characters, to the spirit of Mexico. Likewise, Reed condenses his experience in Jiménez into a few short hours, and he reorders events for dramatic effect.

Reed also makes use of many important stylistic devices in his Mexico writing. For one thing, he transliterates dialogue from Spanish to

English in much the same way Ernest Hemingway was to do several years later, most notably in *For Whom the Bell Tolls*—that is, he translates the Spanish into English in such a way as to communicate the Spanish nuance behind the words as well as their literal meaning. Though formal and stylized, the dialogue proves extremely effective, as in this scene from "Happy Valley" (July 1914), where Reed and his friend Atanacio meet:

> *"Buenos tardes, amigo,"* he murmured, "How do you seat yourself?"
> "Very well, much thanks. And you? How have they treated you?"
> "Delicious. Superlative. Thanks. I have longed to see you again."
> "And your family? How are they?" (It is considered more delicate in Mexico not to ask about one's wife, because so few people are married.)
> "Their health is of the best. Great, great thanks. And your family?"
> *"Bien, bien!* I saw your son with the army at Jiménez. He gave me many, many remembrances of you. Would you desire a cigarette?"
> "Thanks. Permit me a light. You are in Valle Allegre many days?"
> "For the fiesta only, señor."
> "I hope your visit is fortunate, señor. My house is at your orders."

Reed sees Mexico as a land of contradiction, and in order to portray its complexity he juxtaposes images, characters, and events. The resulting irony reminds one once again of Hemingway, especially the Hemingway of *In Our Time* and the early dispatches from the Greco-Turkish war that were published in the *Toronto Star*. However, unlike Hemingway, Reed always tempers his irony with warmth and humor, which allows his characters to seem more human and his readers to sympathize with them. Perhaps the best of many possible examples is Reed's portrait of the former Federalist and the Constitutionalist, both extremely drunk, walking arm in arm in "Happy Valley": Don Priciliano "used to deflower the young women of the village and lend money to the peons at twenty per cent," whereas Don Catarino "is a former schoolmaster, an ardent revolutionist—he lends money at a slightly less rate of usury to the same parties." Earlier the Maderistas had confiscated most of Don Priciliano's property, then strapped him naked on his horse and beat him with the flat of a sword. "Aie!" he says. "The revolution. I have most of the revolution upon my back!"

These accounts are animated by a wonderful sense of humor, a humor derived from absurd or contradictory codes of behavior. In "Jiménez and Beyond" Reed describes two friendly Mexican officers who meet and, after embracing and patting each other on the back, engage in a polite duel to determine which of them will go that night to visit Maria. Or later in the article, when Reed returns to his room in the Station Hotel only to have his sleep interrupted by a drunken lieutenant who breaks down the door and announces, very politely, that he has come to kill the "gringo." Reed writes the scene brilliantly:

"I am Lieutenant Antonio Montoya, at your orders," he said. "I heard there was a gringo in this hotel and I have come to kill you."

"Sit down," said I politely. I saw he was drunkenly in earnest. He took off his hat, bowed politely and drew up a chair. Then he produced another revolver from beneath his coat and laid them both on the table. They were loaded.

"Would you like a cigarette?" I offered him the package. He took one, waved it in thanks and illumined it at the lamp. Then he picked up the guns and pointed them both at me. His fingers tightened slowly on the triggers, but relaxed again. I was too far gone to do anything but just wait.

"My only difficulty," said he, lowering his weapons, "is to determine which revolver I shall use."

"Pardon me," I quavered, "but they both appear a little obsolete. That Colt forty-five is certainly an 1895 model, and as for the Smith and Wesson, between ourselves, it is only a toy."

"True," he answered, looking at them a little ruefully. "If I had only thought I would have brought my new automatic. My apologies, señor." . . .

As it turns out, Reed and Lieutenant Montoya become good friends when the lieutenant takes a liking to Reed's watch and Reed eagerly gives it to him. Though this incident almost certainly did not occur as described here, the scene is dramatically effective and provides a superb portrait of the combination of politeness and *machismo* in the Mexican officer.

Even more explicit codes of behavior can be found in "Happy Valley"—codes that are sometimes ironic, sometimes grotesque, but always warmly and humorously described. "Happy Valley" tells the story of the fiesta of the Santos Reyes and its celebration in Valle Allegre. After a night of drinking, dancing, and several illicit rendezvous, a mysterious stranger appears to sow discord in the otherwise happy valley. Reed and the other remaining revelers at Charlie Chee's hotel are interrupted by Atanacio, who informs them that the stranger has given his wife an anonymous letter that details his "little amusements" when he last went for "recreation" to Juarez. Atanacio says, "I have seen the letter. It is astonishingly accurate! It tells how I went to supper with Maria and then home with her. It tells how I took Ana to the bullfight. It describes the hair, complexion and disposition of all those other ladies and how much money I spent upon them. *Carramba!* It is exact to a cent!" Atanacio has come to elicit support to, as he says, "kill that accursed man in the red blanket who is poisoning our homes and making Valle Allegre a place unfit for a decent woman to live in!" Reed and the others agree to help Atanacio, but they fail to stop the "evil stranger." In fact, the apparition leaves behind yet another note: "Your husband is the father of forty-five young children in the State of Coahiula." It seems that in Valle Allegre infidelity, though expected and even encouraged, must be punished when discovered—either by punishing the offender or, more commonly, the person who exposes the offense.

Of course, these articles have a darker side as well. Repeatedly in the travels described here, Reed encounters scenes of widespread ruin and devastation, the effects of war waged on a civilian population—images that have become all too familiar in the late twentieth century. For example, every station on the train ride from Chihuahua City to Jiménez was "shot to pieces by one army or the other during the three years of revolution." The long-suffering Mexican people have grown so accustomed to war that violence and sudden death have become everyday, domestic affairs. Just as ominous are the American mercenaries who come to Mexico out of greed or love of excitement, or the munitions salesmen and war profiteers who flock to the border hoping to profit from the revolution. Reed describes one such American in "Mac—American" (April 1914), the portrait of a brutal and racist "boss mechanic" who despises both Mexico and the Mexican people. And in "Endymion, or On the Border" (December 1916) Reed describes the collection of misfits gathered in the border town of Presidio, Texas:

> The fortunes of war had thrust greatness upon Presidio. It figured in the news dispatches telephoned to the outer world by way of the single Army wire. Automobiles, gray with desert dust, roared down over the pack-trail from the railroad seventy-five miles north, to corrupt its pristine innocence. A handful of war-correspondents sat there in the sand cursing, and twice a day concocted two-hundred-word stories full of sound and fury. Wealthy *hacendados,* fleeing across the border, paused there to await the battle which should decide the fate of their property. Secret agents of the Constitutionalistas and the Federal plotted and counter-plotted all over the place. Representatives of big American interests distributed retaining fees, and sent incessant telegrams in code. Drummers for munition companies offered to supply arms wholesale and retail to anyone engaged in or planning a revolution.

In Mexico Reed's maturing powers as a writer paralleled his growing political commitment. There he observed, not a single instance, but an historical tide of social and political upheaval that brought his own increasingly radical politics into focus. The columns and analytical articles that Reed published later in *The Masses* demonstrate his commitment to a revolution that he both reported and championed: in "What About Mexico" (June 1914) he argues that the revolution is being fought primarily for a more equal distribution of land; in "The Mexican Tangle" (June 1916) he warns against American intervention in Mexico; in "Persecution of Mexican Refugees" (June 1916) he describes the mistreatment of Mexicans who support the Constitutionalists; and in "The

Legendary Villa" (May 1917) he defends Villa in the face of the general's alleged attack on United States citizens and troops. These works tend to be strident and probably not very convincing to those who do not share Reed's political persuasions, but in the first-person articles he wrote for *The Masses* and *Metropolitan Magazine* Reed managed to merge politics and art in a way that was as effortless as it was natural.

During the summer of 1914, while the world tottered on the brink of the Great War, Reed basked in a well-earned celebrity. He had reached the height of his fame as a war correspondent, and his work was much in demand. He did not know then that he would be sent to the Western Front in the fall and that there, instead of the idealism and political commitment he discovered in Mexico, he would find only slaughter, unimaginable and senseless. The muddy trenches of Europe would make a mockery of an entire civilization.

Mac — American

APRIL 1914

I MET Mac down in Mexico — Chihuahua City — last New Year's Eve. He was a breath from home — an American in the raw. I remember that as we sallied out of the Hotel for a Tom-and-Jerry at Chee Lee's, the cracked bells in the ancient cathedral were ringing wildly for midnight mass. Above us were the hot desert stars. All over the city, from the *cuartels* where Villa's army was quartered, from distant outposts on the naked hills, from the sentries in the streets, came the sound of exultant shots. A drunken officer passed us, and, mistaking the *fiesta*, yelled "Christ is born!" At the next corner down a group of soldiers, wrapped to their eyes in *serapes,* sat around a fire chanting the interminable ballad of the "Morning Song to Francisco Villa." Each singer had to make up a new verse about the exploits of the Great Captain....

At the great doors of the church, through the shady paths of the Plaza, visible and vanishing again at the mouths of dark streets, the silent, sinister figures of black-robed women gathered to wash away their sins. And from the cathedral itself, a pale red light streamed out — and strange Indian voices singing a chant that I had heard only in Spain.

"Let's go in and see the service," I said. "It must be interesting."

"Hell, no," said Mac, in a slightly strained voice. "I don't want to butt in on a man's religion."

"Are you a Catholic?"

"No," he replied. "I don't guess I'm anything. I haven't been to a church for years."

"Bully for you," I cried. "So you're not superstitious either!"

Mac looked at me with some distaste. "I'm not a religious man," and here he spat. "But I don't go around knocking God. There's too much risk in it."

"Risk of what?"

"Why when you die — you know...." Now he was disgusted, and angry.

In Chee Lee's we met up with two more Americans. They were the kind that preface all remarks by "I've been in this country seven years, and I know the people down to the ground!"

"Mexican women," said one, "are the rottenest on earth. Why they never wash more than twice a year. And as for Virtue—it simply doesn't exist! They don't get married even. They just take anybody they happen to like. Mexican women are all——, that's all there is to it!"

"I got a nice little Indian girl down in Torreon," began the other man. "Say, it's a crime. Why she don't even care if I marry her or not! I—"

"That's the way with 'em," broke in the other. "Loose! That's what they are. I've been in this country seven years."

"And do you know," the other man shook his finger severely at me, "you can tell all that to a Mexican Greaser and he'll just laugh at you! That's the kind of dirty skunks they are!"

"They've got no Pride," said Mac, gloomily.

"Imagine," began the first compatriot. "Imagine what would happen if you spoke like that about a woman to an AMERICAN!"

Mac banged his fist on the table. "The American Woman, God bless her!" he said. "If any man dared to dirty the fair name of the American Woman to me, I think I'd kill him." He glared around the table, and, as none of us besmirched the reputation of the Femininity of the Great Republic, he proceeded. "She is a Pure Ideal, and we've got to keep her so. I'd like to hear anybody talk rotten about a woman in my hearing!"

We drank our Tom-and-Jerries in the solemn righteousness of a Convention of Galahads.

"Say Mac," the second man said abruptly. "Do you remember them two little girls you and I had in Kansas City that winter?"

"*Do* I?" glowed Mac. "And remember the awful fix you thought you were in?"

"Will I ever forget it!"

The first man spoke. "Well," said he. "You can crack up your pretty senoritas all you want to. But for *me,* give me a clean little American girl"
. . .

Mac was over six feet tall—a brute of a man, in the magnificent insolence of youth. He was only twenty-five, but he had been many places and done many things. Railroad Foreman, Plantation Overseer in Georgia, Boss Mechanic in a Mexican Mine, Cow-Puncher, and Texas Deputy-Sheriff. He came originally from Vermont. Along about the second Tom-and-Jerry, he lifted the veil of his past.

"When I came down to Burlington to work in the Lumber Mill, I was only a kid about sixteen. My brother had been working there already a year, and he took me up to board at the same house as him. He was four years older than me—a big guy, too; but a little soft ... Always kept bulling around about how wrong it was to fight, and that kind of stuff. Never would hit me—even when he got hot at me; because he said I was smaller.

"Well, there was a girl in the house, that my brother had been carrying on with for a long time. Now I've got the cussedest damn disposition," laughed Mac. "Always did have. Nothing would do me but I should get that girl away from my brother. Pretty soon I did it, too; and when he had to go to town, we certainly just glued ourselves together ... Well, gentlemen, do you know what that devil of a girl did? One time when my brother was kissing her, she suddenly says 'Why you kiss just like Mac does!' ...

"He came to find me. All his ideas about not fighting were gone, of course—not worth a damn anyway with a real man. He was so white around the gills that I hardly knew him—eyes shooting fire like a volcano. He says, '——— —— you, what have you been doing with my girl?' He was a great big fellow, and for a minute I was a little scared. But then I remembered how soft he was, and I was game. 'If you can't hold her,' I says, 'leave her go!'

"It was a bad fight. He was out to kill me. I tried to kill him, too. A big red cloud came over me, and I went raging, tearing mad. See this ear?" Mac indicated the stump of the member alluded to. "He did that. I got him in one eye, though, so he never saw again. We soon quit using fists; we scratched, and choked, and bit, and kicked. They say my brother let out a roar like a bull every few minutes, but I just opened my mouth and screamed all the time ... Pretty soon I landed a kick in—a place where it hurt, and he fell like he was dead" ... Mac finished his Tom-and-Jerry.

Somebody ordered another. Mac went on.

"A little while after that I came away South, and my brother joined the Northwest Mounted Police. You remember that Indian who murdered the fellow out in Victoria in '06? Well, my brother was sent out after him, and got shot in the lung. I happened to be up home visiting the folks— only time I ever went back—when my brother came home to die ... But he got well. I remember the day I went away he was just out of his bed. He walked down to the station with me, begging me to speak just one word to him. He held out his hand for me to shake, but I just turned on him and says "You son of a ——!" A little later he started back to his job, but he died on the way ..."

"Gar!" said the first man. "Northwestern Mounted Police! That must be a job. A good rifle and a good horse and no closed season on Indians! That's what I call Sport!"

"Speaking of Sport," said Mac. "The greatest sport in the world is hunting niggers. After I left Burlington, you remember, I drifted down

South. I was out to see the world from top to bottom, and I had just found out I could scrap. God! The fights I used to get into ... Well anyway, I landed up on a cotton plantation down in Georgia, near a place called Dixville; and they happened to be shy of an overseer, so I stuck.

"I remember the night perfectly, because I was sitting in my cabin writing home to my sister. She and I always hit it off, but we couldn't seem to get along with the rest of the family. Last year she got into a scrape with a drummer—and if I ever catch that— Well, as I say, I was sitting there writing by the light of a little oil lamp. It was a sticky, hot night, the window screen was just a squirming mass of bugs. It made me itch all over just to see 'em crawling around. All of a sudden, I pricked up my ears, and the hair began to stand right up on my head. It was dogs—bloodhounds—coming lickety-split in the dark. I don't know whether you fellows ever heard a hound bay when he's after a human ... Any hound baying at night is about the lonesomest, *doomingest* sound in the world. But this was worse than that. It made you feel like you were standing in the dark, waiting for somebody to strangle you to death—and *you couldn't get away!*

"For about a minute all I heard was the dogs, and then somebody, or some Thing, fell over my fence, and heavy feet running went right past my window, and a sound of breathing. You know how a stubborn horse breathes when they're choking him around the neck with a rope? That way.

"I was out on my porch in one jump, just in time to see the dogs scramble over my fence. Then somebody I couldn't see yelled out, so hoarse he couldn't hardly speak 'Where'd he go?'

"'Past the house and out back!' says I, and started to run. There was about twelve of us. I never *did* find out what that nigger did, and I guess most of the others didn't either. We didn't care. We ran like crazy men, through the cotton field, and the woods swampy from floods, swam the river, dove over fences, in a way that would tire out a man in a hundred yards. And we never felt it. The spit kept dripping out of my mouth, that was the only thing that bothered me. It was full moon, and every once in a while when we came out into an open place somebody would yell 'There he goes!' and we'd think the dogs had made a mistake, and take after a shadow. Always the dogs ahead, baying like bells. Say, did you ever hear a bloodhound when he's after a human? It's like a bugle! I broke my shins on twenty fences, and I banged my head on all the trees in Georgia, but I never felt it ..."

Mac smacked his lips and drank.

"Of course," he said, "when we got up to him, the dogs had just about torn that coon to pieces."

He shook his head in shining reminiscence.

"Did you finish your letter to your sister?" I asked.
"Sure," said Mac, shortly. . . .

"I wouldn't like to live down here in Mexico," Mac volunteered. "The people haven't got any Heart. I like people to be friendly, like Americans."

JUNE, 1914   10 CENTS

The MASSES

IN THIS ISSUE
CLASS WAR IN COLORADO—Max Eastman
WHAT ABOUT MEXICO?—John Reed

What About Mexico?

JUNE 1914

IN THE first place, let's settle the question of whether or not the Mexican people are fighting just because they want to fight — or because they want something that they can get no other way.

It is of course to the interest of those who desire Intervention and Annexation of Mexico to spread the news that this is a "comic opera revolution."

If anybody wants to know the truth at first hand, he must do as I did — go through the country and especially through the Constitutionalist army, asking the people what they are fighting for and whether they like revolution as a way of living.

You will make the astonishing discovery that the peons are sick of war — that, curiously enough, they do not enjoy starvation, thirst, cold, nakedness, and wounds without pay for three years steady; that loss of their homes and years of ignorance as to whether their women and children are alive, does not appeal to them much.

But of course that argument by foreign holders of concessions is like that other which we are familiar with in this country: that the reason employers of labor down there don't pay better wages is that the Mexicans would not know how to spend it, because their standard of living is so low. So you'll find often, when you ask these people why they're fighting, that "It's more fun to fight than work in the mines or as slaves on the great haciendas."

I have seen these mines, where the hovels of the workers are infinitely wretcheder than the slums of Mexican towns. For example, the American Smelting and Refining Company's properties at Santa Eulalia, where they've built a church for the workers to keep them contented, though they crush strikes unmercifully and herd the poor devils into the filthiest huts; where such is the good feeling between miners and operators that the latter don't dare go down into the village at night. And just to prove how different it can be, I've been to Magistnal — where the National Mines and Smelters plant is situated — the happiest village I have seen in Mexico.

There the workmen, though not receiving much more pay than the others, live in their own houses; and hardly a night passes without a *baile,* at which the extremely popular officers of the company are always present. I haven't time to go into the differences between Santa Eulalia and Magistral; but the point is, they are different. The miners at Santa Eulalia join the revolution simply to escape the mines; those at Magistral do not. And any people who would not rather fight than work in most American mines in Mexico are a degraded people.

There is only one book that gives the real facts about the Mexican revolution, and that is the recently published "The Mexican People. Their Struggle for Freedom," by L. Gutierrez de Lara and Edgcumb Pinchon. If you can get hold of that absorbingly interesting book, read it. I am not going to paraphrase it in this article; but I just want to put in a few words the real character of this Revolution. In the first place, it is not a revolution of the middle class; it is a slowly-growing accumulation of grievances of the peons—the lowest class—that has finally burst definitely into expression. There is not one peon out of twenty who cannot tell you exactly what they are all fighting for: Land. In different ways they have been struggling for it for four hundred years, and most of the time, like all simple, half-primitive peoples, they haven't even been able to express this desire consciously. But that they felt it deeply and strongly is shown by the fact that they rose in arms whenever anyone expressed it for them.

This is the strongest underlying cause of the Revolution. Little by little, the untaxed owners of big estates, originally created by Spanish land-grants, have absorbed the common lands of villages, the open ranges, and the small independent farms, leaving the people no choice but to become slaves on the great haciendas and no hope for the future at all. Sometimes it would be the granting of whole valleys as concessions to foreign capitalists by the National Government, or the declaration of areas thrown open to colonization with disregard for those who lived on them, like the lands of the Yaqui Indians in Sonora—an act that turned an agricultural race which had been at peace for three hundred years into a warring tribe that has resisted ever since.

The culmination of this process was the infamous land law of 1896, for which Porfirio Diaz is responsible. This law permitted denunciation of all lands in the Republic not secured by a legal title.

The cynical criminality of this piece of legislation only appears when you consider that three-fourths of the small independent farms and even city property were held by peons too ignorant to know what "title" meant, whose lands had been worked by their ancestors sometimes for four generations, and whose tenure the Government had never questioned. These are the people whom the great land-owners dispossessed of their homes, and turned out to starve or enter virtual slavery. And when they refused to move, regiments of Federal soldiers descended upon them and exterminated whole districts.

I know of one case where 400 families were literally massacred, so that one man who already owned 15,000,000 acres of land might add a few hundred more to his estate. De Lara tells of many more horrible ones.

And the result was that by 1910 the big haciendas touched each other's borders all across the North of Mexico, and the agricultural population were chained to particular haciendas by debt, religious superstition, or the most cunningly calculated mental debauchery. Education was at a standstill; or worse, it was just what the *hacendados* wanted it to be. Public schools could not be established there, because the law said that haciendas were "private property."

But the people, scattered, unable to communicate with one another, deliberately sunk in content and ignorance by their employers, hopeless of change, still nourished a dream.

I have said that the Mexicans are normally an agricultural people. They are more than that. Like all other people, nothing spurs them so much to live as personal ownership of their homes and tools. The peons on the haciendas dreamed of the farms that their grandfathers used to own, and that they themselves desired. Indeed, so strong was this instinct, that the land-owners themselves gave each peon his own little field which he could work Sundays. And so, under such tremendous handicaps, the strange thing is not that the peons rose in such numbers; it is remarkable that they rose at all.

For there is another lie that those interested will tell you—that a very small per cent of the Mexican people are fighting in the Revolution—that out of a population of seventeen million, only some four hundred thousand have been engaged on both sides in the last three years.

It is true that those who originally revolted in 1910 were a small percentage of the people—but that is because news and ideas spread very slowly through the Republic.

Every day more people join the revolution—every day to more and more distant villages far removed from the lines of communication comes the astonishing word that there is hope for the peons. Every state in the Republic is now in revolt, reporting to Carranza at least weekly—and in all these states the revolution steadily gains. The Constitutionalist army in the North now amounts to over fifty thousand men, and a conservative guess at the revolutionists' strength in the rest of the Republic would give them over two hundred thousand in all.

Not all of these are fighting men—yet. But even the *pacificos,* the peons one finds tilling the fields and tending the cattle in the villages and haciendas of the country, are all in favor of the Constitutionalists.

They welcome the rebel entry into their towns; they hate the Federals. Often I asked them why they did not fight.

"They do not need us," came the reply. "The Revolution is going well. When it goes badly and they call to us, then the whole country will rise. But if we fight now, who will raise corn for the army and cattle for the soldiers? And who will make babies that can grow up to be soldiers?"

That is how deep their faith is. They look forward possibly to many years of fighting still, and see the necessity for a growing race of young soldiers to carry on the Revolution.

Zapata was the first leader of the peons in the present revolution to call them to arms for the settlement of the land question. Almost a year afterward Madero issued his famous Plan of San Luis Potosi, which inflamed the people chiefly because it promised a distribution of the great estates among the poor. Zapata joined him, too, nor did he abandon Madero until the latter showed himself unable to settle the question. The rich land-owners bribed Orozco then to start a counter-revolution to embarrass Madero, but the only way Orozco could raise the people was by promising them free farms. And when they discovered that he really did not propose to give them land at all, they deserted Orozco and went back to their homes. At the death of Madero, Carranza took the field, endorsing vaguely the principles of Madero's plan, but placing all the emphasis upon the restoration of constitutionalist government. Zapata denounced Carranza, who refused to commit himself on the land question, but endorsed Villa, because the latter has gone ahead confiscating the great estates and dividing them gratis among the poor. And on that point, I think, the split between Carranza and his General will come—because the Mexican Revolution will not be won until the peons get their land.

And don't let anybody tell you that there are no losses to speak of in a Mexican battle—that the whole affair is a joke, or that Mexicans are not brave. They are perhaps the most recklessly brave people in the world. I saw them charge on foot up a hill two hundred and fifty feet high in the face of *artillery*—saw them do it *seven times,* and get absolutely massacred every time. I saw them on foot again, armed only with hand-bombs, rush a corral defended by twelve hundred men shooting through loopholes and five machine guns—*eight times* they did it, and hardly one of them came back from each charge. And about the sparsity of dead in Mexican battles, let me add that about three thousand of Villa's army were killed and wounded in the first five days' fighting at Torreon; and remember, there have been hundreds of battles in the three years.

Have you ever heard one of your fellow-countrymen talk about the "damned little Greasers," to the effect that "one American was worth twenty Mexicans," or perhaps that they are "a dirty, ignorant, treacherous, cowardly, immoral race"? I was two weeks marching with one hundred ex-bandits, perhaps the most disreputable company in the entire

Constitutionalist army—Gringo-haters, too. Not only did they not steal anything from me—these wretchedly poor, unclothed, unpaid, immoral rascals, but they refused to allow me to buy food or even tobacco. They gave me their horses to ride. They gave me their blankets to sleep in.

Mexicans are notoriously the most warm-hearted and generous of peoples. They are big men, too—good riders, good shots, good dancers and singers. They endure daily what would drive an American soldier to desert. And they never complain. And let me tell you this: *Except in times of war it is almost unknown that foreigners should be killed or even held up in Mexico!* As for outrages to foreigners, they think nothing of killing a Greaser on the American side of the Texas border. There have been enough wanton outrages to Mexican citizens in Texas and California in the last ten years to have justified armed intervention by the Mexican army fifty times. A list will be furnished on request.

And yet the Texan is not a particularly bad man. He's just like all the rest of the Americans—he doesn't understand the Mexican temperament and doesn't want to; but the Texans come into direct contact with Mexicans, and so they are a little more uncivilized than the rest of us farther north. If you will trace the pedigree of Intervention Shouters, you will find that they are either Texans, or somebody with large interests in Mexico, or somebody who hopes to acquire large interests there under the Dear Old Flag. Or perhaps he might be an American Business Man in Mexico, and that is the worst of all.

For American Business Men in Mexico are a degraded race. They have a deep-seated contempt for the Mexicans, because they are different from themselves. They prate of our grand old democratic institutions, and then declare in the same breath that the peons ought to be driven to work *for them* with rifles. They boast in private of the superiority of American courage over Mexican, and then sneakingly truckle to whatever party is in power.

The other foreigners in Mexico usually stand firm on the side of the oppressor, but the American can be found hat in hand in the audience room of the Palace at all seasons of the year, so long as there is some hope of protecting his little investment. And it is for the benefit of these men—who admittedly make forty or fifty per cent on their money, because they say they are taking a "gambler's chance," and then squeal when they lose—that the United States has been pushed to the very brink of conquest.

If you interest yourself much in Mexican affairs you will meet many people who know all about it, because they have "been there for fifteen, or twenty, or thirty years." Do not let them bully you. They know nothing about Mexico at all—no more than the Capitalist who has "employed men for twenty years" knows about Labor.

Whenever you hear anyone refer to Porfirio Diaz as the "Great Educator" or the "Warrior-Statesman," you may know that you have before you one who has "been in Mexico fifteen years," and if you have anything to do, go away and do it. First remarking, however, that the test of Diaz' barbarous regime was that it failed—and that there is *no big South American Republic* which did not progress more in *every way* than Mexico during Diaz' beneficent rule. You may know, too, that this person is probably the owner of a share of stock or so in some concession that Diaz sold for bribes.

At the present time Villa has wisely and calmly refused to say the word which would raise the North against our legions occupying Vera Cruz. He has the promise of the President of the United States that we are not making war against the Mexican people—that we intend to withdraw from Mexico as soon as reparation is made, and he will undoubtedly stick to his neutrality and make half of Mexico stick, too—which he can do with a word—unless we break our promise. The pressure upon President Wilson to force him to break it is fearfully strong. And you may depend upon it that the Border is trying every means in its power to provoke the Mexicans to some act of aggression. I will not dwell upon Mr. Hearst; because of course you remember when he said a few years ago that he intended to invest his family fortunes in Mexico, so as to provide largely and surely for his children.

But if we are forced over the Border—if in any way we inject ourselves into Mexican politics—it will mean the end of the Revolution. For we could never recognize a government there unsuited to the European Powers—indeed, I don't see how we can now; and a government suited to the European Powers would mean the confirmation of foreign concessions, the establishment of the "respectable" element in power, and the subsequent checking of anything like a radical distribution of lands among the peons. We could not sanction a government really elected by the peons, because they would elect a government which would give them what they have been fighting for so long. And that means Confiscation— which the merest school-child knows to be a worse crime than the robbery of peons!

So I think that the United States Government is really headed toward the policy of "civilizing 'em with a Krag"—a process which consists in forcing upon alien races with alien temperaments our own Grand Democratic Institutions: I refer to Trust Government, Unemployment, and Wage Slavery.

Happy Valley

JULY 1914

IT HAPPENED to be the day of the fiesta of the Santos Reyes, and, of course, nobody worked in Valle Allegre. The cock-fight was to take place at high noon in the open space back of Catarino Cabrera's drinking shop—almost directly in front of Dionysio Aguirre's, where the long burro pack-trains rest on their mountain journeys, and the muleteers swap tales over their *tequila*. At one, the sunny side of the dry arroyo that is called a street was lined with double rows of squatting peons—silent, dreamily sucking their cornhusk cigarettes as they waited. The bibulously inclined drifted in and out of Catarino's, whence came a cloud of tobacco smoke and a strong reek of *aguardiente*. Small boys played leap-frog with a large yellow sow, and on opposite sides of the arroyo the competing roosters, tethered by the leg, crowed defiantly. One of the owners, an ingratiating, businesslike professional, wearing sandals and one cerise sock, stalked around with a handful of dirty bank-bills, shouting:

"*Diez pesos,* señores! Only ten dollars!"

It was strange; nobody seemed too poor to bet ten dollars. It came on toward two o'clock, and still no one moved, except to follow the sun a few feet as it swung the black edge of the shadow eastward. The shadow was very cold, and the sun white hot.

On the edge of the shadow lay Ignacio, the violinist, wrapped in a tattered *serape,* sleeping off a drunk. He can play one tune when intoxicated—Tosti's "Good Bye." When very drunk he also remembers fragments of Mendelssohn's "Spring Song." In fact, he is the only high-brow musician in the whole State of Durango, and possesses a just celebrity. Ignacio used to be brilliant and industrious—his sons and daughters are innumerable—but the artistic temperament was too much for him.

The color of the street was red—deep, rich, red clay—and the open space where the burros stood olive drab; there were brown crumbling adobe walls and squat houses, their roofs heaped high with yellow corn-stalks or hung with strings of red peppers. A gigantic green mesquite tree,

85

with roots like a chicken's foot, thatched on every branch with dried hay and corn. Below, the town fell steeply down the arroyo, roofs tumbled together like blocks, with flowers and grass growing on them, blue feather of smoke waving from the chimneys, and occasional palms sticking up between. They fell away to the yellow plain where the horse-races are run, and beyond that the barren mountains crouched, tawny as lions, then faintly blue, then purple and wrinkled, notched and jagged across the fierce, bright sky. Straight down and away through the arroyo one saw a great valley, like an elephant's hide, where the heat-waves buck-jumped.

A lazy smoke of human noises floated up: roosters crowing, pigs grunting, burros giving great racking sobs, the rustling crackle of dried cornstalks being shaken out of the mesquite tree, a woman singing as she mashed her corn on the stones, the wailing of a myriad babies.

The sun fairly blistered. My friend Atanacio sat upon the sidewalk thinking of nothing. His dirty feet were bare except for sandals, his mighty sombrero was of a faded dull brick color, embroidered with tarnished gold braid, and his *serape* was of the pottery blue one sees in Chinese rugs, and decorated with yellow suns. He rose when he saw me. We removed our hats and embraced after the Mexican fashion, patting each other on the back with one hand while we shook the other.

"*Buenos tardes, amigo,*" he murmured, How do you seat your-self?"

"Very well, much thanks. And you? How have they treated you?"

"Delicious. Superlative. Thanks. I have longed to see you again."

"And your family? How are they?" (It is considered more delicate in Mexico not to ask about one's wife, because so few people are married.)

"Their health is of the best. Great, great thanks. And your family?"

"*Bien, bien!* I saw your son with the army at Jiménez. He gave me many, many remembrances of you. Would you desire a cigarette?"

"Thanks. Permit me a light. You are in Valle Allegre many days?"

"For the fiesta only, señor."

"I hope your visit is fortunate, señor. My house is at your orders."

"Thanks. How is it that I did not see you at the *baile* last night, señor? You, who were always such a sympathetic dancer!"

"Unhappily Juanita is gone to visit her mother in El Oro, and now, therefore, I am a *platonico*. I grow too old for the señoritas."

"Ah, no, señor. A *caballero* of your age is in the prime of life. But tell me. Is it true what I hear, that the Maderistas are now at Mapimi?"

"*Si,* señor. Soon Villa will take Torreon, they say, and then it is only a matter of a few months before the revolution is accomplished."

"I think that. Yes. But tell me; I have great respect for your opinion. Which cock would you advise me to bet on?"

We approached the combatants and looked them over, while their

owners clamored in our ears. They sat upon the curbing negligently
herding their birds apart. It was getting toward three of the afternoon.

"But will there be a cock-fight?" I asked them.

"*Quien sabe?*" drawled one.

The other murmured that possibly it would be *manana.* It developed
that the steel spurs had been forgotten in El Oro, and that a small boy had
gone after them on a burro. It was six miles over the mountains to El Oro.

However, no one was in any hurry, so we sat down also. Appeared
then Catarino Cabrera, the saloon-keeper, and also the Constitutionalist
jefe politico of Valle Allegre, very drunk, walking arm in arm with Don
Priciliano Saucedes, the former *jefe* under the Diaz government. Don
Priciliano is a fine-looking, white-haired old Castilian who used to
deflower the young women of the village and lend money to the peons at
twenty per cent. Don Catarino is a former schoolmaster, an ardent
revolutionist – he lends money at a slightly less rate of usury to the same
parties. Don Catarino wears no collar, but he sports a revolver and two
cartridge belts. Don Priciliano during the first revolution was deprived of
most of his property by the Maderistas of the town, and then strapped
naked upon his horse and beaten upon his bare back with the flat of a
sword.

"Aie!" he says to my question. "The revolution! I have most of the
revolution upon my back!"

And the two pass on to Don Priciliano's house, where Catarino is
courting a beautiful daughter.

Then, with the thunder of hoofs, dashes up the gay and gallant
young Jesus Triano, who was a captain under Orozco. But Valle Allegre
is a ten days' ride to the railroad, and politics are not a burning issue
there; so Jesus rides his stolen horse with impunity around the streets. He
is a large young man with shining teeth, a rifle and bandolier and leather
trousers fastened up the side with buttons as big as dollars – his spurs are
twice that big. They say that his dashing ways, and the fact that he shot
Emetario Flores in the back, have won him the hand of Dolores, youngest
daughter of Manuel Paredes, the charcoal contractor. He plunges down
the arroyo at a gallop, his horse tossing bloody froth from the cruel curb.

Captain Adolfo Melendez, of the Constitutionalist army, slouches
around the corner in a new, bottle-green, corduroy uniform. He wears a
handsome gilded sword which once belonged to the Knights of Pythias.
Adolfo came to Valle Allegre on a two weeks' leave, which he prolonged
indefinitely in order to take to himself a wife – the fourteen-year-old
daughter of a village aristocrat. They say that his wedding was magnificent beyond belief, two priests officiating and the service lasting an hour
more than necessary. But this may have been good economy on Adolfo's
part, since he already had one wife in Chihuahua, another in Parral, and

a third in Monterey, and of course had to placate the parents of the bride. He had now been away from his regiment three months, and told me simply that he thought they had forgotten all about him by now.

At half past four a thunder of cheers announced the arrival of the small boy with the steel spurs. It seems that he had got into a card game at El Oro, and had temporarily forgotten his errand.

But of course nothing was said about it. He had arrived, which was the important thing. We formed a wide ring in the open space where the burros stood, and the two owners began to "throw" their birds. But at the first onslaught the fowl upon which we had all bet our money spread its wings, and, to the astonishment of the assembled company, soared screaming over the mesquite tree and disappeared toward the mountains. Ten minutes later the two owners unconcernedly divided the proceeds before our eyes, and we strolled home well content.

Fidencio and I dined at Charlie Chee's hotel. Throughout Mexico, in every little town, you will find Chinamen monopolizing the hotel and restaurant business. Charlie, and his cousin Foo, were both married to the daughters of respectable Mexican villagers. No one seemed to think that strange. Mexicans appear to have no race prejudices whatever. Captain Adolfo, in a bright yellow khaki uniform, and another sword, brought his bride, a faintly pretty brown girl with her hair in a bang, wearing chandelier lustres as earrings. Charlie banged down in front of each of us a quart bottle of *aguardiente,* and, sitting down at the table flirted politely with Señora Melendez; while Foo served dinner, enlivened with gay social chatter in pidgin Mexican.

It seemed that there was to be a *baile* at Don Priciliano's that evening, and Charlie politely offered to teach Adolfo's wife a new step that he had learned in El Paso, called the Turkey Trot. This he did until Adolfo began to look sullen and announced that he didn't think he would go to Don Priciliano's, since he considered it a bad thing for young wives to be seen much in public. Charlie and Foo also tendered their regrets, because several of their countrymen were due in the village that evening from Parral—and said that they would, of course, want to raise a little Chinese hell together.

So Fidencio and I finally departed, after solemnly promising that we would return in time for the Chinese festivities after the dance.

Outside, strong moonlight flooded all the village. The jumbled roofs were so many tipped-up silvery planes, and the tree-tops glistened. Like a frozen cataract the arroyo fell away, and the great valley beyond lay drowned in rich, soft mist. The life-sounds quickened in the dark; excited laughter of young girls, a woman catching her breath at a window to the swift, hot torrent of a man's speech as he leaned against the bars, a dozen guitars syncopating each other, a young buck hurrying to meet his *novia,* spurs ringing clear. It was cold. As we passed Cabrera's door a hot, smoky, alcoholic breath smote us. Beyond that you crossed on stepping-stones the stream where the women wash their clothes. Climbing the other bank we saw the brilliant windows of Don Priciliano's house, and heard the far strains of Valle Allegre's orchestra.

Open doors and windows were choked with men — tall, dark, silent peons, wrapped to the eyes in their blankets, staring at the dance with eager and solemn eyes, a forest of sombreros.

Now Fidencio had just returned to Valle Allegre after a long absence, and as we stood on the outside of the group a tall young fellow caught sight of him, and, whirling his *serape* like a wing, he embraced my friend, crying:

"Happy return, Fidencio! We looked for you many months!"

The crowd swayed and rocked like a windy wheat field, blankets flapped dark against the night. They took up the cry:

"Fidencio! Fidencio is here! Your Carmencita is inside, Fidencio. You had better look out for your sweetheart! You can't stay away as long as that and expect her to remain faithful to you!"

Those inside caught the cry and echoed it, and the dance, which had just begun, stopped suddenly. The peons formed a lane through which we passed, patting us on the back with little words of welcome and affection; and at the door a dozen friends crowded forward to hug us, faces alight with pleasure.

Carmencita, a dumpy, small Indian girl, dressed in a screaming blue ready-made dress that didn't fit, stood over near the corner by the side of a certain Pablito, her partner — a half-breed youth about sixteen years old with a bad complexion. She affected to pay no attention to Fidencio's arrival, but stood dumbly, with her eyes on the ground, as is proper for unmarried Mexican women.

Fidencio swaggered among his *compadres* in true manly fashion for a few minutes, interspersing his conversation with loud virile oaths. Then, in a lordly manner, he went straight across the room to Carmencita, placed her left hand within the hollow of his right arm, and cried: "Well, now; let's dance!" and the grinning, perspiring musicians nodded and fell to.

There were five of them — two violins, a cornet, a flute and a harp. They swung into "Tres Piedras," and the couples fell in line, marching solemnly round the room. After parading round twice they fell to dancing, hopping awkwardly over the rough, hard, packed-dirt floor with jingling spurs; when they had danced around the room two or three times they walked again, then danced, then walked, then danced — so that one number took about an hour.

It was a long, low room, with whitewashed walls and a beamed ceiling wattled with mud above, and at one end was the inevitable sewing-machine, closed now, and converted into a sort of altar by a tiny embroidered cloth upon which burned a perpetual rush flame before a tawdry color print of the Virgin which hung on the wall. Don Priciliano and his wife, who was nursing a baby at her breast, beamed from chairs at the other end. Innumerable candles had been heated on one side and stuck against the wall all around, whence they trailed sooty snakes above them on the white. The men made a prodigious stamping and clinking as they danced, shouting boisterously to one another. The women kept their eyes on the floor and did not speak.

I caught sight of the pimply youth glowering with folded arms upon Fidencio from his corner; and as I stood by the door, fragments of the peons' conversation floated into me:

"Fidencio should not have stayed away so long."

"Carramba! See the way Pablito scowls there. He thought surely Fidencio was dead and that Carmencita was his own!"

And then a hopeful voice:

"Perhaps there will be trouble!"

The dance finally ended and Fidencio led his betrothed correctly back to her seat against the wall. The music stopped. The men poured out into the night where, in the flare of a torch, the owner of the losing rooster sold bottles of strong drink. We toasted each other boisterously in the sharp dark. The mountains around stood dazzling in the moon. And then, for the intervals between dances were very short, we heard the music erupt again, volcanically and exuberantly, into a waltz. The center of twenty curious and enthusiastic youths — for he had traveled — Fidencio strutted back into the room. He went straight to Carmencita, but as he led her out upon the floor, Pablito glided up behind, pulling out a large obsolete revolver. A dozen shouts rang:

"*Cuidado,* Fidencio! Look out!"

He whirled, to see the revolver pointed at his stomach. For a moment no one moved. Fidencio and his rival looked at each other with wrathful eyes. There was a subdued clicking of automatics everywhere as the gentlemen drew and cocked their weapons, for some of them were friends of Pablito's. I heard low voices muttering:

"Porfirio! Go home and get my shot-gun!"

"Victoriano! My new rifle! It lies on the bureau in mother's room."

A shoal of small boys like flying-fish scattered through the moonlight, to get firearms. Meanwhile, the *status quo* was preserved. The peons had squatted out of the range of fire, so that just their eyes showed above the window-sills, where they watched proceedings with joyous interest. Most of the musicians were edging toward the nearest window; the harpist, however, had dropped down behind his instrument. Don

Priciliano and his wife, still nursing the infant, rose and majestically made their way to some interior part of the house. It was none of their business; besides, they did not wish to interfere with the young folks' pleasure.

With one arm Fidencio carefully pushed Carmencita away, holding his other hand poised like a claw. In the dead silence he said:

"You little goat! Don't stand there pointing that thing at me if you're afraid to shoot it! Pull the trigger while I am unarmed! I am not afraid to die, even at the hand of a weak little fool who doesn't know when to use a gun!"

The boy's face twisted hatefully, and I thought he was going to shoot.

"Ah!" murmured the peons. "Now! Now is the time!"

But he didn't. After a few minutes his hand wavered, and with a curse he jammed the pistol back into his pocket. The peons straightened up again and crowded disappointedly around the doors and windows. The harpist got up and began to tune his harp. There was much thrusting back of revolvers into holsters, and sprightly social conversation grew up again. By the time the small boys arrived with a perfect arsenal of rifles and shot-guns, the dance had been resumed. So the guns were stacked in a corner.

As long as Carmencita claimed his amorous attention and there was a prospect of friction, Fidencio stayed. He swaggered among the men and basked in the admiration of the ladies, out-dancing them all in speed, abandon and noise.

But he soon tired of that, and the excitement of meeting Carmencita palled upon him. So we went out into the moonlight again and up the arroyo, to take part in Charlie Chee's celebration.

As we approached the hotel we were conscious of a curious low moaning sound which seemed akin to music. The dinner table had been removed from the dining-room into the street, and around the room Turkey-trotted Foo and another Celestial. A barrel of *aguardiente* had been set up on a trestle in one corner, and beneath it sprawled Charlie himself, in his mouth a glass tube which syphoned up into the barrel. A tremendous wooden box of Mexican cigarettes had been smashed open on one side, the packages tumbling out upon the floor. In other parts of the room two more Chinamen slept the profound sleep of the very drunk, wrapped in blankets. The two who danced sang meanwhile their own version of a once-popular ragtime song called "Dreamy Eyes." Against this marched magnificently "The Pilgrim's Chorus" from Tannhauser, rendered by a phonograph set up in the kitchen. Charlie removed the glass tube from his mouth, put a thumb over it, and welcomed us with a hymn which he sang as follows:

"Pooll for the shore, sailor,
    Pooll for the shore!
Heed not the lowling lave,
    But pooll for the shore!"

He surveyed us with a bleary eye, and remarked:
"Bledlen! Je' Chlist is wid us here toni'."
After which he returned the syphon to his mouth.

We blended into these festivities. Fidencio offered to exhibit the steps of a new Spanish *fandango,* the way it was danced by the damned "grasshoppers" (as Mexicans call the Spaniards). He stamped bellowing around the room, colliding with the Chinamen, and roaring "La Paloma." Finally, out of breath, he collapsed upon a nearby chair, and began to descant upon the many charms of Adolfo's bride, whom he had seen for the first time that day. He declared that it was a shame for so young and blithe a spirit to be tied to a middle-aged man; he said that he himself represented youth, strength and gallantry, and was a much more fitting mate for her. He added that as the evening advanced he found that he desired her more and more. Charlie Chee, with the glass tube in his mouth, nodded intelligently at each of these statements. I had a happy thought. Why not send for Adolfo and his wife and invite them to join our festivities? The Chinamen asleep on the floor were kicked awake and their opinion asked. Since they could understand neither Spanish nor English, they answered fluently in Chinese.

Fidencio translated. "They say that Charlie ought to be sent with the invitation."

We agreed to that. Charlie rose, while Foo took his place at the glass tube. He declared that he would invite them in the most irresistible terms, and, strapping on his revolver, disappeared.

Ten minutes later we heard five shots.... We discussed the matter at length, not understanding why there should be any artillery at that time of night, except, perhaps, that probably two guests returning from the *baile* were murdering each other before going to bed. Charlie took a long time, in the meanwhile, and we were just considering the advisability of sending out an expedition to find him when he returned.

"Well, how about it, Charlie?" I asked. "Will they come?"

"I don't think so," he replied doubtfully, swaying in the doorway.

"Did you hear the shooting?" asked Fidencio.

"Yes, very close," said Charlie. "Foo, if you will kindly get out from under that tube ..."

"What was it?" we asked.

"Well," said Charlie, "I knocked at Adolfo's door and said we were having a party down here and wanted him to come. He shot at me three times and I shot at him twice."

So saying, Charlie seized Foo by the leg and composedly lay down under the glass tube again.

We must have stayed there some hours after that. I remember that toward morning Ignacio came in and played us Tosti's "Good Bye," to which all the Chinamen danced solemnly around.

At about four o'clock Atanacio appeared. He burst open the door and stood there very white, with a gun in one hand.

"Friends," he said, "a most disagreeable thing has happened. My wife, Juanita, returned from her mother's about midnight on an ass. She was stopped on the road by a man muffled up in a *poncho,* who gave her an anonymous letter in which were detailed all my little amusements when I last went for recreation to Juarez. I have seen the letter. It is astonishingly accurate! It tells how I went to supper with Maria and then home with her. It tells how I took Ana to the bullfight. It describes the hair, complexion and disposition of all those other ladies and how much money I spent upon them. *Carramba!* It is exact to a cent!

"When she got home I happened to be down at Catarino's, taking a cup with an old friend. This mysterious stranger appeared at the kitchen door with another letter in which he said I had three more wives in Chihuahua, which, God knows, is not true, since I only have one!

"It is not that I care, *amigos,* but these things have upset Juanita horribly. Of course, I denied these charges, but, *valgame Dios!* women are so unreasonable.

"I hired Dionysio to watch my house, but he has gone to the *baile,* and so, arousing and dressing my small son, that he may carry me word of any further outrages, I have come down to seek your help in preserving my home from this disgrace."

We declared ourselves willing to do anything for Atanacio—anything, that is, that promised excitement. We said that it was horrible—that the evil stranger ought to be exterminated. "Who could it be?"

Atanacio replied that it was probably Flores, who had had a baby by Juanita before he married her, but who had never succeeded in quite capturing her affections. We forced *aguardiente* upon him and he drank moodily. Charlie Chee was pried loose from the glass tube, where Foo took his place, and sent for weapons. And in ten minutes he returned with seven loaded revolvers of different makes.

Almost immediately came a furious pounding on the door, and Atanacio's young son flung himself in.

"Papa!" he cried, holding out a paper. "Here is another one! The man knocked at the back door, and when mamma went to find out who it was, she could only see a big red blanket covering him entirely up to the hair. He gave her a note and ran away, taking a loaf of bread off the window."

With trembling hands Atanacio unfolded the paper and read aloud:

"Your husband is the father of forty-five young children in the State of Coahuila.

(Signed) "SOME ONE WHO KNOWS HIM."

"Mother of God!" cried Atanacio, springing to his feet, in a transport of grief and rage. "Never, never have I been such an animal! I have always discriminated! Forward, my friends! Let us protect our homes!"

Seizing our revolvers we rushed out into the night. We staggered, panting, up the steel hill to Atanacio's house, sticking close together so no one would be mistaken by the others for the Mysterious Stranger. Atanacio's wife was lying on the bed, weeping hysterically. We scattered into the brush and poked into the alleys around the house, but nothing stirred. In a corner of the corral lay Dionysio, the watchman, fast asleep, his rifle by his side. We passed on up the hill until we came to the edge of the town. Already dawn was coming. A never-ending chorus of roosters made the only sound, except the incredibly soft music from the *baile* at Don Priciliano's, which would probably last all that day and the next night. Afar, the big valley was like a great map, quiet, distinct, immense. Every wall corner, tree branch and grass-blade on the roofs of the houses was pricked out in the wonderful clear light of before-dawn.

In the distance, over the shoulder of the red mountain, went a man covered up in a red *serape*.

"Ah, ha!" cried Atanacio, "there he goes!"

And with one accord we opened up on the red blanket. There were five of us, and we had six shots apiece. They echoed fearfully among the houses and clapped from mountain to mountain, reproduced each one a hundred times. Of a sudden the village belched half-dressed men and women and children. They evidently thought that a new revolution was beginning. A very ancient crone came out of a small brown house on the edge of the village, rubbing her eyes.

"*Oyga!*" she shouted. "What are you all shooting at?"

"We are trying to kill that accursed man in the red blanket who is poisoning our homes and making Valle Allegre a place unfit for a decent woman to live in!" shouted Atanacio, taking another shot.

The old woman bent her bleary eyes upon our target.

"But," she said gently, "that is not a bad man. That's only my son going after the goats."

Meanwhile, the red-blanketed figure, never even looking back, continued his placid way over the top of the mountain and disappeared.

Jiménez and Beyond

AUGUST 1914

ALL the long afternoon we ambled slowly south, the western rays of the sun burning as they struck our faces. Every hour or so we stopped at some station, shot to pieces by one army or the other during the three years of revolution; there the train would be besieged by vendors of cigarettes, pinenuts, bottles of milk, *camotes,* and tamales rolled in cornhusks. Old women, gossiping, descended from the train, built themselves a little fire and boiled coffee. Squatting there, smoking their cornhusk cigarettes, they told one another interminable love stories.

It was late in the evening when we pulled into Jiménez. I shouldered through the entire population, come down to meet the train, passed between the flaring torches of the little row of candy booths, and went along the street, where drunken soldiers alternated with painted girls, walking arm in arm, to Dona Louisa's Station Hotel. It was locked. I pounded on the door and a little window opened at the side, showing an incredibly ancient woman's face, crowned with straggly white hair. This being squinted at me through a pair of steel spectacles and remarked, "Well, I guess you're all right!" Then there came a sound of bars being taken down, and the door swung open. Dona Louisa herself, a great bunch of keys at her belt, stood just inside. She held a large Chinaman by the ear, addressing him in fluent and profane Spanish. "*Chango!*" she said, "*Cabron!* What do you mean by telling a guest at this hotel that there wasn't any more hot cakes?" With a final wrench she released the squealing Oriental. She nodded apologetically toward the door. "There's so many damned drunken generals around to-day that I've got to keep the door locked. I don't want the —— ——Mexican —— in here!"

Dona Louisa is a small, dumpy American woman more than eighty years of age—a benevolent-New-England-grandmother sort of person. For forty-five years she has been in Mexico, and thirty or more years ago, when her husband died, she began to keep the Station Hotel. War and peace make no difference to her. The American flag flies over the door and in her house she alone is boss. When Pascual Orozco took Jiménez, his

men began a drunken reign of terror in the town. Orozco himself—
Orozco, the invincible, the fierce, who would as soon kill a person as
not—came drunken to the Station Hotel with two of his officers and
several women. Dona Louisa planted herself across the doorway—
alone—and shook her fist in his face. "Pascual Orozco," she cried, "take
your disreputable friends and go away from here. I'm keeping a decent
hotel!" And Orozco went. . . .

I wandered up the mile-long, incredibly dilapidated street that leads
to the town. A street-car came past, drawn by one galloping mule and
bulging with slightly intoxicated soldiers. Open surreys full of officers
with girls on their laps rolled along. Under the dusty bare alamo trees
each window held its senorita, with a blanket-wrapped *caballero* in
attendance. There were no lights. The night was dry and cold and full of a
subtle exotic excitement; guitars twanged, snatches of song and laughter
and low voices, and shouts from distant streets filled the darkness.

In one quiet stretch of street near the bull-ring, where there are no
houses, I noticed an automobile speeding from the town. At the same
time a galloping horse came from the other direction, and just in front of
me the headlights of the machine illumined the horse and his rider, a
young officer in a Stetson hat. The automobile jarred to a grinding stop
and a voice from it cried, "*Haltoie!*"

"Who speaks?" asked the horseman, pulling his mount to its
haunches.

"I, Guzman!" and the other leaped to the ground and came into the
light, a coarse, fat Mexican, with a sword at his belt.

"*Como le va, mi capitan?*" The officer flung himself from his horse.
They embraced, patting each other on the back with both hands.

"Very well. And you? Where are you going?"

"To see Maria."

The captain laughed. "Don't do it," he said; "I'm going to see Maria
myself, and if I see you there I shall certainly kill you."

"But I am going, just the same. I am as quick with my pistol as you,
señor."

"But you see," returned the other mildly, "we both cannot go!"

"Perfectly!"

"*Oiga!*" said the captain to his chauffeur. "Turn your car so as to
throw the light evenly along the sidewalk. . . . And now we will walk
thirty paces apart and stand with our backs turned until you count three.
Then the man who first puts a bullet through the other man's hat
wins. . . ."

Both men drew immense revolvers and stood a moment in the light,
spinning the chambers.

"*Listo!* Ready!" cried the horseman.

"Hurry it," said the captain. "It is a bad thing to balk love."

Back to back, they had already begun to pace the distance.

"One!" shouted the chauffeur.

"Two!"

But quick as a flash the fat man wheeled in the trembling, uncertain light, threw down his lifted arm, and a mighty roar went soaring slowly into the heavy night. The Stetson of the other man, whose back was still turned, took an odd little leap ten feet beyond him. He spun around, but the captain was already climbing into his machine.

"*Bueno!*" he said cheerfully. "I win. Until tomorrow then, *amigo!*" And the automobile gathered speed and disappeared down the street. The horseman slowly went to where his hat lay, picked it up and examined it. He stood a moment meditating, and then deliberately mounted his horse and he also went away. I had already started some time before. . . .

In the plaza the regimental band was playing "El Pagare," the song which started Orozco's revolution. It was a parody of the original, referring to Madero's payment of his family's $750,000 war claims as soon as he became president, that spread like wildfire over the Republic, and had to be suppressed with police and soldiers. "El Pagare" is even now taboo in most revolutionary circles, and I have heard of men being shot for singing it; but in Jiménez at this time the utmost license prevailed. Moreover, the Mexicans, unlike the French, have absolutely no feeling for symbols. Bitterly antagonistic sides use the same flag; in the plaza of almost every town still stand eulogistic statues of Porfirio Diaz; even at officers' mess in the field I have drunk from glasses stamped with the likeness of the old dictator, while Federal army uniforms are plentiful in the ranks.

There, at the side of the plaza, I came upon a little group of five Americans huddled upon a bench. They were ragged beyond belief, all except a slender youth in leggings and a Federal officer's uniform, who wore a crownless Mexican hat. Feet protruded from their shoes, none had more than the remnants of socks, all were unshaven. One mere boy wore his arm in a sling made out of a torn blanket. They made room for me gladly, stood up, crowded around, cried how good it was to see another American among all these damned greasers.

"What are you fellows doing here?" I asked.

"We're soldiers of fortune!" said the boy with the wounded arm.

"Aw —!" interrupted another. "Soldiers of ——!"

"Ye see it's this way," began the soldierly looking youth. "We've been fighting right along in the Brigada Zaragosa — was at the battle of Ojinaga and everything. And now comes an order from Villa to discharge all the Americans in the ranks and ship 'em back to the border. Ain't that a hell of a note?"

"Last night they gave us our honorable discharges and threw us out of the cuartel," said a one-legged man with red hair.

"And we ain't had any place to sleep and nothing to eat — " broke in a little gray-eyed boy whom they called the major.

"Don't try and panhandle the guy!" rebuked the soldier, indignantly. "Ain't we each going to get fifty Mex. in the morning?"

We adjourned for a short time to a nearby restaurant, and when we returned I asked them what they were going to do?

"The old U.S. for mine," breathed a good-looking black Irishman who hadn't spoken before. "I'm going back to San Fran. and drive a truck again. I'm sick of greasers, bad food and bad fighting."

"I got two honorable discharges from the United States army," announced the soldierly youth proudly. "Served through the Spanish War, I did. I'm the only soldier in this bunch." The others sneered and cursed sullenly. "Guess I'll re-enlist when I get over the border."

"Not for mine," said the one-legged man. "I'm wanted for two murder charges — I didn't do it, swear to God I didn't — it was a frame-up. But a poor guy hasn't got a chance in the United States. When they ain't framing up some fake charge against me, they jail me for a 'vag.' I'm all right though," he went on earnestly. "I'm a hard-working man, only I can't get no job."

The major raised his hard little face and cruel eyes. "I got out of a reform-school in Wisconsin," he said, "and I guess there's some cops waiting for me in El Paso. I always wanted to kill somebody with a gun, and I done it at Ojinaga, and I ain't got a bellyful yet. They told us we could stay if we signed Mex. citizenship papers; I guess I'll sign tomorrow morning."

"The hell you will," cried the others. "That's a rotten thing to do. Suppose we get intervention and you have to shoot against your own people. You won't catch me signing myself away to be a greaser."

"That's easy fixed," said the major. "When I go back to the States I leave my name here. I'm going to stay down here till I get enough of a stake to go back to Georgia and start a child-labor factory."

The other boy had suddenly burst into tears. "I got my arm shot through in Ojinaga," he sobbed, "and now they're turning me loose without any money, and I can't work. When I get to El Paso the cops'll jail me and I'll have to write my dad to come and take me home to California. I run away from there last year," he explained.

"Look here, Major," I advised, "you'd better not stay down here if Villa wants Americans out of the ranks. Being a Mexican citizen won't help you if intervention comes."

"Perhaps you're right," agreed the major thoughtfully. "Aw, quit your bawling, Jack! I guess I'll beat it over to Galveston and get on a

South American boat. They say there's a revolution started in Peru."

The soldier was about thirty, the Irishman twenty-five, and the three others somewhere between sixteen and eighteen.

"What did you fellows come down here for?" I asked.

"Excitement!" answered the soldier and the Irishman, grinning. The three boys looked at me with eager, earnest faces, drawn with hunger and hardship.

"Loot!" they said simultaneously. I cast an eye at their dilapidated garments, at the throngs of tattered volunteers parading around the plaza, who hadn't been paid for three months, and restrained a violent impulse to shout with mirth. Soon I left them, hard, cold misfits in a passionate country, despising the cause for which they were fighting, sneering at the gaiety of the irrepressible Mexicans. And as I went away I said, "By the way; what company did you fellows belong to? What did you call yourselves?"

The red-haired youth answered, "The Foreign Legion!" he said.

It was late night when I finally got back to the hotel. Dona Louisa went ahead to see to my room, and I stopped a moment in the bar. Two or three soldiers, evidently officers, were drinking there—one pretty far gone. He was a pock-marked man with a trace of black mustache; his eyes couldn't seem to focus. But when he saw me he began to sing a pleasant little song:

> *Yo tengo un pistole*
> *Con mango de marfil*
> *Para matar todos los gringos*
> *Que viennen por ferrocarril!*

(I have a pistol with a marble handle
With which to kill all the Americans who come by railroad!)

I thought it diplomatic to leave, because you can never tell what a Mexican will do when he's drunk. His temperament is much too complicated.

Dona Louisa was in my room when I got there. With a mysterious finger to her lips she shut the door and produced from beneath her skirt a last year's copy of the Saturday Evening Post, in an incredible state of dissolution. "I got it out of the safe for you," she said. "The damn thing's worth more than anything in the house. I've been offered fifteen dollars for it by Americans going out to the mines. You see we haven't had any American magazines in a year now."

After that what could I do but read the precious magazine, although I had read it before. I lit the lamp, undressed, and got into bed. Just then came an unsteady step on the gallery outside and my door was flung violently open. Framed in it stood the pock-marked officer who had been drinking in the bar. In one hand he carried a big revolver. For a moment he stood blinking at me malevolently, then stepped inside and closed the door with a bang.

"I am Lieutenant Antonio Montoya, at your orders," he said. "I heard there was a gringo in this hotel and I have come to kill you."

"Sit down," said I politely. I saw he was drunkenly in earnest. He took off his hat, bowed politely and drew up a chair. Then he produced another revolver from beneath his coat and laid them both on the table. They were loaded.

"Would you like a cigarette?" I offered him the package. He took one, waved it in thanks and illumined it at the lamp. Then he picked up the guns and pointed them both at me. His fingers tightened slowly on the triggers, but relaxed again. I was too far gone to do anything but just wait.

"My only difficulty," said he, lowering his weapons, "is to determine which revolver I shall use."

"Pardon me," I quavered, "but they both appear a little obsolete. That Colt forty-five is certainly an 1895 model, and as for the Smith and Wesson, between ourselves it is only a toy."

"True," he answered, looking at them a little ruefully. "If I had only thought I would have brought my new automatic. My apologies, señor." He sighed and again directed the barrels at my chest, with an expression of calm happiness. "However, since it is so, we must make the best of it." I got ready to jump, to duck, to scream. Suddenly his eye fell upon the table, where my two-dollar wrist-watch was lying.

"What is that?" he asked.

"A watch!" Eagerly I demonstrated how to fasten it on. Unconsciously the pistols slowly lowered. With parted lips and absorbed attention he watched it delightedly, as a child watches the operation of some new mechanical toy.

"Ah," he breathed. "*Que esta bonita!* How pretty!"

"It is yours," said I, unstrapping it and offering it to him. He looked at the watch, then at me, slowly brightening and glowing with surprised joy. Into his outstretched hand I placed it. Reverently, carefully, he adjusted the thing to his hairy wrist. Then he rose, beaming down upon me. The revolvers fell unnoticed to the floor. Lieutenant Antonio Montoya threw his arms around me.

"Ah, *compadre!*" he cried emotionally.

The next day I met him at Valiente Adiana's store in the town. We sat amicably in the back room drinking native *aguardiente,* while Lieutenant Montoya, my best friend in the entire Constitutionalist army, told me of the hardships and perils of the campaign.

"Antonio," I said, "I am going on a long journey across the desert tomorrow. I am going to drive to Magistral. I need a *mozo*. I will pay three dollars a week."

" *'Sta bueno!*" cried Lieutenant Montoya. "Whatever you wish, so that I can go with my *amigo!*"

"But you are on active service," said I. "How can you leave your regiment?"

"Oh, that's all right," answered Antonio. "I won't say anything about it to my colonel. They don't need me. Why, they've got five thousand other men here."

In the early dawn, when yet the low gray houses and the dusty trees were stiff with cold, we laid a bull-whip on the backs of our two mules and rattled down the uneven streets of Jiménez and out into the open country. A few soldiers, wrapped to the eyes in their serapes, dozed beside their lanterns. There was a drunken officer sleeping in the gutter.

We drove an ancient buggy, whose broken pole was mended with wire. The harness was made of bits of old iron, rawhide and rope. Antonio and I sat side by side upon the seat, and at our feet dozed a dark, serious-minded youth named Primitivo Aguilar. Primitivo had been hired to open and shut gates, to tie up the harness when it broke, and to keep watch over wagon and mules at night, because bandits were reported to infest the roads.

The country became a vast fertile plain, cut up by irrigating ditches which were overshadowed by long lines of great alamo trees, leafless and gray as ashes. Like a furnace door, the white-hot sun blazed upon us, and the far-stretched barren fields reeked a thin mist. A cloud of white dust moved with us and around us.

That night we made camp beside an irrigation ditch miles from any house, in the middle of the bandit territory.

After a dinner of chopped up meat and peppers, *tortillas,* beans and black coffee, Antonio and I gave Primitivo his instructions. He was to keep watch beside the fire with Antonio's revolver and, if he heard anything, was to wake us. But on no account was he to go to sleep. If he did, we would kill him. Primitivo said, "Si, señor," very gravely, opened his eyes wide, and gripped the pistol. Antonio and I rolled up in our blankets by the fire.

I must have gone to sleep at once, because when I was awakened by Antonio's rising, my watch showed only half an hour later. From the place where Primitivo had been placed on guard came a series of hearty snores. The lieutenant walked over to him.

"Primitivo!" he said.

No answer.

"Primitivo, you cabron!" Our sentinel stirred in his sleep and turned over with noises indicative of comfort.

"Primitivo!" shouted Antonio, violently kicking him.

He gave absolutely no response.

Antonio drew back and launched a kick at his back that lifted him several feet into the air. With a start Primitivo woke. He started up alertly, waving the revolver.

"*Quien vive?*" cried Primitivo.

The next day took us out of the lowlands. We entered the desert, winding over a series of rolling plains, sandy and covered with black mesquit, with here and there an occasional cactus.... Night gathered straight above in the cloudless zenith, while all the skyline still was luminous with clear light, and then the light of day snuffed out, and stars burst out in the dome of heaven like a rocket.

Toward midnight we discovered that the road upon which we were traveling suddenly petered out in a dense mesquit thicket. Somewhere we had turned off the *Camino Real.* The mules were worn out. There seemed nothing for it but a "dry camp."

Now we had unharnessed the mules and fed them, and were lighting our fire, when somewhere in the dense thicket of chaparral stealthy foot-steps sounded. They moved a space and then were still. Our little blaze of greasewood crackled fiercely, lighting up a leaping, glowing radius of about ten feet. Beyond that all was black. Primitivo made one backward leap into the shelter of the wagon; Antonio drew his revolver, and we froze beside the fire. The sound came again.

"Who lives?" said Antonio. There was a little shuffling noise out in the brush, and then a voice.

"What party are you?" it asked hesitantly.

"Maderistas," answered Antonio. "Pass!"

"It is safe for *pacificos?*" queried the invisible one.

"On my word," I cried. "Come out that we may see you."

At that very moment two vague shapes materialized on the edge of the firelight glow, almost without a sound. Two peons, we saw as soon as they came close, wrapped tightly in their torn blankets. One was an old, wrinkled, bent man wearing homemade sandals, his trousers hanging in rags upon his shrunken legs; the other, very tall, barefooted youth, with a face so pure and so simple as to almost verge upon idiocy. Friendly, warm as sunlight, eagerly curious as children, they came forward, holding out their hands. We shook hands with each of them in turn, greeting them with elaborate Mexican courtesy.

At first they politely refused our invitation to dine, but after much urging we finally persuaded them to accept a few tortillas and chile. It was ludicrous and pitiful to see how wretchedly hungry they were, and how they attempted to conceal it from us.

After dinner, when they had brought us a bucket of water out of sheer kindly thoughtfulness, they stood for a while by our fire, smoking our cigarettes and holding out their hands to the blaze. I remember how their serapes hung from their shoulders, open in front so the grateful warmth could reach their thin bodies — and how gnarled and ancient were the old man's outstretched hands, and how the ruddy light glowed upon the other's throat, and kindled fires in his big eyes.... I suddenly conceived these two human beings as symbols of Mexico — courteous, loving, patient, poor, so long slaves, so full of dreams, so soon to be free.

"When we saw your wagon coming here," said the old man, smiling, "our hearts sank within us. We thought you were soldiers, come, perhaps, to take away our last few goats. So many soldiers have come in the last few years — so many. It is mostly the Federals — the Maderistas do not come unless they are hungry themselves. Poor Maderistas!"

"Ay," said the young man, "my brother that I loved very much died in the eleven days' fighting around Torreón. Thousands have died in Mexico, and still more thousands shall fall. Three years — it is long for war in a land. Too long." The old man murmured, "*Valgame Dios!*" and shook his head. "But there shall come a day — "

"It is said," remarked the old man quaveringly, "that the United States of the North covets our country — that gringo soldiers will come and take away my goats in the end...."

"That is a lie," exclaimed the other, animated. "It is the rich Americanos who want to rob us, just as the rich Mexicans want to rob us. It is the rich all over the world who want to rob the poor."

The old man shivered and drew his wasted body nearer to the fire. "I have often wondered," said he mildly, "why the rich, having so much, want so much. The poor, who have nothing, want very little. Just a few goats...."

His *compadre* lifted his chin like a noble, smiling gently. "I have never been out of this little country here — not even to Jiménez," he said. "But they tell me that there are many rich lands to the north and south and east. But this is my land and I love it. For the years of me, and my father and my grandfather, the rich men have gathered in the corn and held it in their clenched fists before our mouths. And only blood will make them open their hands to their brothers."

The fire died down. At his post slept the alert Primitivo. Antonio stared into the embers, a faint glorified smile upon his mouth, his eyes shining like stars.

"Adio!" he said suddenly, as one who sees a vision. "When we get into Mexico City what a *baile* shall be held! How drunk I shall get! ..."

The Mexican Tangle

JUNE 1916

AT last we have got ourselves into the apparently inextricable snarl in Mexico that the interventionists have always wanted. When Villa raided the town of Columbus, New Mexico, there was so much evidence that certain American interests were concerned in inciting him to cross the line and murder American citizens and soldiers, that even President Wilson made a public statement to the people of the United States warning them against "the sinister influences at work in this country" to force intervention on any pretext. The preparedness advocates, equally unscrupulous in their desire to make this a military nation in order that a strong army and navy shall be built up to encourage wholesale exploitation by American business men abroad, and to guard foreign interests of American speculators when they are obtained, do not hesitate to twist the events of the life and death struggle of the Mexican peons for freedom so as to bolster up their arguments. When Wilson refused to recognize Huerta, a treacherous murderer and adventurer, and when Huerta refused to be unrecognized, they told us that America was being "humiliated" and that "Mexico was laughing us to scorn." When an irresponsible minor officer refused to salute our stainless flag, they said again that "Mexico was making a laughing stock of us." When Villa, with a hundred odd followers, came over and shot up Columbus, they talked about the Mexican people "invading" the United States.

Once before the interventionists and the military party forced our army and navy to Vera Cruz, whooping it up for war and conquest all the time; stock in dishonestly obtained American concessions in Mexico flew skyward. But the President managed to get us out of Vera Cruz again without any damage being done.

When the punitive expedition went after Villa a month ago, there was another cry that intervention was coming, and this time those of us who know Mexico believed, and still believe, that they were right.

Things have grown to look more and more sinister down there. First it was our request to be allowed to use the Mexican railways to transport supplies and troops to the "punitive expedition"; refused by Carranza. Then came the rumors from Washington that Carranza had asked Washington to withdraw the American troops from Mexico, since confirmed. All this time a hundred different Mexican sources gave out their scarcely veiled hostile opinion that the Carranza soldiers could capture Villa unaided, and that the Americans never could. It was quite evident that the Mexican army was making very little attempt to do so. This is not astonishing; it looks like a miracle of self-restraint that the armies of the various Mexican generals have not united to attack the Americans before this. That attack is to be expected, for the Mexicans know as well as we do that this is the end of the working out of their revolution.

On April 14th the *de facto* government of Mexico gave out for publication the dispatches in the secret exchange of notes between Carranza and the United States, and revealed Carranza's terrible anxiety in the untenable position in which he now finds himself. If he permits the American army to march all over Mexico and stay months in the illusive chase of a bandit whom even Diaz's ten thousand *rurales* could not capture in twenty years, the Mexican peons will turn against their leader who encourages those *gringoes* whom all Mexicans secretly feel are the enemies of Mexico; if, on the other hand, he orders the American troops to withdraw, why then he knows that we will refuse and that the peons will try to drive us out by force. In either case there is not much chance for the President to accomplish his desire of capturing Villa, and there is not much chance for Mexico.

Such ultimatums as "Huerta must go," "The flag must be saluted," and "Villa dead or alive," leave very few loopholes for us to keep from conquering Mexico. When we don't do what we threaten to, the interventionists find a great opportunity to shout that we are "humiliated." Even after making these stern and dreadful boasts, the President up to now has had the courage to draw out of Mexico before it has been too late. But it looks as if he won't be able to do it this time.

We have refused to order the troops out of Mexico until Villa is captured. And it is almost impossible that Villa should be captured.

This morning (April 15) the papers tell of the second attack upon United States soldiers on the outskirts of the town of Parral. Parral is the center of the old Villa country. Villa himself passed through there a week ago, bound south for the desolate Durango Mountains, where live a race of insolent and independent Indians who have never known oppression, and who are Villa's blood-brothers. Even in the palmiest days of the Diaz regime the rurales kept out of that region. Criminals who escaped into the hills south of Parral were safe from further pursuit. It is an arid country of stony peaks, covered with cactus and sword-plants, without water; of bewildering trails winding through deep canyons and to the far camps of the charcoal-burners, who are Urbanistas and Villistas to a man—and *gringo*-haters as well.

All this part of the country was fed for twenty years by Villa and his band of outlaws, and protected against the rapacity and expropriation of the Diaz government officials and the rich. A large section of Carranza's army, commanded by Luis Herrera, comes from this region. Besides this, most of the Carranza soldiers drawn from Northern Mexico are Villistas at heart, and the rest consider him a half-mythical monster with a charmed life, who is always victorious in battle. The Mexican regular soldiers would probably not aid Villa against Carranza at this stage of the game, because Carranza is now promising all that Villa once promised, and Carranza's party is now the stronger. But when it comes to choosing between Villa and General Pershing, then Villa will get almost every Mexican's adherence.

Remember it was the townspeople of Parral who fired on the American troops. In other words, it is at last the Mexican peons, the workingmen, the *rancheros,* their children and their wives, who are rising against further American advance into Mexico. And as the American troops go farther south they enter more and more deeply the Villa country, the country of the *gringo*-haters, the region where Madero lived and where he first talked to the people, and where after his death the revolution against Huerta began.

Endymion, or On the Border

DECEMBER 1916

PRESIDIO, TEXAS, is a collection of a dozen adobe shacks and a two-story frame store, scattered in the brush in the desolate sand-flat along the Rio Grande. Northward the desert goes rolling gently up against the fierce, quivering blue, a blasted and silent land. The flat brown river writhes among its sand-bars like a lazy snake, not a hundred yards away. Across the river the Mexican town of Ojinaga tops its little *mesa* — a cluster of white walls, flat roofs, the cupolas of its ancient church — an Oriental town without a minaret. South of that the terrible waste flings out in great uptilted planes of sand, mesquite and sage-brush, crumpling at last into a surf of low sharp peaks on the horizon.

In Ojinaga lay the wreck of the Federalista army, driven out of Chihuahua by the victorious advance of Pancho Villa, and apathetically awaiting his coming here, by the friendly border. Thousands of civilians, scourged on by savage legends of the Tiger of the North, had accompanied the retreating soldiers across that ghastly four hundred miles of burning plain. Most of the refugees lay camped in the brush around Presidio, happily destitute, subsisting on the Commissary of the American Cavalry stationed here; sleeping all day, and singing, love-making and fighting all night.

The fortunes of war had thrust greatness upon Presidio. It figured in the news dispatches telephoned to the outer world by way of the single Army wire. Automobiles, gray with desert dust, roared down over the pack-trail from the railroad, seventy-five miles north, to corrupt its pristine innocence. A handful of war-correspondents sat there in the sand, cursing, and twice a day concocted two-hundred-word stories full of sound and fury. Wealthy *hacendados,* fleeing across the border, paused there to await the battle which should decide the fate of their property. Secret agents of the Constitutionalistas and the Federal plotted and counter-plotted all over the place. Representatives of big American interests distributed retaining fees, and sent incessant telegrams in code. Drummers for munition companies offered to supply arms wholesale and retail to anyone engaged in or planning a revolution. Not to mention — as they put it in musical comedy programs — citizens, Rangers, deputy Sheriffs, United States troopers, Huertista officers on furlough, Customs officials, cowpunchers from nearby ranches, miners, etc.

Old Schiller, the German store-keeper, went bellowing around with a large revolver strapped to his waist. Schiller was growing rich. He supplied food and clothing and tools and medicines to the swollen population; he had a monopoly on the freighting business; he was rumored to conduct a poker game and private bar in the back room; and sixty men slept on the floor and counters of his store for twenty-five cents a head.

I went around with a bow-legged, freckle-faced cowboy named Buchanan, who had been working on a ranch down by Santa Rosalia, and was waiting for things to clear up so he could go back. Buck had been three years in Mexico, but I couldn't discover it had left any impression on his mind — except a grievance against Mexicans for not speaking English; all his Spanish being a few words to satisfy his natural appetites. But he occasionally mentioned Dayton, Ohio — from which city he had fled on a freight-train at the age of twelve.

He seemed to be a common-enough type down there; a strong, lusty body, brave, hard, untroubled by any spark of fine feeling. But I hadn't been with him many hours before he began to talk of Doc. According to Buck, Doc was Presidio's first citizen; he was a great surgeon, and more than that, one of the world's best musicians. But more remarkable than everything, to me, was the pride and affection in Buck's voice when he told of his friend.

"He kin set a busted laig with a grease-wood twig and a horse-hair riata," said Buck, earnestly. "And curing up a t'rant'ler bite ain't no more to him than taking a drink is to you or me. . . . And play — say! Doc kin play any kind of a thing. By God. I guess if anybody from New York or Cleveland was to hear him tickle them instruments, he would be a-setting on the Opera House stage right now, instead of in the sand at Presidio!"

I was interested. "Doc who?" I asked.

Buck looked surprised. "Why, just Doc," he said.

After supper that night I plowed through the sand in the direction of Doc's adobe cabin. It was a still night, with great stars. From somewhere up the river floated down the sound of a few lazy shots. All around in the brush flared the fires of the refugee camps; women screamed nasally to their children to come home; girls laughed out in the darkness; men with spurs "ka-junked" past in the sand; and like an accompaniment in the base sounded the insistent mutter of a score of secret agents conspiring on the porch of Schiller's store. Long before I came near, I could hear the familiar strains of the *Tannhauser* overture played on a castrated melodeon; and immediately in front of the house, I almost stumbled over a double row of Mexicans, squatting in the sand, wrapped to the eyes in serapes, rigidly listening.

Within the one white-washed room, two U.S. cavalry officers sat with their eyes closed, pretending to enjoy what they considered "high-brow" entertainment. They had been eight months on the Border, far from the refinements of civilization, and it made them feel "cultured" to hear that kind of music. Buchanan, smoking a corn-cob pipe, lay stretched in an armchair, his feet on the stove, his glistening eyes fixed with frank enjoyment on Doc's fingers as they hopped over the keys. Doc himself sat with his back to us—a pathetic, pudgy, white-haired little figure. Some of the melodeon keys produced no sound at all; others a faint wheeze; and the rest were out of tune. As he played he sang huskily, and swayed back and forth as one rapt in harmony.

It was a remarkable room. At one end stood the wreck of an elaborate glass-topped operating-table. Behind it, a case of rusty surgical instruments—the top shelf full of pill bottles—and a book-case containing five volumes: a book of Operatic Selections scored for the piano, part of a volume of Beethoven's Symphonies arranged for four hands, two volumes on Practical Diagnosis, and The Poems of John Keats, moroccobound, hand-tooled, and worn. There was a desk, too, piled with papers. And all around the rest of the room were musical instruments in various stages of desuetude; concertina, violin, guitar, French horn, cornet, harp. A small Mexican hairless dog, with a cataract in one eye, sat at Doc's feet, his nose lifted to the ceiling, howling continuously.

Doc played more and more furiously, humming as his gnarled fingers jumped over the keyboard. Suddenly, in the midst of a thundering chord, he stopped, turned half around to us, and stretching out his hands, mumbled through his whiskers:

"M' hands are too small! Every damn thing's wrong about me somewheres. Aye!" He sighed. "Franz Liszt had short fingers, too. Hee! Not like mine. No short fingers in the head ..." his words ran off into indistinguishable mumbling.

Buck brought his feet down with a crash, and slapped his knee.

"God, Doc!" he cried. "If you had big hands I don't know what in hell you couldn't do!"

Doc looked dully at the floor. The little dog put his feet upon his lap and whimpered, and the old man laid a trembling hand on his head. The two officers awkwardly took their leave. Presently Doc lit up a great pipe, grumbling and groaning to himself, the smoke oozing out of his mustache, nose, eyes and ears.

With a sort of reverence Buck introduced me. Doc nodded, and looked at me with bleary little eyes that didn't seem to see. His round, puffy face was covered with a white stubble; through a yellow, ragged mustache came indistinctly the ruins of a cultivated articulation. He smelt strongly of brandy.

"Aye—you're not one of these—sand-fleas umbleumbleumble," he said, blinking up at me. "From the great world. From the great world. Tell 'em my name is writ in water umbleumble."

No one knew anything about him except what he had dropped when drunk. He himself seemed to have forgotten his past. The Mexicans, among whom most of his practise was, loved him devotedly, and showed it by paying their bills. He always made the same charge for any medical service—setting a fracture, amputating a limb, delivering a child, or giving a dose of cough-syrup—twenty-five cents. But he had spoken of London, Queen's Hall, the Conservatory of Music, and of being in India and Egypt, and of coming to Galveston as head of a hospital. Beyond that, nothing but the names of Mexican cities, of unknown people. All that Presidio knew of him was that he had come across the border nameless and drunk during the Madero revolution, and had stayed there nameless and drunk ever since.

"On the Maidan!" said Doc suddenly, "Riding in their carriages! And I—here...." He rumbled on for a while, and hiccoughed. "Yes, it killed her, but I wasn't—"

I sat talking with him, trying to strike upon some key that would unlock his life.

"I hear you have been connected with the London Conservatory of Music."

He leaped to his feet, clenching both fists, and glared around. "Who said that?" he roared. Then he sat down again. "And now I am an old tramp doctor in Presidio!" he finished, and chuckled without bitterness.

I tried him with Egypt, and he said, "In those days there was a forest of masts in Alexandria roadstead—thick...." Then I spoke of India, but he only muttered, "In Darjelling—at the big deodar on the law. Oh God ... umbleumble...."

"Galveston!" he cried, and straightened up. "Yes I was in Galveston when the flood—My wife was drowned...." He said this without much feeling, and rising, went unsteadily to the book-case and took down one of the Practical Diagnosis books, which he brought back to me as a child might have done. On the fly-leaf was the date "Galveston, September 18, 1901," and newspaper clippings about the flood were stuck crazily underneath. I took it back to the book-case, and carelessly picking up the Poems of John Keats, opened it. Inside the cover was written, in ink that had almost faded:

June, 1878.
To Endymion—
With my body and soul—
A. deH. K.

Endymion—he! To what woman was that battered old wreck ever Endymion? 1878. In his middle twenties, perhaps—beautiful, a dreamer.

I heard a sort of moaning snarl, and looked up to see Doc upon his feet, bent over and peering at me strangely.

"What have you got? What have you got?" he almost screamed. "Put it down...." As he came lurching at me I slipped the book back in the case. He grasped my two hands and lifted them up to his eyes, then dropped them and turned.

"Nothing," he mumbled. "I had forgotten.... I lost it in Monterey...." He stood still, muttering to himself. "Now what brought her back—drowned for thirty years? Well, drown her all over again!" He went to the corner and got a black bottle and tilted it to his lips. Then he reached down among his instruments and pulled out an old accordion, and sitting down in his chair again, began suddenly to play what could be recognized as Beethoven's Third Symphony. It was startling.

But he played only a minute; stopped, shook his head and sighed. "Eroica!" he said. "Eroica!" Umbleumbleumble. What do you sand-fleas know about high tragedy? I'm getting old and I've hunted all my life and never found—" From what? Fame? Wealth? Love? *Truth?* ...

The next evening we had supper, Buchanan, Doc and I, in a one-room Mexican restaurant, whose proprietor had once owned a little ranch across the river which Enrique Creel sold to William Randolph Hearst and pocketed the proceeds. As big, brown men, booted and spurred, came in, each one stopped at the head of the table to say "Howdye Doc! How ya coming?" The Mexican waiter served Doc first, and when a rich cattleman who had motored in that morning began cursing him for a lazy Greaser, one of the Rangers leaned over and tapped him on the arm.

"Doc gets his first, stranger," he said quietly. "After that you kin put *your* foot in the trough."

Doc had risen late, tormented by the fires of hell; and though he had already gulped down about a quart of *aguardiente,* it hadn't yet taken effect. He was black and silent, answering the greetings with a grunt.

Next to me sat a brisk little man with a retreating chin, a denizen of cities. He was agent for the Crayon Enlargement Home Portrait Company, of Kansas City, Mo., and was greatly pleased with the amount of business he had done in Presidio, taking pictures and getting orders from the Mexicans. The table sat listening to his piping little boasts with grave faces and insides full of mirth. As Buck explained to me afterward, a Mexican loves to get his picture taken; and a Mexican will order anything, or sign his name to anything — but he won't pay for it.

"Mexicans are fine subjects for photography," the agent was saying, enthusiastically. "They will hold a pose for fifteen minutes without moving—"

Doc suddenly lifted his head, rumbled a little and said distinctly,

"That is why I didn't have mine finished. It was hard work to pose for Freddie Watts umbleumbleumble."

"You mean in London?" I asked quickly.

"Hampste'd," answered Doc, absently. "His studio was in Hampste'd...."

So if Doc hadn't been tired of posing, his portrait might be hanging with those of William Morris, Rossetti, George Meredith, Swinburne, Browning, in the National Gallery!

"Did you know William Morris?" I said, breathlessly.

"A damned prig!" shouted Doc suddenly, beating his fist on the table. Eagerly I asked him about the others; but he went on eating, as if he didn't hear. "Dilletantes — an age of petty amateurs!" he cried finally, and would say no more.

The Crayon Enlargement agent tapped his head to the company and jerked a thumb at Doc. "Non-compos, ain't he?" he remarked with a knowing grin. "Bats in his attic, hey?" A prolonged hostile stare met his eyes. Down at the foot of the table a taciturn cowboy pointed a piece of bread at him, and remarked briefly:

"You wooden-headed *cabrito,* you better close up. Doc here's a friend of mine, and he's forgot more'n you'll ever know."

Doc never seemed to notice. But as we went outside afterward I heard him mutter something about "sand-fleas." We walked over toward a little shack where a pool-table had been set up, and I tried to find out just when he had dropped out of "the great world." He responded to the name of Pasteur, but Ehrlich, Freud and the other modern medical names I knew evidently meant nothing to him. In music, Saint-Saens was evidently an interesting youngster and no more; Straus, Debussy, Schoenberg, even Rimsky-Korsakoff, were Greek to him. Brahms he hated, for some reason.

There was a game on in the pool-room when we came in but some one set up a shout "Here comes Doc!" and the players laid down their cues. Doc and Buchanan played on the rickety table, while I sat by. The old man's game was magnificent; he never seemed to miss a shot, no matter how difficult, though he could hardly see the balls. Buck hardly got a chance to shoot. Around the walls on the ground sat a solid belt of Mexicans in high wide sombreros, with *serapes* of magnificent faded colors, great boot buckles and spurs as big as dollars. When Doc made a good shot a chorus of soft applause came from them. When he fumbled and dropped his pipe, ten hands scrambled for the honor of retrieving it. . . .

In the soft, deep, velvety night we started home through the sand. We had gone a little distance when Doc suddenly stopped.

"Here, Tobey! Here, Tobey!" he cried, swaying and peering around in the dark. "I've lost my little dog. I wonder where that little dog is? I guess he must be back at the pool hall. Here, Tobey! I've got to go back and find my little dog."

"Hell, Doc," said Buck impatiently, "your dog'll come back all right. Let me go and get him for you. You're tired."

Doc shook his head, mumbling. "I've got to find my little dog," he said, "nobody can find — anything for me. Each has got to seek — alone umbleumble," and he turned back.

Buck and I squatted down by the trail and lit cigarettes. Around us the thick, exotic night was rich with sounds and smells. Buck abruptly began to speak:

"I don't remember nothing about my father," he said, "except he was a son of a b———. But I thought all old men was like him; in fact, I never met a real man or any other kind of man who wasn't out for himself, until I run across Doc. All that Christian bunk never was nothing to me until now. But that Doc, he's got a kind of combination of awful goodness and just suffering like hell all the time that — well, I don't know but I — I — love that man. And great — he's a great man! I know that. He's big all through. Some damn fools around here say he's crazy; but I sometimes think all the rest of us is. He is drunk all the time, Doc is, but everything he says, even the wildest things, somehow hit me way deep down like God's truth."

Buck stopped, and we saw the chunky little figure of Doc loom up staggering in the dark, with Tobey trotting at his heels. We got up silently and walked along, one on each side of him. He didn't seem to notice us, mumbling and hiccoughing to himself. But suddenly he heaved a tremendous sigh, threw out both arms, and with his poor dim eyes on the sky, said:

"Heigh-ho! Night for the Gentiles is day-time for the Children of Israel!"

III. World War I:
Europe at the Abyss

THE SUMMER of 1914, remembered afterwards as warm and sunny and "idyllic," has remained a symbol of all that has been innocently but irrevocably lost. Though Archduke Francis Ferdinand was assassinated on June 28, actual hostilities between the great powers did not occur until August 3, when Germany declared war on France and invaded Belgium and Luxembourg. England responded the next day with a declaration of war on Germany, and the Great War had officially begun. When the fighting ceased, four years later, an estimated ten million people had died, and another twenty million had been wounded in what John Reed referred to as a "trader's war," a "falling out among commercial rivals."

Reed was bitterly opposed to the war. He regarded it not as an aberration, but as a natural outgrowth of the competition between capitalist nations whose nationalism and imperialism forever brought them into conflict. He wrote in an unpublished article, "Rule Britannia," that "this war seems to be the supreme expression of European civilization," the inevitable result of the militarism which was the "crowning fact" of our time.[15] "We, who are socialists, must hope," he wrote in "The Trader's War," "that out of this horror of destruction will come far-reaching social changes." In this Reed, and international socialism in general, would be disappointed.

Nevertheless, Reed agreed to cover the war for *Metropolitan Magazine* for the highly respectable salary of $500 per month. He arrived in Europe in late August, and by early September he was in Paris, where defeated English and French soldiers straggled into the city and rumors circulated that German troops were advancing on the French capital. On September 9, while the Battle of the Marne raged, Reed and Robert Dunn of the *New York Evening Post* hired a car to take them to the front. Outside of Paris they found confusion and chaos: army units advanced and retreated, while refugees clotted the roads, bringing with them whatever possessions they could carry. Before Reed and Dunn reached the front, they were arrested by French gendarmes and forced to sign a written promise to keep out of the military zone. Meanwhile, at the Marne, unknown to Reed, the British and French forces managed to stop the German advance on Paris — at a cost of half a million casualties on each side.

117

After a brief trip to London, Reed returned to France and again attempted to reach the front. Again he was arrested and forced to return to Paris empty-handed. When he tried to write, he could produce only abstract denunciations of the war, nothing suitable for publication in *Metropolitan Magazine* or *The Masses*. Where he had always written so effortlessly, now his writing was forced, labored. He could not write about this "ghastly" war as he had about Mexico, for the European war had "none of the spontaneity, none of the idealism of the Mexican revolution. It was a war of the workshops, and the trenches were factories turning out ruin—ruin of the spirit as well as of the body, the real and only death," he wrote.[16]

In December Reed traveled to Berlin, where he interviewed the socialist Karl Liebknecht, who was one of the few members of the Reichstag to oppose the war. Liebknecht held on to the belief that out of the war would come a worldwide socialist revolution, but Reed was not so optimistic.

Finally, on January 11, Reed and Robert Dunn visited the German front lines a few miles south of Ypres, traversing a countryside laid to waste by relentless artillery barrages—a ghostly land of craters, broken tree trunks, and ruined villages. They found the trenches a nightmare of mud and disease, where the German soldiers crouched like beasts in the darkness, waiting for the next attack or counterattack. Before leaving, Reed and Dunn, half-jokingly, fired a rifle in the general direction of the Allied lines. The gesture would come back to haunt them later; when Dunn published his account of the incident, both correspondents were barred from the Western Front.

Reed returned to America toward the end of January with virtually nothing to show for his five months in Europe. His contribution to the February 1915 issue of *The Masses,* "A Daughter of the Revolution," was the first article whose quality equaled that of the work he had done in Mexico. However, in the very next issue he returned to angry polemics in "The Worst Thing in Europe," an article that only *The Masses* would print as the editorial policies of magazines and newspapers, reflecting the mood of the nation, moved closer to open support of the Allies and, finally, intervention. Even *Metropolitan Magazine* expressed dissatisfaction with Reed's work; in a last effort to employ him as their correspondent, they sent him in late March to the Balkans to cover the war on the Eastern Front (where he was not regarded as a traitor and an assassin, as the French *Le Temps* had branded him after the rifle incident in the German trenches became public).

Reed fared better on the Eastern Front. Though he still found the war senseless, it was at least senseless on a smaller, more human scale; there were no great military machines here, only ragged, demoralized armies fighting inefficiently. In Serbia he interviewed an artillery captain who had been a socialist leader before the war and who had, he confessed to Reed, lost his faith in a better world. The experience became the material for "The World Well Lost," published in the February 1916 issue of *The Masses*. Reed also visited Goutchevo Mountain, where the Austrian and Serbian armies had fought each other for fifty-four days in trenches twenty yards apart, and where parts of ten thousand human bodies protruded from mounds of churned-up earth between the trenches. Reed described the horrible scene: "We walked on the dead, so thick were they—sometimes our feet sank through into pits of rotting flesh, crunching bones. Little holes opened suddenly, leading deep down and swarming with gray maggots. Most of the bodies were covered only with a film of earth, partly washed away by the rain—many were not buried at all."[17]

Reed remained in the Balkans until early October, traveling in Hungary and Romania and Russia, where he was arrested again for entering a war zone. He returned to New York suffering from a kidney ailment and spent the next several months writing from his notes. The ensuing articles, written for *Metropolitan Magazine,* were generally better than the work he had done, or had attempted to do, on the Western Front. In April 1916, he collected the articles and published them with Scribner's as *The War in Eastern Europe*. The book received favorable reviews, but by this time, as war fever began sweeping America, his audience was more interested in what was happening in western Europe. As a result, *The War in Eastern Europe* sold considerably fewer copies than *Insurgent Mexico*.

Of the articles that Reed published in *The Masses* during this time, the two most important are "A Daughter of the Revolution" (February 1915) and "The World Well Lost" (February 1916). The first and longer of the two articles involves a woman—here called Marcelle—whom Reed had met at a Paris cafe in November 1914. Reed sets the scene in such a way as to evoke a sense of melancholy and loss: he and Marcelle sit on the *terrasse* of the Rotonde, while outside soldiers march by in the rain. Responding to talk of the revolution to come, Marcelle laughs bitterly and interrupts the speaker by singing, or mocking, the last lines of the *Internationale*. Three generations of her "worthless family" have been socialists, and she wants nothing more to do with those "villains" who wish to overthrow everything, she explains to Reed. However, after some encouragement, she tells the story of her family and provides a fascinating chronicle of the struggle of socialism in France. Her grandfather had been shot against a wall at Père Lachaise for carrying a red flag in the Commune of 1870, and her father was a veteran of many strikes and as many beatings by the police. Marcelle's description of her father conjures up in Reed's imagination "the picture of this coarse, narrow, sturdy old warrior, scarred with the marks of a hundred vain, ignoble fights with the police, reeling home through squalid streets after union meetings, his eyes blazing with visions of a regenerated humanity."

And her brother, Marcelle laughs, was even worse than her father. He, too, would organize and lead strikes, but he had a "lashing, gallant way that made all the comrades love him." He would do things such as go to a cabaret or music hall after work and burst out singing the *Internationale,* shouting down whatever entertainers happened to be performing. Marcelle explains that

> When he had finished, he would cry: "How do you like that?" and then they would cheer and applaud him. Then he would shout "Everybody say with me 'Down with the capitalists! *A bas* the police! To the Lanterne with the *flics!*'" Then there would be some cheers and some whistles. "Did I hear somebody whistle me?" he'd cry. "I'll meet anybody at the door outside who dared to whistle me!" And afterward he would fight ten or fifteen men in a furious mob in the street outside, until the police came....

When her brother did his military service and became a corporal, he refused to command the soldiers in his squad. "Why should I give orders to these comrades? . . . One orders me to command them to dig a trench. *Voyons,* are they slaves?" he asked. When his superiors demoted him to the ranks, he organized a revolt and advised his comrades to shoot their officers. And now, ironically, her brother once again has been conscripted into the army and shipped off to the trenches with all the other young men of Paris, Marcelle says. She does not know if he is alive or dead.

Marcelle's attitude toward her family is crucial to an understanding of this article. As she tells her tale, she remains "half-ashamed, half-pleased, wholly ironical." She professes to be estranged from her father, who disowned her because of her desire for fine clothes and jewelry, and because of her decision to become a mistress and lover. And yet it gradually becomes clear to Reed (and his readers) that Marcelle loves and respects them all. In fact, her desire for "freedom," which she mentions many times, springs from the same "dim dream of liberty" that guided the actions and the socialist politics of her grandfather, her father, and her brother. Ironically, Reed and his readers understand this, but Marcelle only half-consciously makes the connection when, asked whether she regrets her life, she responds proudly: "*Dame,* no! I'm free!"

Reed's portrait of international socialism in "A Daughter of the Revolution" remains hopeful, if realistic. Though he acknowledges, through his personifications, that socialists had sacrificed and suffered for generations, he finds their struggle against repression and economic exploitation to be, if not transcendent, at least enduring. Marcelle and her brother especially, as Reed describes them, maintain a spirit, a sense of humor, and a love of freedom that continue to inspire, even in defeat. Here there is still the shared belief in the possibility of a better world.

In contrast, "The World Well Lost" (February 1916) offers a much darker view of the future of socialism—its power to resist, or even to survive the war. One can chart Reed's deepening pessimism from "A Daughter of the Revolution" to "The World Well Lost," published exactly one year later. After a year and a half of trench warfare, the Serbian town of Obrenovatz looks as though it belongs in a different century from the Paris of November 1914. Here, mocking the very idea of freedom, thousands of human corpses lie unburied on the mountain summits, among the powdered remains of the mountainsides, where "half-starved dogs battle . . . ghoulishly with vultures." The war, the dull, monotonous business of killing, has become the only reality for the Serbian soldiers, who have forgotten what life was like before the war.

One such Serbian, a former socialist by the name of Takits, speaks with a bitter sense of loss that Reed obviously shares. Takits tells Reed that he has come to believe that civilization will have to be rebuilt after the war. He says:

> . . . Again we must learn to till the soil, to live together under a common government, to make friends across frontiers among other races who have become once more only dark, evil faces and speakers of tongues not our own. This world has become a place of chaos, as it was in the Dark Ages. . . . Afterward will come the long pull up from barbarism to a time when men think and reason and consciously organize their lives again. . . . But that will not be in our time. I shall die without seeing it, —the world we loved and lost.

However, with "extraordinary emotion," Takits confesses to Reed that he has lost faith in the possibility of such regeneration. The war, he says, has become his entire life—when he goes home on leave to visit his wife and children, their existence seems so "tame" that he becomes restless and longs to return to "my friends here, my work, —my guns." As Takits finishes his speech, rifle-shots again ring out on the mountain, providing an ominous conclusion to an already pessimistic article.

Subsequent events did not change Reed's pessimistic view of the war. By mid-1916, after the disastrous Allied attack on the Somme in which at least 60,000 men were killed in a single day, the war settled into a stalemate where first one side attacked, advanced a few hundred yards at the cost of thousands of lives, then the other side attacked, etc. Both sides began to realize that the war could not be won. But neither could it be stopped.

A Daughter of the Revolution

FEBRUARY 1915

THAT night there was one of those Paris rains, which never seem to wet one as other rains do. We sat on the *terrasse* of the Rotonde, at the corner table—it was a warm night, though November—Fred, Marcelle and I, sipping a Dubonnet. The cafés all closed at eight sharp because of the war, and we used to stay until then almost every night before we went to dinner.

Next to us was a young French officer with his head done up in a bandage, and his arm comfortably around Jeanne's green-caped shoulder. Beatrice and Alice were farther down along under the glare of the yellow lights. Behind us we could peek through a slit in the window-curtain and survey the smoke-filled room inside, an uproarious band of men sandwiched between girls, beating on the table and singing, the two old Frenchmen at their tranquil chess-game, an absorbed student writing a letter home, his *amie's* head on his shoulder, five utter strangers and the waiter listening breathlessly to the tales of a muddy-legged soldier back from the front....

The yellow lights flooded us, and splashed the shining black pavement with gold; human beings with umbrellas flowed by in a steady stream; a ragged old wreck of a man poked furtively for cigarette-butts under our feet; out in the roadway the shuffling feet of men marching fell unheeded upon our accustomed ears, and dripping slanted bayonets passed athwart a beam of light from across the Boulevard Montparnasse.

This year all the girls at the Rotonde dressed alike. They had little round hats, hair cut short, low-throated waists and long capes down to their feet, the ends tossed over their shoulders Spanish-fashion. Marcelle was the image of the others. Besides, her lips were painted scarlet, her cheeks dead white, and she talked obscenities when she wasn't on her dignity, and sentimentalities when she was. She had regaled us both with the history of her very rich and highly respectable family, of the manner of her tragic seduction by a Duke, of her innate virtue—and had remarked proudly that she was no common ordinary street-walker....

At this particular instant she was interlarding a running fire of highly-flavored comment upon what passed before her eyes, with appeals for money in a harshened little voice; and I thought to myself that we had got to the bottom of Marcelle. Her comments upon things and persons were pungent, vigorous, original — but they palled after while; a strain of recklessness and unashamed love of life held only a little longer. Marcelle was already soiled with too much handling. . . .

We heard a violent altercation, and a tall girl with a bright orange sweater came out from the café, followed by a waiter gesticulating and exclaiming:

"But the eight anisettes which you ordered, *nom de Dieu!*"

"I have told you I would pay," she shrilled over her shoulder. "I am going to the Dome for some money," and she ran across the shiny street. The waiter stood looking after her, moodily jingling the change in his pockets.

"No use waiting," shouted Marcelle, "There is another door to the Dome on the Rue Delambre!" But the waiter paid no attention; he had paid the *caisse* for the drinks. And, as a matter of fact, the girl never re-appeared.

"That is an old trick," said Marcelle to us. "It is easy when you have no money to get a drink from the waiters, for they dare not ask for your money until afterward. It is a good thing to know now in time of war, when the men are so few and so poor. . . ."

"But the waiter!" objected Fred. "He must make his living!"

Marcelle shrugged. "And we ours," she said.

"There used to be a *belle type* around the Quarter," she continued after a minute, "who called herself Marie. She had beautiful hair — *épatante,* — and she loved travelling. . . . Once she found herself on a Mediterranean boat bound for Egypt without a *sou,* — nothing except the clothes on her back. A monsieur passed her as she leaned against the rail, and said, 'You have marvellous hair, mademoiselle.'

"'I will sell it to you for a hundred francs,' she flashed back. And she cut off all her beautiful hair and went to Cairo, where she met an English lord. . . ."

The waiter heaved a prodigious sigh, shook his head sadly, and went indoors. We were silent, and thought of dinner. The rain fell.

I don't know how it happened, but Fred began to whistle absent-mindedly the *Carmagnole*. I wouldn't have noticed it, except that I heard a voice chime in, and looked around to see the wounded French officer, whose arm had fallen idly from the shoulder of Jeanne, staring blankly across the pavement, and humming the *Carmagnole*. What visions was he seeing, this sensitive-faced youth in the uniform of his country's army, singing the song of revolt! Even as I looked, he caught himself up short, looked conscious and startled, glanced swiftly at us, and rose quickly to his feet, dragging Jeanne with him.

At the same instant Marcelle clutched Fred roughly by the arm.

"It's *défendu*—you'll have us all pinched," she cried, with something so much stronger than fear in her eyes that I was interested. "And, besides, don't sing those dirty songs. They are revolutionary—they are sung by *voyous*—poor people—ragged men—"

"Then you are not a revolutionist yourself?" I asked.

"I? *B'en* no, I swear to you!" she shook her head passionately. "The *méchants,* the villains, who want to overturn everything—!" Marcelle shivered.

"Look here, Marcelle! Are you happy in this world the way it is? What does the System do for you, except to turn you out on the street to sell yourself?" Fred was launched now on a boiling flood of propaganda. "When the red day comes, I know which side of the Barricades I shall be on—!"

Marcelle began to laugh. It was a bitter laugh. It was the first time I had ever seen her un–self-conscious.

"*Ta gueule,* my friend," she interrupted rudely. "I know that talk! I have heard it since I was so high.... I *know!*" She stopped and laughed to herself, and wrenched out—"My grandfather was shot against a wall at Père Lachaise for carrying a red flag in the Commune in 1870." She started, looked at us shame-facedly, and grinned. "There, you see I come of a worthless family...."

"Your grandfather!" shouted Fred.

"Pass for my grandfather," said Marcelle indifferently. "Let the crazy, dirty-handed old fool rest in his grave. I have never spoken of him before, and I shall burn no candles for his soul...."

Fred seized her hand. He was exalted. "God bless your grandfather!"

With the quick wit of her profession, she divined that, for some mysterious reason, she had pleased. For answer she began to sing in a low voice the last lines of the *Internationale.*

"*C'est la lutte finale*—" She coquetted with Fred.

"Tell us more about your grandfather," I asked.

"There is no more to tell," said Marcelle, half-ashamed, half-pleased, wholly ironical. "He was a wild man from God knows where. He had no father and mother. He was a stone-mason, and people say a fine work-man. But he wasted his time in reading books, and he was always on strike. He was a savage, and always roaring 'Down with the Government and the rich!' People called him 'Le Farou.' I remember my father telling how the soldiers came to take him from his house to be shot. My father was a lad of fourteen, and he hid my grandfather under a mattress of the bed. But the soldiers poked their bayonets in there and one went through his shoulder – so they saw the blood. Then my grandfather made a speech to the soldiers – he was always making speeches – and asked them not to murder the Commune.... But they only laughed at him – " And Marcelle laughed, for it was amusing.

"But my father – " she went on; "Heavens! He was even worse. I can remember the big strike at the Creusot works, – wait a minute, – it was the year of the Great Exposition. My father helped to make that strike. My brother was then just a baby, – eight years he had, and he was already working as poor children do. And in the parade of all the strikers, suddenly my father heard a little voice shouting to him across the ranks, – it was my little brother, marching with a red flag, like one of the comrades!

"'Hello, old boy!' he called to my father. *'Ca ira!'*

"They shot many workmen in that strike." Marcelle shook her head viciously. "Ugh! The scum!"

Fred and I stirred, and found that we had been chilled from resting in one position. We beat on the window and ordered cognac.

"And now you have heard enough of my miserable family," said Marcelle, with an attempt at lightness.

"Go on," said Fred hoarsely, fixing her with gleaming eyes.

"But you're going to take me to dinner, *n'est-ce pas?*" insinuated Marcelle. I nodded. *"Pardié!"* she went on, with a grin. "It was not like this that my father dined – he! After my grandfather died, my old man could get no work. He was starving, and went from house to house begging food. But they shut the door in his face, the women of my grandfather's comrades, saying 'Give him nothing, the *salaud;* he is the son of Le Farrou, who was shot.' And my father sneaked around the café tables, like a dog, picking up crusts to keep his soul and body together. It has taught me much," said Marcelle, shaking her short hair. "To keep always in good relations with those who feed you. It is why I do not steal from the waiter like that girl did; and I tell everybody that my family was respectable. They might make me suffer for the sins of my father, as he did for his father's."

Light broke upon me, and once more the puzzling baseness of humanity justified itself. Here was the key to Marcelle, her weakness, her vileness. It was not vice, then, that had twisted her, but the intolerable degradation of the human spirit by the masters of the earth, the terrible punishment of those who thirst for liberty.

"I can remember," she said, "how, after the Creusot strike was ended, the bosses got rid of their troublesome workmen. It was winter, and for weeks we had had only wood that my mother gathered in the fields, to keep us warm – and a little bread and coffee that the Union gave us. I wasn't but four years old. My father decided to go to Paris, and we started—walking. He carried me on his shoulder, and with the other a little bundle of clothes. My mother carried another—but she had already tuberculosis, and had to rest every hour. My brother came behind.... We went along the white, straight road, with the light snow lying on it, between the high naked poplars. Two days and a night.... We huddled down in a deserted road-mender's hut, my mother coughing, coughing. Then out again before the sun rose, tramping along through the snow, my father and my brother shouting revolutionary cries, and singing

> 'Dansons la Carmagnole
> 'Vive le son—Vive le son—
> 'Dansons la Carmagnole
> 'Vive le son du canon!'"

Marcelle had raised her voice unconsciously as she sang the forbidden song; her cheeks flushed, her eyes snapped, she stamped her foot. Suddenly she broke off and looked fearfully around. No one had noticed, however.

"My brother had a high, little voice like a girl, and my father used to break off laughing as he looked down at his son stamping sturdily along beside him, and roaring out songs of hate like an old striker.

"'Allons! Petit cheminot,—you little tramp you! I'll bet the police will know you some day!' And he would slap him on the back. It made my mother turn pale, and sometimes at night she would slip out of bed and go to the corner where my brother slept, and wake him up to tell him, weeping, that he must always grow up to be a good man. Once my father woke up and caught her.... But that was later, at Paris....

"And they would sing—

> 'Debout freres de misere!
> (Up! Brothers of misery!)
> 'Ne voulons plus de frontieres
> (We want no more frontiers)
> 'Pour egorger la bourgeoisie
> (To loot the bourgeoisie)
> 'Et supprimer la tyrranie
> (And suppress tyranny)
> 'Il faut avoir du coeur
> (We must have heart)
> 'Et de l'energie!'
> (And energy!)

"And then my father would look ahead with flashing eyes, marching as if he were an army. Every time his eyes flashed like that, my mother would tremble, — for it meant some reckless and terrible fight with the police, or a bloody strike, and she feared for him. . . . And I know how she must have felt, for she was law-abiding, like me — and my father, he was no good." Marcelle shuddered, and gulped her cognac at one swallow.

"I really did not begin myself to know things until we came to Paris," she went on, "because then I began to grow up. My first memory, almost, is when my father led the big strike at Thirion's, the coal-yard down there on the avenue de Maine, and came home with his arm broken where the police had struck him. After that it was work, strike, — work, strike — with little to eat at our house and my mother growing weaker until she died. My father married again, a religious woman, who finally took to going continually to church and praying for his immortal soul. . . .

"Because she knew how fiercely he hated God. He used to come home at night every week after the meeting of the Union, his eyes shining like stars, roaring blasphemies through the streets. He was a terrible man. He was always the leader. I remember when he went out to assist at a demonstration on Montmartre. It was before the Sacré Coeur, the big white church you see up there on the top of the mountain, looking over all Paris. You know the statue of the Chevalier de la Barre just below it? It is of a young man in ancient times who refused to salute a religious procession; a priest broke his arm with the cross they carried, and he was burned to death by the Inquisition. He stands there in chains, his broken arm hanging by his side, his head lifted so, — proudly. *Eh b'en,* the working-men were demonstrating against the Church, or something, I don't know what. They had speeches. My father stood upon the steps of the basilica and suddenly the *curé* of the church appeared. My father cried, in a voice of thunder, '*A bas* the priests! That pig burned *him* to death!' he pointed to the statue. 'To the Lanterne with him! Hang him!' Then they all began to shout and surge toward the steps, — and the police charged the crowd with revolvers. . . . Well, my father came home that night all covered with blood, and hardly able to drag himself along the street.

"My step-mother met him at the door, very angry, and said, 'Well, where have you been, you good-for-nothing?'

"'At a manifestation, *quoi!*' he growled.

"'It serves you right,' she said. 'I hope you're cured now.'

" 'Cured?' he shouted, roaring through the bloody toothlessness of his mouth. 'Until the next time. *Ca ira!*'

"And true enough, it was at the guillotining of Leboeuf that the cuirassiers charged the Socialists, and they carried my father home with a sabre cut in his head."

Marcelle leaned over with a cigarette in her mouth to light it from Fred's.

"They called him *Casse-téte* Poisot—the Head-breaker, and he was a hard man.... How he hated the Government! ... Once I came home from school and told him that they had taught us to sing the Marseillaise.

"'If I ever catch you singing that damned traitors' song around here,' he cried at me, doubling up his fist, 'I'll crack your face open.'"

To my eyes came the picture of this coarse, narrow, sturdy old warrior, scarred with the marks of a hundred vain, ignoble fights with the police, reeling home through squalid streets after Union meetings, his eyes blazing with visions of a regenerated humanity.

"And your brother?" asked Fred.

"Oh, he was even worse than my father," said Marcelle, laughing. "You could talk to my father about some things, but there were things that you could not talk to my brother about at all. Even when he was a little boy he did dreadful things. He would say, 'After school come to meet me at such and such a church,—I want to pray.' I would meet him on the steps and we would go in together and kneel down. And when I was praying, he would suddenly jump up and run shouting around the church, kicking over the chairs and smashing the candles burning in the chapels.... And whenever he saw a *curé* in the street, he marched along right behind him crying, '*A bas les calottes! A bas les calottes!*' Twenty times he was arrested, and even put in the Reformatory. But he always escaped. When he had but fifteen years he ran away from the house and did not come back for a year. One day he walked into the kitchen where we were all having breakfast.

"'Good morning,' he said, as if he had never gone away. 'Cold morning, isn't it?'

"My step-mother screamed.

"'I have been to see the world,' he went on. 'I came back because I didn't have any money and was hungry.' My father never scolded him, but just let him stay. In the daytime he hung around the cafés on the corner, and did not come home at night until after midnight. Then one morning he disappeared again, without a word to anyone. In three months he was back again, starving. My step-mother told my father that he ought to make the boy work, that it was hard enough with a lazy, fighting man to provide for. But my father only laughed.

"'Leave him alone,' he said. 'He knows what he's doing. There's good fighting blood in him.'

"My brother went off and came back like that until he was almost eighteen. In the last period, before he settled down in Paris, he would most always work until he had collected enough money to go away. Then he finally got a steady job in a factory here, and married....

"He had a fine voice for singing, and could hold people dumb with the way he sang revolutionary songs. At night, after his work was finished, he used to tie a big red handkerchief around his neck and go to some music hall or cabaret. He would enter, and while some singer was giving a song from the stage, he would suddenly lift up his voice and burst out into the *Ca ira* or the *Internationale.* The singer on the stage would be forced to stop, and all the audience would turn and watch my brother, up there in the top benches of the theatre.

"When he had finished, he would cry 'How do you like that?' and then they would cheer and applaud him. Then he would shout 'Everybody say with me "Down with the Capitalists! *A bas* the police! To the Lanterne with the *flics!*"' Then there would be some cheers and some whistles. 'Did I hear somebody whistle me?' he'd cry. 'I'll meet anybody at the door outside who dared to whistle me!' And afterward he would fight ten or fifteen men in a furious mob in the street outside, until the police came. . . .

"He, too, was always leading strikes, but had a laughing, gallant way that made all the comrades love him. . . . He might perhaps some day have been a deputy, if my father had not taught him lawlessness when he was young—"

"Where is he now?" asked Fred.

"Down there in the trenches somewhere." She waved her arm vaguely Eastward. "He had to go with the others when the war broke out, though he hated the Army so. When he did his military service, it was awful. He would never obey. For almost a year he was in prison. Once he decided to be promoted, and within a month they made him corporal, he was so intelligent. . . . But the very first day he refused to command the soldiers of his squad. . . . 'Why should I give orders to these comrades?' he shouted. 'One orders me to command them to dig a trench. *Voyons,* are they slaves?' So they degraded him to the ranks. Then he organized a revolt, and advised them to shoot their officers. . . . The men themselves were so insulted, they threw him over a wall.—So terribly he hated war! When the Three Year Military Law was up in the Chamber, it was he who led the mob to the Palais Bourbon. . . . And now he must go to kill the *Bóches,* like the others. Perhaps he himself is dead,—I do not know, I have heard nothing." And then irrelevantly, "He has a little son five years old."

Three generations of fierce, free blood, struggling indefatigably for a dim dream of liberty. And now a fourth in the cradle! Did they know why they struggled? No matter. It was a thing deeper than reason, an instinct of the human spirit which neither force nor persuasion could ever uproot.

"And you, Marcelle?" I asked.

"I?" She laughed. "Shall I tell you that I was not seduced by a Duke?" She gave a bitter little chuckle. "Then you will not respect me,—for I notice that you friends of passage want your vice seasoned with romance.

But it is true. It has not been romantic. In that hideousness and earnest-
ness of our life, I always craved joy and happiness. I always wanted to
laugh, be gay, even when I was a baby. I used to imagine drinking
champagne, and going to the theatre, and I wanted jewels, fine dresses,
automobiles. Very early my father noticed that my tastes led that way; he
said, 'I see that you want to throw everything over and sell yourself to the
rich. Let me tell you now, that the first fault you commit, I'll put you out
the door and call you my daughter no more.'

"It became intolerable at home. My father could not forgive women
who had lovers without being married. He kept saying that I was on the
way to sin — and when I grew older, I wasn't permitted to leave the house
without my step-mother. As soon as I was old enough, he hurried to find
me a husband, to save me. One day he came home and said that he had
found one, — a pale young man who limped, the son of a restaurant-
keeper on the same street. I knew him; he was not bad, but I couldn't bear
to think of marrying. I wanted so much to be free." We started, Fred and
I. "Free!" Wasn't that what the old man had fought for so bitterly?

"So that night," she said, "I got out of bed and put on my Sunday
dress, and my everyday dress over that, and ran away. All night I walked
around the streets, and all the next day. That evening, trembling, I went
to the factory where my brother worked and waited for him to come out.
I did not know whether or not he would give me up to my father. But
soon he came along, shouting and singing with some comrades. He spied
me.

"'Well, old girl, what brings you here?' he cried, taking my arm.
'Trouble?' I told him I had run away. He stood off and looked at me. 'You
haven't eaten,' he said. 'Come home with me and meet my wife. You'll
like her. We'll all have dinner together!' So I did. His wife was wonderful.
She met me with open arms, and they showed me the baby, just a month
old.... And so fat! All was warm and happy there in that house. I
remember that she cooked the dinner herself, and never have I eaten such
a dinner! They did not ask me anything until I had eaten, and then my
brother lighted a cigarette and gave me one. I was afraid to smoke, for my
step-mother had said it was to bring hell on a woman.... But the wife
smiled at me and took one herself.

"'Now,' said my brother. 'Well, what are your plans?'

"'I have none,' I answered. 'I must be free. I want gaiety, and lovely
clothes. I want to go to the theatre. I want to drink champagne.'

"His wife shook her head sadly.

"'I have never heard of any work for a woman that will give her those
things,' she said.

"'Do you think I want work?' I burst out. 'Do you think I want to
slave out my life in a factory for ten francs a week, or strut around in

other women's gowns at some *couturière's* on the Rue de la Paix? Do you think I will take orders from anyone? No, I want to be free!'

"My brother looked at me gravely for a long time. Then he said, 'We are of the same blood. It would do no good to argue with you, or to force you. Each human being must work out his own life. You shall go and do whatever you want. But I want you to know that whenever you are hungry, or discouraged, or deserted, that my house is always open to you, — that you will always be welcome here, for as long as you want'.
. . ."

Marcelle wiped her eyes roughly with the back of her hand.

"I stayed there that night, and the next day I went around the city and talked with girls in the cafés, — like I am now. They advised me to work, if I wanted a steady lover; so I went into a big Department-store for a month. Then I had a lover, an Argentine, who gave me beautiful clothes and took me to the theatre. Never have I been so happy!

"One night when we were going to the theatre, — as we passed by my brother's house, I thought I would stop in and let him know how wonderful I found life. I had on a blue charmeuse gown, — I remember it now, it was lovely! Slippers with very high heels and brilliants on the buckles, white gloves, a big hat with a black ostrich feather, and a veil. Luckily the veil was down; for as I entered the door of my brother's tenement, my father stood there on the steps! He looked at me. I stopped. My heart stood still. But I could see he did not recognize me.

" '*Va t'en!*' he shouted. 'What is your kind doing here, in a workingman's house? What do you mean by coming here to insult us with your silks and your feathers, sweated out of poor men in mills and their consumptive wives, their dying children? Go away, you whore!'

"I was terrified that he might recognize me!

"It was only once more that I saw him. My lover left me, and I had other lovers. . . . My brother and his wife went out to live near my father, in St. Denis. I used sometimes to go out and spend the night with them, to play with the baby, who grew so fast. Those were really happy times. And I used to leave again at dawn, to avoid meeting my father. One morning I left my brother's house, and as I came onto the street, I saw my father, going to work at dawn with his lunch pail! He had not seen my face. There was nothing to do but walk down the street ahead of him. It was about five o'clock, — few people were about. He came along behind me, and soon I noticed that he was walking faster. Then he said in a low voice, 'Mademoiselle, wait for me. We are going the same direction, *hein?*' I hurried. 'You are pretty, mademoiselle. And I am not old. Can't we go together some place?' I was in a panic. I was so full of horror and fear that he might see my face. I did not dare to turn up a side-street, for he would have seen my profile. So I walked straight ahead, — straight ahead for hours, for miles.... I do not know when he stopped.... I do not know if now he might be dead.... My brother said he never spoke of me...."

She ceased, and the noises of the street became again apparent to our ears, that had been so long deaf to them, with double their former loudness. Fred was excited.

"Marvelous, by God!" he cried, thumping the table. "The same blood, the same spirit! And see how the revolution becomes sweeter, broader, from generation to generation! See how the brother understood freedom in a way which the old father was blind to!"

Marcelle shot him an astonished look. "What do you mean?" she asked.

"Your father,—fighting all his life for liberty,—yet turned you out because you wanted *your liberty*."

"Oh, but you don't understand," said Marcelle. "I did wrong. I am bad. If I had a daughter who was like me, I should do the same thing, if she had a frivolous character."

"Can't you *see?*" cried Fred. "Your father wanted liberty for men, but not for women!"

"Naturally," she shrugged. "Men and women are different. My father was right. Women must be—*respectable!*"

"The women need another generation," sighed Fred, sadly.

I took Marcelle's hand.

"Do you regret it?" I asked her.

"Regret my life?" she flashed back, tossing her head proudly, "*Dame,* no! I'm *free!* ..."

The Worst Thing in Europe

MARCH 1915

IN a city of Northern France occupied by the Germans, we were met at the train by several officers and the Royal automobiles. The officers, genial, pleasant, rather formal young fellows in the smart Prussian uniform, were to be our guides and hosts in that part of the German front. They spoke English well, as so many of them do; and we were charmed by their friendliness and affability. As we left the station and got into the machines, a group of private soldiers off duty loitered about, looking at us with lazy curiosity. Suddenly one of the officers sprang at them, striking at their throats with his little "swagger stick."

"*Schweinhunde!*" he shouted with sudden ferocity. "Be off about your business and don't stare at us!"

They fell back silently, docilely, before the blows and the curses, and dispersed....

Another time a photographer of our party was interrupted, while taking moving pictures, by a sentry with a rifle.

"My orders are that no photographs shall be taken here!" said the soldier.

The photographer appealed to the Staff Lieutenant who accompanied us.

"It's all right," said the officer. "I am Lieutenant Herrmann of the General Staff in Berlin. He has my permission to photograph."

The sentry saluted, looked at Herrmann's papers, and withdrew. And I asked the Lieutenant by what right he could countermand a soldier's orders from his own superior.

"Because I am that soldier's commanding officer. The fact that I have a Lieutenant's shoulder-straps makes me the superior of every soldier in the army. A German soldier must obey every officer's orders, no matter what they may be."

"So that if a soldier were doing sentry duty on an important fort in time of war, and you came along and told him to go and get you a drink, he would have to obey?"

133

He nodded. "He would have to obey me unquestioningly, no matter what I ordered, no matter how it conflicted with his previous orders, no matter whether I even belonged to his regiment. But of course I should be held responsible."

That is an Army. That is what it means to be a soldier. Plenty of people have pointed to the indisputable fact that the German army is the most perfect military machine in the world. But there are also other armies in the present war.

Consider the French army, rent with politics, badly clothed, badly provisioned, and with an inadequate ambulance service; opposed always to militarism, and long since sickened with fighting. The French army has not been fighting well. But it has been fighting, and the slaughter is appalling. There remains no effective reserve in France; and the available youth of the nation down to seventeen years of age is under arms. For my part, all other considerations aside, I should not care to live half-frozen in a trench, up to my middle in water, for three or four months, because someone in authority said I ought to shoot Germans. But if I were a Frenchman, I should do it, because I would have been accustomed to the idea by my compulsory military service.

The Russian army, inexhaustible hordes of simple peasants torn from their farms, blessed by a priest, and knouted into battle for a cause they never heard of, appeals to me even less. Of all the armies in this war, I might make a secondary choice between the Belgians, doing England's dirty work, and the Servians, doing Russia's; but I hesitate at the sight of two hundred thousand Belgians who made a fierce, short resistance at Liege, Namur and Brussels, practically wiped off the face of the earth. "The Belgian army does not exist!" All that remains of that drilled and disciplined flower of Belgium are a few regiments restoring their shattered nerves in barracks, and quarreling with their Allies. The Servian army is still making heroic last stands, but that is no fun.

And crossing over to the Austrian side, I call to mind that hideous persistent story about the first days of the war, when Austria sent her unequipped regiments against the Russians. Only the first ranks had rifles and ammunition; the ranks behind were instructed to pick up the guns when the first ranks were killed — and so on.

But I could fill pages with the super-Mexican horrors that civilized Europe is inflicting upon itself. I could describe to you the quiet, dark, saddened streets of Paris, where every ten feet you are confronted with some miserable wreck of a human being, or a madman who lost his reason in the trenches, being led around by his wife. I could tell you of the big hospital in Berlin full of German soldiers who went crazy from merely hearing the cries of the thirty thousand Russians drowning in the swamps of East Prussia after the battle of Tannenburg. Or of Galician peasants dropping out of their regiments to die along the roads of cholera. Or of the numbness and incalculable demoralization among men in the trenches. Or of holes torn in bodies with jagged pieces of melanite shells, of sounds that make deaf, of gases that destroy eye-sight, of wounded men dying day by day and hour by hour within forty yards of twenty thousand human beings, who won't stop killing each other long enough to gather them up. . . .

But that is not my purpose in this brief article. I want to try and indicate the effect of military obedience and discipline upon human beings. Disease, death, wounds on the battle-field, Philosophical Anarchism, and International Socialism, seem to be futile as incentives to Peace. Why? As for the bloody side of war, that shocks people less than they think; we're so accustomed to half a million a year maimed and killed in mines and factories. As for Socialism, Anarchism, any democratic or individualist faith—I don't speak of Christianity, which is completely bankrupt—the Socialists, Anarchists, et al. *were all trained soldiers!*

I seem to hear shouts of "England! Look at England! England has no conscript army!" Well, if England has no conscript army now, England is going soon to have one. The Englishman has been prepared for this war by adroit press alarms for years. Hardly one ordinary Briton—of the class that fills the ranks of her far-flung regiments—who did not admit that war with Germany was coming, and that he would have to fight. I could digress here for pages to tell you the terrible means by which England filled her "volunteer" army; how workingmen of enlistable age were fired from their jobs, and relief refused their wives and children until the men joined; how others were intimidated, bullied, shamed into fighting for a cause they had no interest in, nor affection for; how Harrods' great department-store loaded a truck with young clerks and sent them to the recruiting-office, with a big sign on the side, "Harrods' Gift to the Empire."

You have perhaps said to yourself, "In the English army an officer is not allowed to strike an enlisted man." That is perfectly true. When an English soldier gets impudent to his superior, the latter orders the nearest non-commissioned officer to "Hit him." But the English soldier is seldom insubordinate. *He knows his place.* The officer caste is a caste above him, to which he can never attain. There are *rankers* in the British army—men who rise from the ranks—but they are not accepted by the army aristocracy, nor respected by the men. They float, like Mohammed's coffin, between heaven and earth. I bring to your notice the advertisement which appeared lately in the London *Times:* "Wanted—Two thousand young *Gentlemen* for Officers in Kitchener's Army." I have seen the English army in the field in France; I have noticed the apparent democracy of intercourse between men and officers—it is the kind of thing that takes place between a gentleman and his butler. Yes, the English soldier knows his place, and there's no Revolution in him. In Germany there is a little hope from the people—they do not think for themselves, but they are corrupted and coerced; in England, the people do not have to be coerced —they obey of their own free will.

And if you want to see those whom the Germans themselves call "an army of non-commissioned officers"—the best soldiers in the world—look at the first British Expeditionary Force, two hundred and fifty thousand men who have served seven years or more from India to Bermuda, and around the world again. These are the real Tommy Atkinses that Kipling sung. They are usually undersized, debauched, diseased little men, with a moral sense fertilized by years of slaughtering yellow, brown and black men with dum-dum bullets. Their reward consists of bronze medals and colored strips of ribbon—and their ruined lives, after they are mustered out, if they are not maimed and useless, are spent opening and shutting carriage-doors in front of theatres and hotels.

No, I'm afraid we must leave England out of this discussion. England breeds men that know their place, that become obedient soldiers whenever their social superiors order them to. The harm does not lie in joining Kitchener's army; it lies in being an Englishman. In no other self-governing nation in the world would the people acquiesce in the complete suppression of representative government at the order of a military dictator like Kitchener.

At the beginning of this article I gave two instances of what a German must become to be a good soldier. But since Germany has for more than forty years armed and trained her entire manhood, the consequences of the system must appear in her national life. They do. The Germans are politically cowed. They do what they are told. They learn by rote, and their "Kultur" has become a mechanical incubator for sterile Doctors of Philosophy, whose pedantry is the despair of all Youth except German youth. Nietzsche is the last German genius, and 1848 the last date in their vain struggle for political self-expression. Then comes Bismarck, and the German spirit is chained with comfortable chains, fed with uniforms, decorations, and the outworn claptrap of military glory, so that today small business men and fat peasants think like Joachim Murat and talk like General Bernhardi. Allow me to point out that the party of "Revolution," the German Social-Democrats, is as autocratic as the Kaiser's government; and that the crime for which a member is expelled from the Party is "insubordination to the Party leaders." I was informed proudly by a Social-Democratic Deputy in the Reichstag that the Party was now *collecting Party dues in the trenches;* and that, when requested, the *Government deducts the dues from the men's pay and hands it over to the Party organization!*

The German people — *Cannonen-fütter* ("Cannon-food") they are jocularly called — went to war almost without a protest. And today, from top to bottom of Germany, the investigator must seek hard before he finds a single dissenting voice. Germany is practically solid; when the Government has an official opinion, the street-cleaners have that same opinion in three days. That is the logical result of universal military service in a country where the classes are not inalterably fixed, as they are in England. And that, let me insist, is what is absolutely required for an efficient army. There is no choice. Thorough efficiency can only be attained at this time by an Autocracy, and so only can an army be attained; in a Democracy, neither efficiency in government, nor an efficient army is possible.

I hate soldiers. I hate to see a man with a bayonet fixed on his rifle, who can order me off the street. I hate to belong to an organization that is proud of obeying a caste of superior beings, that is proud of killing free ideas, so that it may the more efficiently kill human beings in cold blood. They will tell you that a conscript army is Democratic, because everybody has to serve; but they won't tell you that military service plants in your blood the germ of blind obedience, of blind irresponsibility, that it produces one class of Commanders in your state and your industries, and accustoms you to do what they tell you even in time of peace.

Here in America we have our chance to construct someday a Democracy, unhampered by the stupid docility of a people who run to salute when the band plays. They are talking now about building up an immense standing army, to combat the Japs, or the Germans, or the Mexicans. I, for one, refuse to join. You ask me how I am going to combat a whole world thirsting for our blood? And I reply, not by creating a counter-thirst for the blood of the Japs, Germans, or Mexicans. There is no such thing as a "moderate army" or an "army of defense." Once we begin that, Japan, Germany, or Mexico, whichever it is, will begin to build up a defense against us. We will raise them one, and so on. And the logical end of all that is Germany; and the logical end of Germany is, and always will be, War. And you, gentle reader, you will be the first to get shot.

The World Well Lost

THE Serbian town of Obrenovatz is a cluster of red tile roofs and white bulbous towers, hidden in green trees on a belt of land, around which sweeps the river Sava in a wide curve. Behind rise the green hills of Serbia, toppling up to blue ranges of mountains upon whose summit heaps of dead bodies lie still unburied, among the stumps of trees riddled down by machine-gun fire; and half-starved dogs battle there ghoulishly with vultures. Half a mile away on the bank of the yellow river, the peasant soldiers stand knee-deep in inundated trenches, firing at the Austrians three hundred yards away on the other side. Between, the rich hills of Bosnia sweep westward forever like sea-swells, hiding the big guns that cover Obrenovatz with a menace of destruction. The town itself is built on a little rise of ground, surrounded by flooded marshes when the river is high, where the sacred storks stalk seriously among the rushes, contemptuous of battles. All the hills are bursting with vivid new leaves and plum tree blossoms like smoke. The earth rustles with a million tiny thrills, the pushing of pale green shoots and the bursting of buds; the world steams with spring. And regular as clockwork, the crack of desultory shots rises unnoticed into the lazy air. For nine months it has been so, and the sounds of war have become a part of the great chorus of nature.

We had dinner with the officers of the Staff, — good-natured giants, who were peasants and sons of peasants. The orderly who fell upon his knees to brush our shoes and stood so stiffly pouring water over our hands while we washed, and the private soldiers who waited on us at dinner with such smart civility, came in and sat down when coffee was served, and were introduced all round. They were intimate friends of the Colonel.

After dinner somebody produced a bottle of cognac and a box of real Havana cigars, which Iovanovitch laughingly said had been captured from the Austrians two weeks before, and we strolled out to visit the Serbian batteries.

Westward over the Bosnian hills a pale spring sun hung low in a shallow sky of turquoise green. Line after line of little clouds burned red-golden, scarlet, vermilion, pale pink and gray, all up the tremendous arch of sky. Drowsy birds twittered, and a soft fresh wind came up out of the west.

Iovanovitch turned to me:

"You wanted to talk to a Serbian Socialist," he said. "Well, you'll have the chance. The captain in command of the battery we are going to see is a leader of the Serbian Socialist parties, — or at least he was in the days of peace. No, I don't know what his doctrines are; I am a Young Radical myself," he laughed. "We believe in a great Serbian Empire."

"If all the Socialists were like Takits," said the Colonel, puffing comfortably at his cigar, "I wouldn't have a thing to say against Socialism. He is a good soldier."

In a deep trench, curved in half-moon shape across the corner of a field, four six-inch guns crouched behind a screen of young willows. There was a roof over them almost on the level with the field, and on this roof sods had been laid and grass and bushes were growing, to hide them from aeroplanes. At the sentry's staccato challenge the Colonel answered, and hailed "Takits!" Out of the gun-pits came a man, muddy to the knees and without a hat. He was tall and broad; his faded uniform hung upon him as if once he had been stout; a thick, unkempt beard covered his face to the cheekbones, and his eyes were quiet and direct.

They said something to him in Serbian, and he laughed.

"So," he said, turning to me with a twinkle in his eye, and speaking French that halted and hesitated like a thing long unused. "So. You are interested in Socialism?"

I said I was. "They tell me you were a Socialist leader in this country."

"I *was*," he said, emphasizing the past tense. "And now — "

"Now," interrupted the Colonel, "he is a patriot and a good soldier."

"Just say 'a good soldier,'" said Takits, and I thought there was a shade of bitterness in his voice. "Forgive me if I speak bad French. It is long since I have talked to foreigners, — though I once made speeches in French — "

"And Socialism?" I asked.

"Well, I will tell you," he began slowly. "Walk with me a little." He put his arm under mine and scowled at the earth. Suddenly he turned swiftly, preoccupied, and shouted to some one invisible in the pit: "Peter! Oil breechblock number one gun!"

The others strolled on ahead, laughing and throwing remarks over their shoulders the way men do who have dined and are content. Night rushed up the west and quenched those shining clouds, drawing her train of stars like a robe to cover all heaven. Somewhere in the distant trenches voices sang a quavering Macedonian song about the glories of the Empire of the Tsar Stefan Dooshan, and an accompanying violin scratched and squeaked under the hand of a gypsy "gooslar." On the dim slope of a hill far across the river in the enemy's country a spark of flame quivered red. . . .

"You see, in our country it is different than in yours," began Takits. "Here we have no rich men and no industrial population, so we are not ready, I think, for the immense combining of the workers to oppose the concentration of capital in the hands of the few." He stopped a minute, and then chuckled, "You have no idea how strange it feels to be talking like this again! . . .

"Our party was formed then to combat the regular Socialists, to apply the principles of Socialism to the conditions of this country, — a country of peasants who all own their land. We are naturally communists, we Serbians. In every village you will see the houses of the rich *zadrugas,* — many generations of the same family, with all their connections by marriage, who have pooled their property and hold it in common. We didn't want to waste time with the International. It would hinder us, — block our program, which was, to get into the hands of the people who produced everything and owned all the means of production, the means of distribution too. The political program was simpler; we aimed at a real democracy by means of the widest possible suffrage, initiative, referendum and recall. You see, in the Balkans, a great gulf separates the ambitious politicians in power and the mass of the people who elect them. Politics is getting to be a separate profession, closed to all but scheming lawyers. This class we wanted to destroy. We did not believe in the General Strike, and the great oppressed industrial populations of the world could do nothing with us, except use us for the furtherance of their economic programs, which had nothing to do with conditions in Serbia."

"You opposed war?"

He nodded. "We were against war — " he began, then stopped short and burst out laughing. "Do you know, I had forgotten all that. It seems so silly now! We thought that the peasants, the people of Serbia, could stop war any time if they wanted to, by simply refusing to fight. God! There were only a few of us, — not a great solid working-class as in Germany and France, — but we thought it could be done. Why on God's earth did no one in Europe realize what a conscript army means? We thought war was brutal, bloody, useless, horrible. Imagine anyone who could not see how much better war is than peace and the slavery of industry! Think of the thousands of people killed, maimed and made unfit every year by the terrible conditions in which they must live to support the rich, even in prosperous times. No. In war, a man dies with a sense of ideal sacrifice, — and his wife and mother and family miss him less, because he fell on the field of honor! Besides, in peace-time they were left to starve when the machines got him, — and now there is a pension. They are taken care of." He spoke vehemently.

"And now, — after the war?"

Takits turned slowly to me, and his eyes were tragic and bitter. "I don't know. I don't know. It was myself before the war who spoke to you just now. What a shock it was to me to hear my voice saying those old, outworn things! They are so meaningless now! I have come to think that it has all to be done over again, — the upbuilding of civilization. Again we must learn to till the soil, to live together under a common government, to make friends across frontiers among other races who have become once more only dark, evil faces and speakers of tongues not our own. This world has become a place of chaos, as it was in the Dark Ages; and yet we live, have our work to do, feel happiness on a clear day and sadness when it rains. These are more important than anything just now. Afterward will come the long pull up from barbarism to a time when men think and reason and consciously organize their lives again.... But that will not be in our time. I shall die without seeing it, — the world we loved and lost."

He turned to me with extraordinary emotion, eyes blazing and dark, and gripped my arm tersely. "Here is the point, — the tragic point. Once I was a lawyer. The other day the Colonel asked me about some common legal point, and *I had forgotten it.* When I talked with you about my party, I discovered again that all was vague, — nebulous. You noticed how obscure and general it was, didn't you? Well, *I have forgotten my arguments, and I have lost my faith!*

"For four years now I have been fighting in the Serbian army. At first I hated it, wanted to stop, was oppressed by the *unreasonableness* of it all. Now it is my job, my life. I spend all day thinking of the position of those guns, — I lie awake at night worrying about the men of the battery, whether So-and-So will stand his watch without carelessness, whether I shall need fresh horses in place of the lame ones in the gun-teams, what can be done to correct the slight recoiling-fault of number three. These things and my food, my bed, the weather, — that is life to me. When I go home on leave to visit my wife and children, their existence seems so tame, so removed from the realities. I get bored very soon, and am relieved when the time comes to return to my friends here, my work, — my guns.... That is the horrible thing."

He ceased, and we walked along in silence. A stork on great pinions came flapping down upon the roof of the cottage where he had his nest. From far down the river a sudden ripple of rifle-shots broke out inexplicably, and ended with sharp silence.

IV. World War I: Opposition and Repression at Home

In DECEMBER 1915, shortly after he returned to America, Reed took a train west to Portland for a visit with his family. He was exhausted from his travels in Europe and suffering from the kidney ailment that continued to plague him. Disillusioned with the war, and with politics in general, Reed turned to personal matters. The coming year was to be a time of quiet and introspection for Reed, a time when he began to think about settling down — probably the most serene period in all of his short but tumultuous career.

Contributing to this new desire for permanence was his relationship with Louise Bryant. Reed met Bryant in Portland, and they were immediately and mutually attracted; when he returned to New York, she followed close behind. By summer they were living together in Provincetown, Massachusetts, in a colony of writers and artists that included Eugene O'Neill and George Cram Cook, with whom Reed founded the Provincetown Players. Reed directed most of his time and energy into his relationship with Louise, and into writing, directing, and acting for the Players. Writing seemed less important here, amid the flurry of social and theatrical activity. In March he turned down an offer from *Metropolitan Magazine* to cover one of the biggest events of the year — Pancho Villa's attack on Columbus, New Mexico, and the resulting American intervention in Mexico. He was too preoccupied, and not well enough physically, to undertake the trip.

Reed's few contributions to *The Masses* during 1916 were of mixed quality. He interviewed Henry Ford in Detroit, out of which came "Why They Hate Ford" (October 1916), an article that explained — and praised — Ford's progressive industrial policies, especially the profit-sharing plan that he offered his employees (as well as an eight-hour working day and a $5 a day minimum wage). Such concessions to his workers, and statements such as "The world's wealth is concentrated in too few hands," created misgivings, sometimes outright panic, on the part of most wealthy industrialists. "That is why the capitalists hate Henry Ford," Reed wrote. "That is why the Steel Trust would like to cut off his steel — and Wall Street curb his power under the cold tyranny of the little financial geniuses who own all the rest of America."

On the same three-week swing through the Midwest, Reed stopped off in Chicago and St. Louis to cover the national political conventions for *Metropolitan Magazine*. But the most interesting story, as Reed discovered, was at the Progressive Convention in Chicago, which offered its nomination to Teddy Roosevelt, only to have the Colonel refuse and — contemptuously, it seemed to many — suggest that the conservative Henry Cabot Lodge be nominated in his place. Once the champion of the Progressive Party, a leader who represented "democracy" and "justice and fairness and the cause of the poor," Roosevelt had by 1916 reversed himself and become a conservative advocate of militarism and preparedness, openly espousing intervention in the Mexican Revolution and the war in Europe. Reed disagreed with nearly everything Roosevelt stood for, and he presented the old Rough Rider as a Judas who had sold his own constituency for "thirty pieces of political silver."

The article, "Roosevelt Sold Them Out," appeared in the August 1916 issue of *The Masses* and was more important for its description of the Progressives than for its attack on Roosevelt. Reed composed a timeless portrait of an American political convention, half politics and half circus:

> I looked down from the platform of the Auditorium in Chicago upon that turbulent sea of almost holy emotion; upon men and women from great cities and little towns, from villages and farms, from the deserts and the mountains and the cattle ranches, wherever the wind had carried to the ears of the poor and the oppressed that a leader and a mighty warrior had risen up to champion the Square Deal. The love of Teddy filled those people. Blind and exalted, they sang "Onward Christian Soldiers!" and "We Will Follow, Follow Teddy!" There was virility, enthusiasm, youth in that assembly; there were great fighters there, men who all their lives had given battle alone against frightful odds to right the wrongs of the sixty per cent. of the people of this country who own five per cent. of its wealth.

Reed was moved by the passion of these ordinary men and women "of little vision and no plan" — moved in spite of himself. Though he doubted the political wisdom of the Progressives and "sneered" (as he himself wrote) at their hysterical worship of Roosevelt, he could still write that "when I saw the Progressive Convention, I realized that among those delegates lay the hope of this country's peaceful evolution, and the material for heroes of the people."

By November Reed's kidney ailment had grown markably worse, and doctors informed him that surgery would be needed. Reed immediately began to put his affairs in order; he and Louise were married on the morning of November 9 so that she would be his legal heir. The surgery, which was performed at Johns Hopkins Hospital in Baltimore on November 22, involved the removal of one kidney and left him in severe pain for two weeks after. Not until January did the doctors pronounce his recovery complete, and by that time world events were once again pressing in on him, even in his secluded cottage at Croton, New York, which he and Louise had recently purchased.

In January, Woodrow Wilson severed diplomatic relations with Germany after the German ambassador to Washington informed him that, beginning February 1, German submarines would attack all ships proceeding to and from the Allied nations. When, on March 18, news arrived that three American ships had been sunk on the Atlantic, Wilson called a special session of Congress for April 2, a turn of events that could mean only one thing—war. In a last, desperate attempt to protest the inevitable, pacifists and radicals of all sorts, including John Reed, gathered in Washington on April 2. That evening Reed attended an anti-war rally, but before he could speak the announcement came—the president had called for war. Reed stepped to the platform nevertheless and shouted, "This is not my war, and I will not support it. This is not my war, and I will have nothing to do with it."[18]

After the official declaration of war, Reed worked even harder for peace. He appeared before the House Judiciary Committee to speak against the Espionage Act, and before the House Committee on Military Affairs to speak against conscription. And in an article for *The Masses,* "Whose War?" (April 1917), he argued a point that few Americans wanted to hear—that the war, and the fanatic patriotism that it spawned, would lead to a curtailment of artistic, social, and political freedom. Henceforth America would be "less tolerant, less hospitable," for "war means an ugly mob-madness, crucifying the truth-tellers, choking the artists, sidetracking reforms, revolutions, and the working of social forces. Already in America those citizens who oppose the entrance of their country into the European melée are called 'traitors,'" Reed wrote. He concluded by reiterating that, quite simply, "It is not our war."

However, the world seemed to close in on the few radical groups that remained opposed to the war. In cities across the nation, police and angry demonstrators disrupted socialist meetings, and radical publications were censored by the U.S. government. Anarchists Emma Goldman and Alexander Berkman, both friends of Reed, were arrested for organizing No-Conscription League meetings, charged with conspiring "to induce persons not to register," found guilty and sentenced to two years in prison and $10,000 fines. In response to the escalating repression at home, Reed contributed numerous notes and short articles to what would be, though no one knew it at the time, the last issues of *The Masses*. Beginning with the August number, *The Masses* was denied mailing privileges by the United States Postmaster on the grounds that articles like Reed's "Whose War?" hampered the war effort. The three subsequent issues met the same fate.

Reed's articles for these last issues vary in tone. Some are well-reasoned appeals to all rational Americans, and others are bitter harangues that denounce government, military, and business leaders for involving America in an imperialist war abroad and suppressing basic civil liberties at home. The best of these articles, "One Solid Month of Liberty" (September 1917), begins: "In America the month just past has been the blackest month for freemen our generation has known. With a sort of hideous apathy the country has acquiesed in a regime of judicial tyranny, bureaucratic suppression and industrial barbarism, which followed inevitably the first fine careless rapture of militarism." Reed continues angrily, listing the government's repression of pacifist, socialist, and labor groups in what reads like a catalogue of lost freedom in America. "All of which goes to prove that in America law is merely the instrument for good or evil of the most powerful interest," Reed writes, "and there are no Constitutional safeguards worth the powder to blow them to hell."

Reed had traveled an enormous distance — both artistically and politically — since joining *The Masses*. He gradually moved away from the literary or first-person journalism that he began with back in Greenwich Village and became a political journalist, or a "polemicist" as his detractors have argued. However, even if his late work can be criticized for its didacticism, it is also important to remember that this didacticism grew out of a genuine (and frustrated) concern for all those whom Reed felt were exploited by a vicious capitalist system, and out of a passionate commitment to changing that system, through either evolutionary or revolutionary means. Perhaps his commitment can best be illustrated by a passage from an unpublished autobiographical essay entitled "Almost Thirty": "As for me, I don't know what I can do to help — I don't know yet. All I know is that my happiness is built on the misery of other people, that I eat because others go hungry, that I am clothed when other people go almost naked through the frozen cities in winter; *and that fact poisons me, disturbs my serenity, makes me write propaganda when I would rather play*" [italics added].[19]

Reed's drift toward "propaganda" all but ended his career as a working journalist in America. Once the United States had actually entered the war, commercial magazines and newspapers refused to print anything critical of the war effort. And in the autumn of 1917, as *The Masses* and ultimately more than seventy other radical publications were closed down by the government, Reed found himself without an outlet for his work, at least for the kind of political journalism that he wanted to write. America had lost its way, he felt — and now he had lost the means by which to support himself.

Roosevelt Sold Them Out

AUGUST 1916

THE Editor of the *New York Evening Mail* was advising the German-Americans to vote for Roosevelt. Someone asked him why. He replied, "I know he is anti–German, but the Germans should support Roosevelt because he is the only exponent of German Kultur in the United States."

When Theodore Roosevelt was President, a delegation from the State of Michigan went to Washington to plead with him the cause of the Boer Republic, then fighting for its life against the British Government. One of the delegates told me that Roosevelt answered them, cold as ice: "No, the weaker nations must yield to the stronger, even if they perish off the face of the earth."

When Germany invaded Belgium, Colonel Roosevelt, in *The Outlook,* told us that was none of our business and that our policy of isolation must be maintained even at the expense of the Belgian people.

These instances showed the peculiar Prussian trend of the Colonel's mind, and we were at a loss when he subsequently took up cudgels for that same Belgium which he had so profoundly damned, and came forward as the champion of the "weak nations." Could it be chivalry? Could it be a sympathy with the cause of democracy? We held off and waited, skeptical as we were, and soon the Snake was discerned gliding through the Colonel's grass. All this talk about Belgium insensibly changed into an impassioned pleading for enormous armies and navies in order that we might live up to our international obligations, and into a violent attack upon the Wilson administration for not doing what the Colonel had told it to in the first place. And the particular point he kept emphasizing was the administration's cowardly refusal to crush the Mexican people!

After General Leonard Wood and the ambitious military caste in this country had whispered in the Colonel's ear, and after the munitions makers and the imperialist financiers had given the Colonel a dinner, and after the predatory plutocrats he fought so nobly in the past had told him

149

they would support him for President of the United States, "Our Teddy" came out for the protection of weak nations abroad and the suppression of weak nations at home; for the crushing of Prussian militarism and the encouragement of American militarism; for all the liberalism, including Russia's, financed by the Anglo-French loan, and all the conservatism of the gentlemen who financed it.

We were not fooled by the Colonel's brand of patriotism. Neither were the munitions makers and the money trust; the Colonel was working for their benefit, so they backed him. But large numbers of sincere people in this country who remembered Armageddon and "Social Justice" imagined that Roosevelt was still on the side of the people. Most of these persons had flocked to his standard in 1912 flushed with a vision of re-generated humanity, and had given up a good deal of their time, money and position to follow Democracy's new Messiah. Four years of dictator-ship by George W. Perkins and the Steel Trust, four years in which the Colonel had patently allowed his crusaders to perish politically in droves, four years of contradiction and change until he was screaming at the top of his lungs for blood-thirstiness, obedience and efficiency, had not dimmed their faith. These people were not militarists; they were for peace, not war; they were not for universal service of any kind, nor obedience to corporations. They were for Roosevelt; they thought that, after all, he stood for Social Justice. So they blindly swallowed what he advocated and shouted, "We want Teddy!"

In 1912 Theodore Roosevelt issued his Covenant with the American People, assuring them that he would never desert them, and affirming the unalterable principle of Social Justice for which he stood. This Covenant was the Progressive Party's reason for being. Indeed, if they had not believed the Covenant with the American people would be resuscitated, I doubt if the Progressives, after those four long years of silence and neglect, would have risen to blindly follow Colonel Roosevelt again. They had had their knocks. They had made their sacrifices. They knew that as Progressives they could not come to power in 1916. But when that call came, all over the country in a million hearts the spark of almost extinct enthusiasm burst into flame, and the feeling of a holy crusade of democ-racy which had stirred men and women four years ago, again swept the country.

Not the intelligent radicals — no matter how much they wanted Teddy, they knew he would betray them when it suited him — but the common, ordinary, unenlightened people, the backwoods idealists, as it were, — they trusted Teddy. Hadn't he said he would never desert them? It was to be another Armageddon, and they would sacrifice to the cause as they had sacrificed before.

Little did they know that Theodore Roosevelt, in New York, was referring to them as "rabble," and planning how he could shake himself free from enthusiasts, from idealists, from the dirty and stupid lower classes. Little did they know that he was saying impatiently about them "You can't build a political party out of cranks. I have got to get rid of the 'lunatic fringe.'" And by "lunatic fringe" he meant those people who believed in Social Justice and wanted to put it into effect.

The call to the Progressive Convention spoke of trying to reach a basis of understanding with the Republican Party. To this the Progressives assented; some because they wanted to get back into the Republican fold, and others because they wanted to force Roosevelt and Social Justice upon the Republicans and upon the country. And if the Republicans would not take Teddy and Progressivism why then hadn't Teddy made a covenant with them? They would go it alone again as they had in 1912 — the Party of Protest, the noble forlorn hope. And so they came to Chicago, inarticulate, full of faith, stirred by a vague aspiration which they would put into words later. Teddy was not Teddy to them; he was Democracy — he was justice and fairness and the cause of the poor. Also he was Preparedness; but if Teddy said Preparedness meant Justice and Liberty, then Teddy must be right. The platform of the party shows how completely these crusaders of 1913 had replaced principles with Roosevelt — there is no social justice in it.

I looked down from the platform of the Auditorium in Chicago upon that turbulent sea of almost holy emotion; upon men and women from great cities and little towns, from villages and farms, from the deserts and the mountains and the cattle ranches, wherever the wind had carried to the ears of the poor and the oppressed that a leader and a mighty warrior had risen up to champion the Square Deal. The love of Teddy filled those people. Blind and exalted, they sang "Onward Christian Soldiers!" and "We Will Follow, Follow Teddy!" There was virility, enthusiasm, youth in that assembly; there were great fighters there, men who all their lives had given battle alone against frightful odds to right the wrongs of the sixty per cent. of the people of this country who own five per cent. of its wealth. These were not Revolutionists; for the most part they were people of little vision and no plan — merely ordinary men who were raw from the horrible injustice and oppression they saw on every side. Without a leader to express them, they were no good. We, Socialists and Revolutionists, laughed and sneered at the Progressives; we ridiculed their worship of a Personality; we derided their hysterical singing of Revival Hymns; but when I saw the Progressive Convention, I realized that among those delegates lay the hope of this country's peaceful evolution, and the material for heroes of the people.

On the platform was another crowd — the Progressive leaders. Now at the Republican Convention I had seen Barnes and Reed, Smoot and

Penrose, and W. Murray Crane and those other sinister figures who fight
to the death against the people. Well, the crowd on the platform of the
Progressive Convention looked much the same to me; George Perkins of
Wall Street, James Garfield, Charles Bonaparte, etc. Among this furtive,
cold group of men there was no spark of enthusiasm, no sympathy for
Democracy. Indeed, I passed close to them once and I heard them talking
about the delegates on the floor. They called them "the cheap skates!"
And yet this inner circle, whose task it was to use the Progressives as a
threat to the Republicans, but not to permit them to embarrass the
Colonel, were, as I knew, Theodore Roosevelt's confidants, his lieuten-
ants in the Convention.

The Republican Convention was sitting only a few blocks away,
thoroughly controlled by Penrose, Smoot, Crane, Barnes, et al. This the
Progressive delegates learned; and they learned that Theodore Roosevelt
could not under any circumstances be nominated there. They clamored
for Teddy. Roaring waves of sound swept the house, "We want Teddy!
Let's nominate Teddy now!" Only with the greatest difficulty did the Gang
persuade them to wait. "The call for a Convention," they said, "had
emphasized the necessity of getting together with the Republicans in order
to save the country. We ought to appoint a Committee to confer with the
Republican Convention as to a possible candidate that both parties might
support."

"We want Teddy. We want Teddy!"

"Wait," counseled Perkins, Penrose, Garfield and the rest of the
Gang, "it will do no harm to talk with them."

Governor Hiram Johnson of California thundered to the delegates:
"Remember Barnes, Penrose and Crane in 1912! We left the Republican
Convention because the bosses were in control. They are still in control.
The only word we should send to the Republican Convention is the
nomination of Theodore Roosevelt!"

"It won't do any harm to talk it over with them," counseled the Gang.
"We have here a telegram from Theodore Roosevelt recommending that
we discuss matters with the Republicans." And they read it aloud.

Flaming Victor Murdock leaped to the stage. "You want Teddy!" he
cried. "Well, the only way you will get him is to nominate him now!"

"I will tell you the message we ought to send to the Republican Convention," shouted William J. McDonald. "Tell them to go to Hell!"

Well did they know—Murdock, McDonald and Johnson—that the
Colonel was liable to sell them out. Well did they know that the only way
to put it up squarely to Roosevelt was to nominate him immediately,
before the Republicans had taken action.

"Wait!" counseled the Gang, cold, logical, polished and afraid. "It
will do no harm to appoint a Committee to consult with the Republicans.

If we go it alone, Theodore Roosevelt and Social Justice cannot be elected."

And so the Committee of Conference was appointed, because the delegates trusted Perkins, Garfield, Bonaparte — and Roosevelt. What the Republicans thought about it was indicated in the composition of *their* Conference Committee: *Reed Smoot, W. Murray Crane, Nicholas Murray Butler,* Borah and Johnson.

"God help us!" cried Governor Hiram Johnson. "Tonight we sit at the feet of Reed Smoot and Murray Crane!"

And literally he did; for he was appointed as one of the Progressive Committee upon which sat *George W. Perkins* and *Charles J. Bonaparte.*

Upon the platform of the Progressive Convention the next morning word was spread quietly around that the Colonel, over the telephone, had requested that his name not be put in nomination until the Republicans had nominated their man. The Committee made its report, inconclusive from every point of view, and little by little the feeling that Roosevelt must be nominated grew as the time went on. Only the Gang held the Convention in check by insisting that the Committee must have another session with the Republicans. And then, like a thunderbolt, came Roosevelt's second message from Oyster Bay, recommending as a compromise candidate the name of Senator Henry Cabot Lodge of Massachusetts! Henry Cabot Lodge, the heartless reactionary, who is as far from the people as any man could be! It threw a chill over the assembly. They could not understand. And now the nominations had begun in the Republican Convention, and the Gang in control of the Progressives could control no longer. Bainbridge Colby of New York was recognized and nominated Theodore Roosevelt; Hiram Johnson seconded the nomination; and in three minutes the rules had been suspended and Roosevelt was adopted by acclamation. "Now," said Chairman Raymond Robins, "the responsibility rests with Colonel Roosevelt, and I have never known him to shirk any responsibility, no matter how insignificant or tremendous it might be. I believe that Colonel Roosevelt will accept." And the convention adjourned until three o'clock.

How the Republicans nominated Hughes by an overwhelming majority is now ancient history; and how the Progressives, full of hope and enthusiasm and girding themselves for the great fight, returned to receive Roosevelt's acceptance, I saw. The bands played, and exultingly, like children, the standards moved up and down the aisles. Prof. Albert Bushnell Hart of Harvard raved about the hall waving a huge American flag.

"No one man or two men or three men can own the Progressive Party," shouted Chairman Robins, referring directly to George W. Perkins. "This is to be a people's party, financed by the people. I call for subscriptions to the campaign fund from the floor." In twenty minutes, with a burst of tremendous enthusiasm, $100,000 had been pledged by the delegates in the gallery. It was a magnificent tribute to the spirit of the "cheap skates."

And then it began to be whispered about the platform that Theodore Roosevelt's answer had arrived; it said that if the Convention insisted upon an answer at once, he must decline—that before accepting the Progressive nomination Colonel Roosevelt must hear Justice Hughes' statement; that he would give the Progressive National Committee his answer on June 26th; that if the Committee thought Justice Hughes' position on Preparedness and Americanism was adequate he would decline the Progressive nomination; however, if the Committee thought Justice Hughes' position inadequate, he would consult with them upon what was best to be done. This we, the newspapermen, and George Perkins and the Gang knew for an hour before the Convention adjourned, yet not one word was allowed to reach the delegates on the floor. Skilfully, Chairman Robins announced that in accordance with the will of the delegates, he was going to see that the Convention adjourned at five o'clock sharp—though no one had asked for this. The collection of money went merrily on, and those who gave did so because they thought Theodore Roosevelt was going to lead them in another fight. Only Governor Hiram Johnson and Victor Murdock sounded the note of bitterness and the certainty of betrayal.

"God forgive us," cried Governor Johnson, "for not acting the first day as we ought to have acted!"

Victor Murdock was even more disillusioned. "The steam roller has run over us," he cried. "We must never again delay making our decisions."

And then, at four minutes to five o'clock, Chairman Robins announced perfunctorily another communication from Theodore Roosevelt, and read it; and before the Convention had time to grasp its meaning, it had been adjourned and was pouring, stunned and puzzled, out through the many doors into the street. It took several hours for the truth to get into those people's heads that their Messiah had sold them for thirty pieces of political silver. But they did understand finally, I think.

That night I was in the Progressive Headquarters. Big bronzed men were openly weeping. Others wandered around as if they were dazed. It was an atmosphere full of shock and disaster. Yes, the intelligent radicals had known it would come, but they did not think it would come this way, so contemptuously, so utterly. They thought that the Colonel would have left them some loophole as he left himself one. They did not realize that the Colonel was not that kind of a man, that his object was to break irrevocably with the "cranks" and the "rabble"—to slap them in the face by the suggestion of Henry Cabot Lodge as a Progressive candidate. But now they were left, as one of them expressed it, "out on a limb and the limb sawed off."

As for Colonel Roosevelt, he is back with the people among whom alone he is comfortable, "the predatory plutocrats." At least he is no longer tied to Democracy. For that he undoubtedly breathes a sigh of relief. And as for Democracy, we can only hope that some day it will cease to put its trust in men.

Why They Hate Ford

OCTOBER 1916

Henry FORD started with the idea that everyone ought to be able to own an automobile; and it has led him far. He saw that the only way an automobile could be put in the reach of all was to manufacture it in great quantities and all of one kind. In order to do this, Ford spent years simplifying his machinery, increasing the swiftness of production, and organizing the efficiency of his workmen.

Then he turned his attention to the people themselves. He had been a poorly-paid mechanic himself, and, unlike other self-made men, he had not forgotten that low wages, overwork, and no leisure, make bad work-men and bad human beings. Moreover, he was absolutely ignorant of the economic theories of the seventeenth century — which was lucky. He said: "It costs as much for a poor man to bring up a family as it does for a rich man.... The world's wealth is concentrated in too few hands.... A workman has the right to what he produces, — as nearly as that can be determined.... The only way to mend a bad world is to create a right one; and the only way to create a right one is to give men enough to live on so they won't be driven into destruction."

This is Sunday School stuff, of course, — if he had not made up his mind to act on it. That is what bothered the other employers of labor: Ford's acting on his beliefs. With such ideas as that, if he really believes in them, you can readily see how far a man would go. And when Ford says a thing he means it, in the most literal sense. For example, many men cried out that the European War was a horror, and that peace must be brought as soon as possible. But only Henry Ford chartered that amazing Peace Ship and naively started out to bring peace with his own two hands.

When he talked of the profit-sharing plan, a roar of protest went up from manufacturers all over the country. Ford was going to disrupt the labor market, raise the wage standard, create chaos in the industrial world. Even his own business associates were horrified and opposed him with all their strength in his mad efforts to ruin the Ford Motor Company. But he simply answered: "It will make them work better. Don't you worry about that. I know how they feel about it."

One hears a great deal about the "benevolent despotism" exercised by the Ford Company over its employees — and there is something in it, as I intend to show; but it remains a fact that, if Fordism were as effective as is, for example, German industrial paternalism, in keeping workmen down, our most far-sighted industrial barons would not fear it as they undoubtedly do. No. The truth is that this new Ford plan is turning into something dangerously like a real experiment in democracy, and from it may spring a real menace to capitalism.

In inaugurating his profit-sharing plan, Henry Ford upset several of our most sacred industrial and economic laws: for instance, "that no manufacturing institution can successfully employ more than 5,000 men in a single unit." Ford increased that number to 30,000, and now plans to triple that number. Next, he smashed the doctrine which says that the more hours you work a man the more work you get out of him; he voluntarily reduced his workmen's hours from 10 to 8 a day. And finally, the *Times'* pet theory, "low wages are necessary to keep laborers at their work," he violated by establishing a $5 a day minimum wage. Let us see how this worked out:

> Number of motor cars made and shipped in February, 1913, by 16,000 men working 10 hours a day 16,000
> Number of cars made and shipped in February, 1914 (after the new plan went into effect), by 15,800 men working 8 hours a day 26,000
> Number of cars made during the year 1915–1916 by 30,000 men working 8 hours a day, 550,000 — about 50,000 a month.

Before the inauguration of the plan, a social survey of the company's 16,000 employees was made, followed, five months later, by a second survey including only the beneficiaries of profit-sharing, then numbering 9,251. Of 16,000 men at the start, 5,872 had bank accounts totaling $996,418, — an average of $62.12. Of the 9,251 *profit-sharers* at the second survey, 7,540 had bank accounts totaling $1,603,768 — an average of $173.86. In January, 1915, Ford employees had $3,046,301 in banks. In January, 1916, $5,968,936. In 1914 Ford employees carried about $2,500,000 in life insurance; in 1916, just under $15,000,000. In 1914 they owned a little over $500,000 worth of homes and lots; in 1916, $3,500,000. In 1914 homes and lots on contract came to a little over $3,500,000; in 1916 they had increased to about $25,000,000.

In January, 1914, about 47 per cent. of the employees had good home conditions, and 41½ per cent. lived in good neighborhoods; 30 per cent. had fair home conditions and, 40 per cent. lived in fair neighborhoods; 23 per cent. had poor home conditions, and 19 per cent. lived in poor neighborhoods. In January, 1916, 87 per cent. had good home conditions, and 81 per cent. lived in good neighborhoods; 11 per cent. had fair home conditions and 18 per cent. lived in fair neighborhoods; less than 2 per cent. had poor home conditions, and less than 1 per cent. lived in poor neighborhoods. The Chiefs of Police of Highland Park and of Hamtramck, where most of the Ford employees live, state that since the profit-sharing plan went into effect Ford employees have been almost never arrested, and that the improvement in homes and rooming-houses is incredible.

Since the profit-sharing plan went into effect, no Union has ever tried to organize the Ford plant, and no complaint of a Union man working at the Ford plant has ever been made to the Union headquarters in Detroit.

It seems remarkable, then, that there should be such hostility to Ford Industrialism on the part of employers of labor. The reason, however, is obvious. It lies in the stark simplicity of Henry Ford's mental processes. For Mr. Ford is only secondarily interested in making money.

It must be remembered that in paying a minimum wage of $5 a day Henry Ford felt that his workmen had a right to it. But his advisers and business associates managed to persuade him that it was ruinous to pour out such a flood of wealth upon the unprepared laboring classes. So they elaborated a plan by which, above the regular wages per hour, a "share of the profits" was added to bring the minimum stipend of unskilled workmen up to $5 a day; and the Sociological Department of the Ford plant took charge of the distribution. A smug clergyman's morality was set up as a standard to which profit-sharers must attain. Profit-sharing was made a charity.

In order to share profits a man had to lead "a clean, sober and industrious life, and be of thrifty habits." Every unmarried male employee over 21 who could so qualify was eligible. Every married man over 22 who could so qualify, and "whose domestic relations were satisfactory," was eligible. Boys over 18 years of age (the age of employment at the Ford) who had relatives directly dependent upon them, were eligible. But no woman was eligible, no matter what her age, unless she was the sole support of relatives; and this was because, as the chief of the Sociological Department recently informed me, *"We find here that women are not forced into the labor market. Women usually go to work because they want to get a little more to put on their backs to swell around with, hunting for a man."* Needless to say, this view of womankind was not Mr. Ford's — he was simply ignorant.

The paid investigators of the Sociological Department went from home to home, investigating the employee's manner of living, his management of his income, the way he and his wife got along together, his habits and tastes. A system of spying was elaborated all over the city, to report lapses of morality, smoking, drinking, playing pool, and attending burlesque shows. Children were brought before the inquisition to testify against their fathers, and wives were made spies on their husbands. The profit-sharing was arbitrarily given and taken away from men upon the report of investigators as to whether these men were living up to the required conditions or not. The most abominable system of petty tyranny grew up; one case, for instance, being the forcing of an employee's wife to submit to the amorous attentions of the investigator, on pain of his profits being taken away from him.

Sanitary and other improvements were suggested — and even ordered — in the home, and whole families were plucked up from what the investigator decided were "undesirable" neighborhoods and set down in another part of town. In some cases, even, nagging mothers-in-law who caused domestic troubles and a resultant loss of efficiency on the part of the worker, were removed and ordered to live elsewhere!

The main emphasis, however, was placed on domestic relations. No married man could share profits unless he was living amicably with his wife. Conjugal difficulties were settled by the investigators by negotiation, if possible — and if not, by the threat of taking away the profits. If a man instituted divorce proceedings against his wife his profits were taken away from him; and if a divorce decree was handed down by any Court blaming that man, he was discharged.

Now it was Henry Ford and Henry Ford's influence which put a stop to this state of affairs. The spy system was abolished. Several investigators were summarily dismissed. And Mr. Ford and the officers of the company made it plain that they could be reached at any time by any employee who wished to make a complaint. The "clean, sober and industrious" clause in the profit-sharing qualification was removed. The qualifications for profit-sharing were simplified to such a degree that, while a year ago only about 15,000 out of 25,000 men were paid the $5 a day minimum, now more than 25,000 out of 30,000 men qualify, and the remainder are, without exception, new employees, who are not eligible for profit-sharing anyway until after six months' probation.

Henry Ford said to me: "Most people want others to decide for them in the organization of their work as far as making a living is concerned. But every one is here to get his own experience in his own way; and he ought not to be interfered with." This explains Ford's real feeling about the profit-sharing plan. He has resolutely set his face against "welfare work." There are no company houses, company stores, endowed schools for workingmen's children, recreation grounds, no compulsory Mutual Benefit Associations or Employees' Clubs; and no interference in the workmen's social, economic and religious beliefs. But the plan has only been in operation for two years; and in that time all of the objectionable features have not yet been remedied. Women are still barred from profit-sharing—though I can confidently predict that this will be remedied in a short time. The Sociological Department's investigators still supervise the workmen's savings and expenditures, although with constantly diminishing thoroughness. Marital relations are still considered important enough for the investigators to offer their friendly services in domestic disagreements; though no man's profits are taken away from him because of a Court divorce decision, and he cannot be discharged for anything that happens in his private life. If a profit-sharer flagrantly fails to live up to the conditions for one month, his profits are withheld and repaid to him if he makes good the second time. If he falls down for two months, 75 per cent. of the accumulated profits are paid to him, and 25 per cent. handed over to some charity picked out by the Sociological Department. For three months he gets 60 per cent. and 40 per cent. goes to charity; four months, 40 per cent., and 60 per cent. to charity; five months, 25 per cent., and 75 per cent. goes to charity, and six months all his accrued profits go to charity and he is brought up before the council of the Sociological Department to show cause why he should not be discharged.

But Henry Ford has made it almost impossible for a Ford employee to lose his job; a man's position is more sacred in the Ford Company than it is in the Civil Service. No man can be discharged without the personal order of Mr. Ford himself or of the general superintendent. Any man who has trouble with his foreman can apply for and get a transfer to some other department—as can also any man who is tired of the monotony of any particular line of work. A newspaper man whom I know—a well-paid, rising and influential journalist—broke down nervously and afterward got an unskilled job in the Ford plant. "No more damned slavery for me!" he said enthusiastically when I saw him. "I get more money, live cheaper and better, have more leisure and a bigger chance to get on right here."

To illustrate the tendency of the Ford plan, it is interesting to know what Henry Ford did to preserve his workmen from exploitation by outside interests. When the profit-sharing plan first went into operation, a cloud of real estate speculators, loan sharks and goldbrick vendors descended on the men. There was already in existence a model hospital and a highly efficient Medical Department to preserve the men, free of charge, from the attacks of hostile bacilli. Now to preserve them against purely human ills, Ford established the Legal Aid Department and the Real Estate and Investment Department—formed of the best legal and financial talent he could obtain, and also free of charge. When I spoke of these services as "free," Ford objected. "I don't like that word 'free,'" he said impatiently. "Nothing is free. We don't give anything away in this plant. These services are part of the wages we pay the men." And a little later he gave me the key to the whole vast plan of profit-sharing. "This thing is changing all the time," he said. "It started as a kind of paternalism, if you want to call it that; because I didn't know any other way to give people what they have a right to, and to see that they used it to make themselves happy. But it has developed. And it is changing automatically into a system of advice — just as the Medical Department, the Legal Aid Department and the Real Estate and Investment Department are systems of advice. The Education Department, which includes all these, and also the old Sociological Department, will some day be nothing but a great system of advice which our employees can come to when they want it, and don't have to have when they don't want it."

It must be remembered that this $5 a day wage plan was promulgated by Mr. Ford within an hour after it had first taken shape in his mind. It originated in Ford's wish to pay people what belonged to them, and was not carefully planned out with an eye to increasing the profits of Henry Ford. Of course he knew the simple fact that an adequate income, freedom from anxiety about unemployment, and leisure, would make better workmen, but how could he know, for example, that the sweepers and scrubbers who clean the factory, whose wage scale at $5 a day amounts to over $600,000 a year, would save $600,000 to the Ford Company by retrieving that much worth of vanadium steel dust and scraps from under the machines? How could he realize that highly-paid workmen would take a new interest in the business, and spontaneously invent new methods of manufacturing, and new labor-saving devices? How could he have prophesied that the first effect of the new scheme would be to create rivalry of achievement in the plant, that made it immediately a great training school from which he might draw for all branches of the business?

Let us consider this man Henry Ford. He stood alone in his ideas — opposed by the solid hostility of other manufacturers, by the shocked conservatism of his own business associates, by public opinion; and even labor was apathetic and suspicious. At a recent meeting of the Central Committee of the Detroit branch of the American Federation of Labor, the paternalistic activities of the Sociological Department were endorsed, *because workingmen were not fit to take care of themselves!* And at the present time an officer of the Federation is a Sociological Department Investigator!

The Ford plan of manufacturing, which includes profit-sharing, is in its infancy. This year more than half a million automobiles were manufactured in the home plant at Detroit, 50,000 in the Canadian factory, and 25,000 in the works at Manchester, England. On the strength of this production Ford lopped $95 from the price of the car. In two or three years the home plant will be making more than a million cars annually, and there will be immense new plants turning out Fords by the hundred thousand in Kansas City, Chicago, Duluth, Hoboken, Long Island City, etc. The nineteen immense assembling plants all over the United States will be doubled or tripled. The Ford car will some day cost $100 or less.

In Dearborn, Mich., is the nucleus of Ford's immense new plant for manufacturing the Ford farm tractor, which will be made in millions and sold by weight for about 10¢ a pound. With this Ford plans to make the farmer independent of railroad short-haul freight rates, to free him from the burden of horses and draft cattle, to supply him with cheap power. He says that the tractor is going to plow up the Siberian steppe, the wastes of Mesopotamia and Persia, the Australian bush. To run it he has invented a cheap motor fuel which can be manufactured out of a farmer's growing crops, without destroying their food value, for a few cents a gallon.

He dreams of an aeroplane that can also be manufactured in vast quantities, and very cheaply.

And how about the Ford workman? In all the Ford enterprises at present established the Ford profit-sharing plan has gone into effect; and in all Ford's future dreams profit-sharing is an integral part. The shares of profits will not remain fixed—they will rise as the profits of the Ford Company rise and as the price of Ford products declines. Think of it! Millions of men—for his vision embraces millions—for ever gaining an increasing share in an industrial empire whose extent may well be almost boundless! And the man who founded all this, who hates to be considered a philanthropist, who will not give charity, realizing more and more that material ease increases strength and intelligence, and that when a man gets the value of what he produces, he loves his work.

But let us not fool ourselves. The Ford workmen can get more and more of the profits and still be slaves—for, after all, their well-being depends upon the benevolent intelligence of one man. Ford profit-sharing is still in the form of a gift, not as a right to do with as the recipient pleases. It is so because Henry Ford is not yet sure of his own theory; though he is getting more sure of it every day. And yet, even were profit-sharing made legal wages, Ford workmen will not be self-respecting human beings until they have self-government. And Henry Ford himself knows this. I am sure that he thinks of it and is coming to that point of view—though I cannot tell here what makes me sure.

Some day Henry Ford will die. That he knows, and he knows, too, that with his death the great Ford empire, like the Empire of Alexander the Great, may be divided among squabbling captains. Above everything he wants to keep the Ford empire intact—not the money part of it, but the Ford Idea. The only way he can do this is to give the Ford employees a voice in the government of the great community they have made. And I think Henry Ford is aware of that fact.

That is why the capitalists hate Henry Ford. That is why the Steel

Trust would like to cut off his steel — and Wall Street curb his power under the cold tyranny of the little financial geniuses who own all the rest of America.

Whose War?

APRIL 1917

"The current ebullition of patriotism is wonderful."
— Rev. Dr. Parkhurst.

BY the time this goes to press the United States may be at war. The day the German note arrived, Wall Street flung the American flag to the breeze, the brokers on the floor of the Stock Exchange sang "The Star-spangled Banner" with tears rolling down their cheeks, and the stockmarket went up. In the theaters they are singing "patriotic" ballads of the George M. Cohan–Irving Berlin variety, playing the national anthem, and flashing the flag and the portrait of long-suffering Lincoln—while the tired suburbanite who has just been scalped by a ticket-speculator goes into hysterics. Exclusive ladies whose husbands own banks are rolling bandages for the wounded, just like they do in Europe; a million-dollar fund for Ice in Field-hospitals has been started; and the Boston Budget for Conveying Virgins Inland has grown enormously. The directors of the British, French and Belgian Permanent Blind Relief Fund have added "American" to the name of the organization, in gruesome anticipation. Our soldier boys, guarding the aqueducts and bridges, are shooting each other by mistake for Teutonic spies. There is talk of "conscription," "war-brides," and "On to Berlin." . . .

I know what war means. I have been with the armies of all the belligerents except one, and I have seen men die, and go mad, and lie in hospitals suffering hell; but there is a worse thing than that. War means an ugly mob-madness, crucifying the truth-tellers, choking the artists, sidetracking reforms, revolutions, and the working of social forces. Already in America those citizens who oppose the entrance of their country into the European melée are called "traitors," and those who protest against the curtailing of our meagre rights of free speech are spoken of as "dangerous lunatics." We have had a forecast of the censorship—when the naval authorities in charge of the Sayville wireless cut off American news from Germany, and only the wildest fictions reached Berlin via

164

London, creating a perilous situation.... The press is howling for war. The church is howling for war. Lawyers, politicians, stock-brokers, social leaders are all howling for war. Roosevelt is again recruiting his thrice-thwarted family regiment.

But whether it comes to actual hostilities or not, some damage has been done. The militarists have proved their point. I know of at least two valuable social movements that have suspended functioning because no one cares. For many years this country is going to be a worse place for free men to live in; less tolerant, less hospitable. Maybe it is too late, but I want to put down what I think about it all.

Whose war is this? Not mine. I know that hundreds of thousands of American workingmen employed by our great financial "patriots" are not paid a living wage. I have seen poor men sent to jail for long terms without trial, and even without any charge. Peaceful strikers, and their wives and children, have been shot to death, burned to death, by private detectives and militiamen. The rich has steadily become richer, and the cost of living higher, and the workers proportionally poorer. These toilers don't want war — not even civil war. But the speculators, the employers, the plutocracy — they want it, just as they did in Germany and in England; and with lies and sophistries they will whip up our blood until we are savage — and then we'll fight and die for them.

I am one of a vast number of ordinary people who read the daily papers, and occasionally *The New Republic,* and want to be fair. We don't know much about international politics; but we want our country to keep off the necks of little nations, to refuse to back up American beasts of prey who invest abroad and get their fingers burned, and to stay out of quarrels not our own. We've got an idea that international law is the crystallized common-sense of nations, distilled from their experiences with each other, and that it holds good for all of them, and can be understood by anybody.

We are simple folk. Prussian militarism seemed to us insufferable; we thought the invasion of Belgium a crime; German atrocities horrified us, and also the idea of German submarines exploding ships full of peaceful people without warning. But then we began to hear about England and France jailing, fining, exiling and even shooting men who refused to go out and kill; the Allied armies invaded and seized a part of neutral Greece, and a French admiral forced upon her an ultimatum as shameful as Austria's to Serbia; Russian atrocities were shown to be more dreadful than German; and hidden mines sown by England in the open sea exploded ships full of peaceful people without warning.

Other things disturbed us. For instance, why was it a violation of international law for the Germans to establish a "war-zone" around the British Isles, and perfectly legal for England to close the North Sea? Why is it we submitted to the British order forbidding the shipment of non-contraband to Germany, and insisted upon our right to ship contraband to the Allies? If our "national honor" was smirched by Germany's refusal to allow war-materials to be shipped to the Allies, what happened to our national honor when England refused to let us ship non-contraband food and even *Red Cross hospital supplies* to Germany? Why is England allowed to attempt the avowed starvation of German civilians, in violation of international law, when the Germans cannot attempt the same thing without our horrified protest? How is it that the British can arbitrarily regulate our commerce with neutral nations, while we raise a howl whenever the Germans "threaten to restrict our merchant ships going about their business?" Why does our Government insist that Americans should not be molested while traveling on Allied ships armed against submarines?

We have shipped and are shipping vast quantities of war-materials to the Allies, we have floated the Allied loans. We have been strictly neutral toward the Teutonic powers only. Hence the inevitable desperation of the last German note. Hence this war we are on the brink of.

Those of us who voted for Woodrow Wilson did so because we felt his mind and his eyes were open, because he had kept us out of the mad-dog-fight of Europe, and because the plutocracy opposed him. We had learned enough about the war to lose some of our illusions, and we wanted to be neutral. We grant that the President, considering the position he'd got himself into, couldn't do anything else but answer the German note as he did—but if we had been neutral, that note wouldn't have been sent. The President didn't ask us; he won't ask us if we want war or not. The fault is not ours. It is not our war.

A Friend at Court

THERE is a man in the United States Senate who has been a friend of democracy all his life—Robert M. La Follette. Almost alone he restored the government of the State of Wisconsin to the people. Almost alone he went down to Washington and tried to restore the government of the United States to the people. The birth and growth of the Progressive movement are due to this man's courage and intelligence more than to any one other thing. He staggered the world by bucking an economic despotism and shaking it on its foundation. Then along came the arch-compromiser, Theodore Roosevelt, and varnished himself with the shellac of Progressivism, and stole the mantle from La Follette's shoulders, and betrayed the cause. And since that time La Follette has stayed in the Senate, stubbornly believing in the virtue and intelligence of the people, doggedly fighting their battle. The world has moved past him—backward to where it was when he first began his fight. The tide of Progressivism petered out with Hughes in the backwaters of Wall Street and Oyster Bay. Wisconsin is in the hands of the Stalwarts. I was present at the Republican convention in Chicago last summer, when La Follette's delegate read that brave, hopeless liberal platform of his, to the accompaniment of sneers and laughter. He is sixty-two years old, again alone in the Senate, absolutely undismayed, his spirit youthful, his mind more powerful than ever. And for a splendid climax to his life, La Follette has smashed the Armed Ship Bill, and stood up against the will of the strongest President since Lincoln, the desperate resolve of the great financial interests, and the organized hate of all America.

The so-called Armed Ship Bill authorized the President to supply guns for arming American merchant ships fore and aft, and to equip these guns with sailors from the United States Navy. Besides, it told him to go ahead and use whatever other *"instrumentalities and methods"* he saw fit to protect these ships in the "barred zone," and handed him $100,000,000 of the people's money to do it with. That means that these ships may fire on submarines at sight. That means that merchantmen so armed, if they

167

resist "the public armed vessel of a nation with which we are at amity" (I quote the United States statute on the matter), are nothing more than pirates. The manning of the guns with American naval gunners makes them ships of war. The uncontrolled use by the President of *"instrumentalities and methods"* means that he could declare war and send the Navy out without Congress's permission, if he chooses. And the $100,000,000 — well, that means the smile on the face of the tiger.

And it was not only that this Armed Ship Bill was a war-measure which moved La Follette and the rest. Although the President admitted, when he came before Congress on February 27th, that the submarine situation had not changed since February 3d, nevertheless he waited until six days before the close of the Congressional session to ask for these powers. The Naval Appropriation Bill, carrying colossal and hasty expenditures of half a billion dollars, was held back until the last few days. The Army Appropriation Bill, the largest Army Bill which ever came before Congress, carrying a form of compulsory military service; the Sundry Civil Appropriation Bill, providing for the expenses of the entire federal government; the Espionage Bill, practically abolishing the free institutions of the republic at the President's will; and the Revenue Bill, voting enormous bond issues to pay for all this, and saddling uncounted future generations with the payment — all these came up together, and an attempt was made to jam them through, the Armed Ship Bill among them. And anyone who tried adequately to discuss these measures, anyone who questioned an appropriation bill, was threatened with being called "filibuster."

La Follette fought the Navy Bill. He fought the Revenue Bill, and the Espionage Bill. They passed, over his head, and the press was silent concerning the bitter and searching truths he told there, unafraid, on the floor of the Senate. But when he opposed the Armed Ship Bill, and not being allowed to speak, refused to let it come to a vote, a burst of public wrath poured upon his head, and he and his companions were compared unfavorably with Benedict Arnold.

The Congressional Record silently tells the story of the Armed Ship Bill in the Senate. It was introduced on February 27th, but the majority fiddled along, hearing conference reports and discussing other measures, until March 2nd at 4:30 o'clock — just 43½ hours before the close of the session. This time Senator Hitchcock, in charge of the bill, still further reduced to 35 hours by moving that the Senate recess from 12:40 a.m. March 3d to 10 a.m. The opposition, accused of filibustering, had nothing to do with all this delay. Indeed they protested against it on the floor. *And of the 35 hours consumed in debate on the Armed Ship Bill, more than twenty-four hours were taken by the Senators who favored it, and less than eleven hours by the opposition.* Senator Stone, who was willing at all times to let the bill come to a vote, spoke for a little more than four hours; Senators Works and Norris, about two hours each; Senators Cummins and Clapp, about one hour each; Senator Lane, about thirty minutes. Senator La Follette, and several others, were not permitted to speak at all, being absolutely refused recognition by the Chair. A more disgraceful piece of political trickery has never been seen in the Senate.

The most powerful supporters of the bill believed it meant war, and said so in public debate. Senator Lodge, Senator Fall and Senator Brandegee, all war-shouters, declared that the effect of arming the merchant ships would be war against Germany. The war party in the Senate was jubilant when the President came before Congress to ask for authority to do this thing, and predicted war in two weeks. And even the pacifists among them admitted that they favored the bill only "because they trusted the President to keep peace."

This trusting the President! Has there ever been a President so trusted as Woodrow Wilson? Half the liberal-minded people I know are always "trusting the President." And yet his course of action with regard to this bill was not very reassuring. He made no bones of his anxiety to get this power of making war into his own hands, and then sending Congress home. He held back the news of the Zimmermann note until March 1st, the day the bill came up in the Senate, and then let it out — to the Senate? No, to the press! And when La Follette and his friends succeeded in preventing a vote without reasonable discussion, he called them "a little group of wilful men, representing no opinion but their own," and declared that they had rendered the United States "helpless and contemptible" before the world. And with the angry reaction of the whole country beating upon the Senate, he used the opportunity to force a change in the rules which would make that body as subservient to his wishes as the House of Representatives.

There remains only the "round-robin," that statement signed by seventy-six Senators declaring that they were in favor of the bill — a bludgeon to still further coerce those "wilful men." And with a storm of denunciation lashing him such as no public man has experienced in our time, La Follette cried stubbornly, "I object!"

La Follette doesn't believe that we should plunge into the European maelstrom because Germany, in her bitter desperation, has incidentally inconvenienced us. He doesn't believe that we should go to war to protect our unneutral traffic in munitions, and to safeguard our ships full of food for England, when our own people are rioting for bread. He thinks that the United States should keep out of it so as to bring her mighty uninterested influence to bear in the consideration of peace terms, for the future of liberty and justice in the world.

Is it true then that he "represents no opinion but his own"? Is it true that the American people are unanimously in favor of going to war — or anyway, of unreservedly trusting the President? Write to him at Washington, so he may know that all the world has not gone mad.

One Solid Month of Liberty

SEPTEMBER 1917

IN America the month just past has been the blackest month for freemen our generation has known. With a sort of hideous apathy the country has acquiesced in a regime of judicial tyranny, bureaucratic suppression and industrial barbarism, which followed inevitably the first fine careless rapture of militarism.

Who that heard it will ever forget the feeling of despair he experienced when Judge Mayer charged the jury in the Berkman-Goldman trial:

"This is not a question of free speech," he said, "for *free speech is guaranteed under the Constitution.* No American worthy of the name believes in anything else than free speech, *but free speech does not mean license......* Free speech means that frank, free, clear and orderly expression in which every man and woman in the land, citizen or alien, may engage in *lawful and orderly fashion......"*

The italics are ours. The definition is the new American definition of freedom — the freedom for which countless millions have died in the long uphill pull of civilization — which is, in effect, "freedom is the right to do what nobody in power can possibly object to."

Emma Goldman and Alexander Berkman were not convicted of the charges upon which they were ostensibly tried; they were convicted by the Assistant District Attorney's constant stress of the term "Anarchist," and by the careful definition of that term, brought out by both Judge and Prosecutor, as one who wishes wantonly to overthrow society by violence.

After conviction the prisoners were brutally hustled from the court to the trains which whirled them to their prisons, without even the customary respite granted to prisoners to settle their affairs. Moreover, not only was their bank account seized, including money belonging to other persons, but part of their bail was held up *while its sources were investigated* — ostensibly to find out if any of it belonged to the defendants, but actually with the effect of intimidating those who put up the bail. And last outrage of all, the clerk of the court claimed and took out of the amount of bail some $500 as his rightful fee!

171

Next in order is the wholesale suppression of the radical press by the Post Office, some eighteen periodicals, among them THE MASSES, being denounced as "unmailable" under the Espionage Act, without any specific grounds being specified.

"Because," Solicitor Lamar is reported to have said to the representative of one paper, "if I told you what we objected to, you'd manage to get around the law some way."

Now I happen to have been one of those who lost a good many pounds fighting the original censorship provision of the Espionage Bill in Washington. And we licked it, finally, in the face of the whole Administration. But what did the Administration care? It does what it pleases, and finds a law to back it up. If the entire Espionage Act had been defeated, some obscure statute passed in 1796 would have been exhumed, and the radical press suppressed just the same.

All of which goes to prove that in America law is merely the instrument for good or evil of the most powerful interest, and there are no Constitutional safeguards worth the powder to blow them to hell.

The attack of soldiers and sailors in Boston upon the July first parade and the Socialist headquarters, which sent a thrill of rage through the heart of every lover of liberty in this country, was followed by two horrors more sinisterly suggestive.

The first was the race riot in East Saint Louis, where the large negro town was sacked and burned, and more than thirty black people, men and women, were butchered. Eye-witnesses tell how innocent negro passers-by were pursued by white men with smoking guns, who shot them down in the streets and then kicked their dead faces to jelly; how white women with streaming hair and foaming lips dragged negresses from street cars and cut them mortally in the breasts with knives.

All this of course outdoes the feeble German atrocities. It rivals the abominations of Putumayo and the Congo. The "war for civilization" begins to lose its drawing power. And the spirit of our own American soldiers in battle is beginning to appal those who know it. Read Arthur Guy Empey's "Over the Top" if you want to know how barbarians revel in sheer butchery. I met a friend who had served in the British army. "I have killed eight Huns with my own hands," he boasted, "and I want to kill ten more. Greatest sport in the world." Killing niggers is, of course, also great sport.

Anent this matter, Colonel Roosevelt and Colonel Samuel Gompers had a tiff upon the platform at Carnegie Hall, where both were patronizing the Russian revolutionary mission from the standpoint of our superior democracy. Colonel Roosevelt thought that the workingmen who killed the negroes that were brought in to take away their jobs ought to be hung. Colonel Gompers seemed to think that the negroes were to blame for allowing themselves to be brought in to take the jobs. Neither of the Colonels referred to the gentlemen who had brought the negroes north in order to smash trades-unionism forever.

The second mile-stone in the history of the New Freedom was the wholesale deportation, at the point of a gun, of some hundreds of striking workingmen from the mines in Bisbee, Arizona, into the American desert. These strikers were loudly heralded as "I. W. W.'s" in an attempt to bemuse the truth; but it is slowly leaking out that the mining company deported from Bisbee all the men who were striking in an orderly fashion for decent living wages and conditions, whether I. W. W.'s or not. And not only that, but all sympathizers with the strikers, *and even the strikers' attorney!* Many of these men lived in Bisbee, owned property there; some of them were torn from the arms of their wives and children. They were loaded on cattle-cars and sent to Columbus, N. M., whose outraged citizens promptly shipped them back north, until they halted in the middle of the desert — foodless, waterless, homeless.

At the present writing the United States Army is feeding these dangerous characters, and there is talk of interning them for the balance of the war — on the ground that they have been subsidized by German gold. And in the meanwhile, the Phelps-Dodge Corporation, which owns the mines — and Bisbee — is not allowing any one to enter the town without a passport!

Samuel Gompers protested to the German trades-unions against the deportation of Belgian workingmen. But even the Germans didn't deport Belgians into the middle of a desert, without food or water, as Bisbee did — and yet Gompers hasn't uttered a single peep about Bisbee.

Out in San Francisco, the bomb trials go merrily on. In spite of the exposure of Oxman, the utter contradiction and discrediting of the state's witnesses, Mooney is still going to die. Mrs. Mooney has only with the greatest difficulty been acquitted, and District Attorney Fickert asserts that the other prisoners will be vigorously prosecuted. Alexander Berkman has been indicted in the same case, and Bob Minor is threatened with indictment.

District Attorney Fickert no longer relies upon the evidence. Like Prosecutor Content, he cries, "This woman is an anarchist. Either you must destroy anarchy, or the anarchists will destroy the state!" And so the most patent frame-up ever conceived by a Chamber of Commerce to extirpate union labor goes on, and indictments rain upon all who have dared to defend the Mooneys.

This country-wide movement to wipe out organized labor, which was launched a year ago in Wall Street with such a flourish of trumpets, and which Mr. Gompers defied at Baltimore with quotations from Shakespeare, is developing quietly but powerfully. An investigation recently made in Omaha, Nebraska, by Carl Sandburg, shows the business men of that community organizing along the lines of San Francisco, sending out invitations to scabs everywhere, and evidently framing up something on which a union man can be railroaded to the electric chair, as they railroaded Tom Mooney on the coast.

Meanwhile, organized labor lies down and takes it—nay, in San Francisco, connives at it. Gompers is so busy running the war that he has time for nothing except to appoint upon his committees labor's bitterest enemies. I suppose that as soon as Tom Mooney and his wife are executed, Gompers will invite District Attorney Fickert to serve upon the Committee on Labor.

The suffrage pickets in front of the White House, set upon by mobs of government clerks, then by the police, arrested time and time again upon no charge, and finally committed to the work-house for sixty days, were, as the world knows, hurriedly pardoned by the President as soon as it was evident how prominent they and their husbands were. But at the same time that he pardoned them for their "crime," he intimated that he was too busy over his "War for Democracy" to give any attention to their petition—which was a petition for the fundamental rights of citizens.

It is the blackest month for freemen our generation has known.

V. The Russian Revolution

THE RUSSIAN REVOLUTION was the salvation of John Reed. If World War I had been the long dark night of his soul, the revolution in Russia was his apotheosis—both as a journalist and radical. Professionally, the revolution brought him the opportunity to write the biggest story of his career and the biggest story of his time. Personally, the triumph of the Bolsheviks renewed his faith that socialism could survive the war and create a new international order. In Russia as in Mexico, Reed's sympathetic vision enabled him to record the vast historical forces at work, forces that were reshaping the modern world.

Events in Russia had proceeded ever more rapidly and inexorably since February 1917, when the Czar had been overthrown and a provisional government established in his place. At first Reed dismissed the revolution as "middle-class." In "Russia" (May 1917), he argued that "this is a middle-class revolution, led by business men, publishers, and the progressive country nobles." However, subsequent events made it increasingly obvious that a power struggle had developed between the provisional government on one side, and the Councils of Workingmen's and Soldiers' Delegates (or "Soviets") on the other. By summer, as the balance of power began to shift to the Soviets, Reed changed his mind completely. In "The Russian Peace" (July 1917), he acknowledged that "the Councils of Workingmen's and Soldiers' Delegates, which is the real revolutionary heart of the new Russia, grows stronger hourly as the power of the awakened proletariat bursts up through the veneer of capitalism smeared thinly over the face of things." The Soviets wanted and needed peace with Germany in order to consummate the revolution, whose purpose was "the establishment of a new human society upon the earth," Reed argues.

By late summer Reed had decided to go to Russia to witness the coming revolution. But again he could not find an editor willing to hire a correspondent with his reputation as an antiwar radical. *The Masses* and the *New York Call* (a socialist daily) provided credentials, but neither could pay him or advance money for the trip. Finally Max Eastman solved the problem by soliciting $2,000 from a wealthy acquaintance, and in August Reed and Louise Bryant sailed together on the Danish ship *United States*. Before leaving, they wrote a long article for *The Masses*

177

entitled "News from France" (October 1917), based on Bryant's recent
experience in Europe. "Events grand and terrible are brewing in Europe,
such as only the imagination of a revolutionary poet could have conceived," they wrote. The "great bust-up" approaches, as discipline breaks
down in the armies of the combatants, and the masses of people all across
Europe grow weary of the fighting. And in Russia events promise to be
the grandest and most terrible of all: "Russia has shaken off the evil spell
that bound her, and arises slowly, a gentle giant, hope of the world."

Reed's last article for *The Masses,* "A Letter from John Reed,"
published in the final (Nov./Dec. 1917) issue, describes his crossing to
Halifax on board the *United States.* Here Russia has become a symbol of
hope for Reed and the other passengers, who are a "strange blend" of
nationalities and political persuasions, all returning to Russia for various
undisclosed purposes. Rumors add to the sense of intrigue on the ship:
"Almost every one is suspicious of every one else, and rumors fly about
that so-and-so is a German spy, another an American Socialist in disguise
going to the Stockholm conference, and most of the steerage really
I.W.W.'s." One passenger in particular fascinates Reed—a Russian
diplomat, a member of the aristocracy, who expresses admiration for the
revolution even though it has marked the end of his former way of life.
To a question about the revolution, the diplomat, whom Reed calls
"Tamberley" responds:

> "It was worthy of Russia," he answered, seriously. "If it had been
> done in another way I should be ashamed. I am not a socialist, I despise
> all those swarming, methodical democracies, like your country, where
> the mediocre comes to the top and beauty is always destroyed. But the
> Russian people, they have the art instinct. They have done it grandly,
> magnificently. They have made what the French call the *grand geste* —
> the grand gesture. It is all I care for in life. The ballet, the opera, the
> grand extravagances of the rich—what are these beside this epic? I am
> no proletarian—my family is one of the most ancient in Russia, but I
> am prouder now to be alive, to be Russian, than to be Tamberley . . ."

So here Reed's work for *The Masses* comes to an end, with Reed on
his way to Russia, where he would record the history of those who, as he
writes in his final sentence, "overthrew an empire—and perhaps a world."

Ten Days That Shook the World, published in 1919, was Reed's personal contribution to the Russian Revolution. Unfortunately Reed did
not live long enough to enjoy the celebrity that the book occasioned; he
died of typhus the following year in Moscow and was buried in Red
Square.

The Masses' articles collected here demonstrate that Reed was much
more than a "polemicist" or "propagandist"—that he was an extremely
talented writer who, because of his commitment to socialism, gradually

and perhaps even a bit reluctantly chose politics over literature. Above all else, John Reed was a writer who surrendered the many pleasures of Greenwich Village and middle-class America and instead chose to follow, as Waldo Frank wrote, "the lady of his sonnets, the Revolution" to his final encounter with history.

Russia

MAY 1917

I HATE to set up as a prophet, but it seems to me I diagnosed the situation leading to the present revolution in Russia pretty well in my book, "The War in Eastern Europe," published a year ago.

I quote from Part III:

> For the last ten years Russia has become more and more a German commercial colony. Every embarrassment of Russia was taken advantage of by Germany to increase her trade advantages in the empire; as, for example, in 1905, German interests exacted enormous concessions by overt threats of aiding the revolutionists. The Germans also crept into government offices, even into the army administration. They dictated the plans of the Russian strategic railways on the German frontier. And in the Imperial Court, in the entourage of the Tsarina — herself a German — they exercised a sinister and powerful influence.
>
> Russian merchants, manufacturers, and bankers have long bitterly opposed the German power in their country, and this has made them enemies of the corrupt and tyrannical Russian Government — which is bound up with the Germans — and allies of the revolutionists. So in this war we have the curious spectacle of the Russian proletariat and the middle class both intensely patriotic, and both opposing the government of their country. And to understand Russia now one must realize the paradox that to make war on Germany is to make war on the Russian Bureaucracy.

This is not the first manifestation of that internal struggle which has been going on in Russia since the very commencement of the war. In the summer and fall of 1915, the treachery of Soukomlinov, Minister of War, of General Masdeiev; the dismissal of the Grand Duke Nicholas from command of the western armies; the wholesale corruption of the Intendancy; the traitorous activities of the Tsarina's German entourage; and the cynical ascendancy of the reactionary party, with wholesale deportations to Siberia, massacres of Jews, and repression of the Duma — all this had forced the Liberal elements of the Russian people into a defensive alliance. Moreover, it was the scarcely-veiled purpose of the autocracy to make a separate peace with Germany, a move which was bitterly opposed by both the [proletariat and] the Russian middle class.

In the face of the wholesale corruption of the purchasing department of the government, the Association of Zemstvos, or county councils, undertook to buy army supplies for the government—a job which it accomplished with real ability. This is an important fact, as the Association represented to a large extent the Russian middle class.

All this time the Duma, limited as it was, had been getting more and more frankly critical. For example, one speaker said that Russia had a government which was extraordinarily inefficient, extraordinarily corrupt, and extraordinarily traitorous. In addition, it began to name specific grafters and traitors and hinted where the trail led, and it recommended that committees of the Duma be put in charge of the buying of supplies, in conjunction with the Zemstov, and also the manufacture of munitions. Besides all this, there was rapidly growing popular unrest manifested all over the empire. And it was the discontent of patriots that determined Russia should win the war.

In September a premature revolution broke out in the form of a strike at the Peteelov Armament Works at Petrograd which was ruthlessly suppressed. Thirty leaders were sent to Siberia, and many pickets shot in the streets. The Tsar suddenly dissolved the Duma. Widespread strikes of transport-workers, railroad and public service employees followed in Moscow, Kiev, Odessa, and other cities. The Association of Zemstvos and the Association of Cities sent a joint committee, headed by Prince Lvov (who is said to be the head of the new government), to the Tsar direct, threatening that unless he liberalized the Government they would favor revolution. The Tsar refused to receive this delegation.

Then the Allied censorship settled down on the situation, and I wrote:

Is there a powerful and destructive fire working in the bowels of Russia, or is it quenched? Rigid censorship and the suppression of news within the empire make it very difficult to know; but even after the prorogation of the Duma there were wholesale dismissals of Intendancy officials, and a complete military reorganization of the western armies, and even as I write this same powerful, quiet menace, as yet vaguely defined, has forced the Tsar to reopen the Duma with Imperial pomp. And Boris Sturmer, the new premier, though a Reactionary of the worst type, has assured the Duma that 'Even in war time the work of internal organization must go on.'

Since then Russia has swung back again to reaction, and through the shifting clouds of the censorship we have caught glimpses of the autocracy more and more tightening its hold. The result was inevitable.

I repeat that this is a middle-class revolution, led by business men, publishers, and the progressive country nobles. The army is with them, because they are in favor of continuing the war against Germany; the Duma, because they stand for untrammeled representative government; the workingmen, peasants and Jews, because they have proclaimed the most democratic program since the French Revolution. Some people may be skeptical of bourgeois promises; but it is a fact that the new Russian middle class has ideas which antedate the ideas of bourgeois Western Europe and America by a hundred years. If the Russian revolutionary program fails, indeed, it will be because the French and English middle classes are afraid to allow it, on the ground that it might interfere with the value of their Russian investments.

It is interesting to note that the powers that be in England and France have abandoned their policy of whitewashing Russia, of explaining how "liberal" the Tsar's government was and of suppressing all news that reflected upon it. In the last few months these gentlemen have been strangely silent; and now we suddenly wake to find the taboo gone. That in itself is to me proof enough of the tremendous power of Russia's house-cleaning.

The Russian Peace

JULY 1917

AT this writing the bourgeois press is alarmed at the prospect of a Russian separate peace with Germany. The Council of Workingmen's and Soldiers' Delegates, which is the real revolutionary heart of the new Russia, grows stronger hourly as the power of the awakened proletariat bursts up through the veneer of capitalism smeared thinly over the face of things. And the Council of Workingmen's and Soldiers' Delegates wants peace.

Premier Miliukov sent a message to the Allies assuring them that Russia would fight until the Allied end. The Russian people responded with a demand for Miliukov's resignation, and the Council of Workingmen's and Soldiers' Delegates rebuked the Provisional Government by establishing its own Department of Foreign Affairs. Guchkov has resigned, then Miliukov. It looks as if the Russian Peace were coming.

We make our apologies to the Russian proletariat for speaking of this as a "bourgeois revolution." It was only the "front" we saw, the wished-for consummation of Kapitaltum. The real thing was the long-thwarted rise of the Russian masses, as now we see with increasing plainness; and the purpose of it is the establishment of a new human society upon the earth. For this, it is necessary that Russia have peace from without; indeed, every other consideration, whether of honor or profit, sinks into insignificance beside it.

The cumbersome medieval tyranny that ruled Russia has vanished like smoke before the wind. The bright framework of the complicated modern capitalistic tyranny that rules us all is crumbling from the face of Russia. And from the leaden sea of dumb and driven conscripts, the rivers of workers bent with hideous fatigue, the nations of mujiks mud-colored and voiceless, something is taking shape—something grand, and simple, and human. Do you remember in Dostoievsky's "Idiot," where the boy prophesies about the Russia of the future—Russia with her gyves stricken off, Russia ruling the world with love?

What will follow the Russian peace? We profess to fear it, seeing nothing but the German victory, and with it the strengthening of German autocracy. To make Germany democratic, it is said, the German nation must be crushed. Kick her into self-government.

That seems fallacious to us. Whoever heard of a great civilized people bullied by outsiders into changing its form of government? Even Greece, with Venizelos set up as liberator by the Allied troops, is loyal to her weak king in the face of insults.

But what the Hohenzollerns need never fear from an Allied victory, deeply should they dread from the Russian Peace. To be a hard-driven military despotism in the shadow of a great free commonwealth—that is impossible. With Russia free, Russia at peace, autocracy disappears from Europe.

News from France

OCTOBER 1917

Louise Bryant and John Reed

THE uninteresting war begins to be interesting to liberals. Out of the dull twilight that has hung over the world these three years like a winter mist in Flanders, tremendous flames begin to leap, like bursting shells. Events grand and terrible are brewing in Europe, such as only the imagination of a revolutionary poet could have conceived. The great bust-up is coming.

Russia has shaken off the evil spell that bound her, and arises slowly, a gentle giant, hope of the world. Not a day passes without revolt in Germany, though every day revolts are put down there with cannon. British labor and British soldiers are chafing under the platitudes of Lloyd George. In Italy people talk openly of refusing to suffer another winter without coal, for the doubtful rewards of imperialism. And France is at the end of her men, resources and patience.

Stephen Lausanne and André Tardieu keep reiterating monotonously that France is in "better condition now than at the beginning of the war"; but the French people themselves greet such phrases with bitter anger. Intelligent Frenchmen know that there are no more men in France from which to build new armies; that food is shockingly lacking, and fuel too; that formidable strikes are occurring all over the country, wherein soldiers on leave join with the strikers against the police; that the women swarm to the railway stations and try to prevent their men from returning to the front.

As always, the French are the first of the peoples to face the truth — and the truth is, that the world is defeated. There is and can be no victor in this war. There can be no decisive military success. The French realize this, and they also realize that no ambiguous "democracy," as mouthed so glibly by the exploiters of mankind, is worth the extermination of the

Louise Bryant has just returned from a trip to France where she has been gathering material for the Bell Syndicate.

185

race. Alone among all the belligerent peoples the French can be depended upon to meet the truth magnificently, as they did in 1789, in 1815, 1830, and 1871.

Splendid in defeat, the French, whose clear skeptical intelligence always ultimately conquers sentimentalities and shams, are beginning to probe the depths of this world madness. Go to France to-day—or even read the much-censored French papers. You will find there sublime ridicule of jingoism, military glory, patriotic twaddle; immense satire upon the tremendous stupidity of war; a low, bitter growl against diplomats, financiers, statesmen, and all the respectable powers which plunge peoples into war on false pretenses; and a growing fury about the profiteers whose patriotism never has prevented them from preying upon the masses of the people, whether as workers or soldiers. How is it that these insatiable beasts have been allowed to cook up this horrible thing? Of course when a people like the French—and there is no people like them— begin to think about such things, then there is trouble coming. When the French are defeated they look searchingly into themselves, and then they proceed to remove the cankers.

Suppose there is public announcement that France bleeds for Alsace-Lorraine—well, the ordinary Frenchman on the street candidly admits that Alsace-Lorraine isn't sure that it wants to return to France, and that the people ought to have the say. Suppose the French figureheads gush about the Belgians; the French people don't like the Belgians, as everyone knows who has been in France since the beginning of the war. The brutal fact is that all the French care about is the expulsion of the Germans from French territory. France officially may deny it, but the truth remains that the French army and the French workers, male and female, are ready to accept the Russian peace terms, and even less. If the Germans were simply to offer to withdraw from France, the government which dared to reject that offer would go down in a whirl of bloody dust.

The proof of all this lies in a book, "Le Feu," by Henri Barbusse, which to my mind is the biggest thing next to the Russian revolution that the war has so far produced. In France it has run into an edition of more than three hundred thousand copies; literally every Frenchman has read it or talks about it.

It is the story of a squad of poilus, simple soldiers, who have been through it; it is a fearful biography of the war. The book opens, with the effect of an immense curtain rising upon a stage as big as the world, to music grander than any known:

> The great pale sky is peopled with claps of thunder; each explosion exhibits, falling from harsh lightning, at once a column of fire in the remainder of night and a column of smoke in what there is of day.

Up there, very high, very distant, a flight of terrible birds, of powerful and staccato breath, heard and not seen, who circle up to observe the
earth . . ."

Then the earth! The vast sterile plain, glistening with wet mud
heaped in little masses, with shell-holes full of water, and the trenches,
soaking, filthy, where from little holes and caves creep forth the soldiers
at daybreak, covered with lice, stinking, broken with fatigue.

The book shows these poilus in the trenches, relieved, sent back for a
period of rest, under bombardment, on leave, in an assault, at their
frightful work of digging trenches out on the plain between the lines at
night, and the final dawn. It tells how they act, what they say and how,
without any circumlocutions whatever. There are descriptions of the
dead, what bursting shells do to the human body, how men and women
you know and love look when they are rotting; and there are tales of how
men die.

When the soldiers are sent back of the lines to some little village for a
few days' rest, quartered in some leaky old barn full of vermin, without
fuel, often hungry, the civilian population preys upon them, overcharging
them hideously. They see the rich men and their friends in gay uniforms,
who have managed by hook or crook to escape the actual fighting. The
townspeople patronize them, look down upon them because they are
filthy, and stink. Yet these humble men of the people endure all, complain
not.

In the trenches one time they make way for the African troops to
pass, and someone comments upon their fighting fury.

"These boys are real soldiers," says one.

A big peasant speaks up. "*We're* not soldiers," he says, proudly,
"we're *men!*"

Yes, they are men — clerks, farmers, students, storekeepers — and
they do not like to kill. "Ignorant," Barbusse describes them, "narrow-
minded, full of common sense . . . ; inclined to be led and to do what they
are told to do, hardly resistant, capable of immense suffering." Just
ordinary men.

"And so each one sets himself, according to his intelligence, his
activity, resources and audacity, to combat the frightful discomfort. Each
one seems, in showing himself, to be confessing: 'This is all I have known
how, could, dared to do, in the great misery into which I have fallen.'"

But like a thin scarlet thread through the story runs the theme of
coming change. The preface ends like this:

"The future is in the hands of the slaves, and one sees well that the
old world will be changed by the alliance which will be built between them
by those whose number and whose misery are infinite."

It is never absent, that note. And there is little socialist doctrine preached, for these men are not socialists. They are, as the peasant said, men. They speak of the "peoples of the world (not the masters), joining hands." They talk of Liebknecht as the bravest man in the whole world. They tell how they have been thinking it out, and it is not really the Prussians who are to blame, but the system which keeps wars going, and makes sudden enemies out of friendly peoples. One man complains that the German poison gas is not sportsmanlike, and the rest of the squad turn on him fiercely and call him a fool. Does he think it any more sportsmanlike to blow a man to the worst death possible with a steel shell? Of course there are fools, — men who say, "the Kaiser is a vile criminal, but Napoleon, — ah, *there* was a great man!"—But it is astonishing what mordant intelligence is working everywhere, everywhere.

There is not one page without at least one little picture of war, of death, disease, torture, misery, the beauty and the ghastliness but always the pitifulness of the human spirit. There is painted, against the background of the vanished peaceful life of simple people the immensity of war, too vast for the human spirit to stand. One can never, for example, forget the field where the deserter was shot, with his comrades standing in the dark about his dishonorable grave and pitying him, calling him brave, writing loving messages on the wooden cross they have put up over him. And at the last, that awful dawn, where the poor human wrecks gather in the midst of that sea of sterile mud, on the vast plain, and cry aloud that there must be no more war.

Every line of this book is a horrible exposure of the colossal idiocy of war — nor are the Germans blamed altogether for it. War is what must be defeated, not the Germans. And that thought leads inevitably to other thoughts, to an examination of how war is caused. We are all familiar with the logical outcome of that chain of reasoning. We have watched the process of war-making in this country, and like Henri Barbusse, we know who is the common enemy — ours and the French and the Germans and the British.

Why did the French government allow "Le Feu" to be published? Because all France has begun to think as Barbusse thinks. Because the French people are facing the truth. Because even the truth about this war, that there are really no great ideas in it which any simple man cares to fight for, is running like wildfire over the world.

" 'All men ought finally to be equal' " said one.

" 'The word seemed to come to us like a rescue.'

" 'Equal ... Yes, yes ... There are the great ideas of justice, truth. There are things one believes in, toward which one turns always to fix upon like a kind of light. Above all there is equality.'

" 'There is also liberty and fraternity....'

"'But above all equality. . . .'

"I told them that fraternity is a dream, a cloudy sentiment, inconsistent; that it is contrary to a man's nature to hate an unknown, but equally contrary to love him. One can base nothing on fraternity. Nor upon liberty, either; it is too relative in a society where all the groups prey upon each other.

"But equality is always the same. Liberty and fraternity are only words, while equality is a thing. Equality (social, for individuals have each different values, but each ought to participate in society in the same measure — and that is justice, because the life of one human being is as big as the life of any other), equality is the great formula of mankind. . . ."

A Letter from John Reed

NOVEMBER/DECEMBER 1917

For five days the steamer has been lying quietly here in Halifax harbor while the British authorities go over her inch by inch — and over the passengers as well — looking for contraband, spies, or any person or thing which for any reason should not be allowed to go to Scandinavia now. To-day the examination was finished, and now we are only waiting permission from London to go to sea.

My shipmates are a strange blend of various sorts of Scandinavians, Russians, a knot of young college boys from the States going to Russia as clerks in the Petrograd branch of an American bank, a Hughes Republican who was born in Venezuela of Dutch parents and is the most patriotic man on board, and a few morose-looking foreigners who walk alone and talk to no one. Almost every one is suspicious of every one else, and rumors fly about that so-and-so is a German spy, another an American Socialist in disguise going to the Stockholm conference, and most of the steerage really I. W. W.'s.

To-day a trainload of Russians — most of them Jews — arrived from New York and came on board with wives, children, innumerable trunks and bundles, containing largely food and books. These the British sailors examined with painful care, even going through their pockets, for Russians, especially those from the United States, are considered dangerous since Charles Edward Russell brought back news of their baneful activities in undermining the Root mission in Russia. Indeed, I have been told both by the Americans on board and by some of the British searchers here that if it hadn't been for the returning Russian-Americans the revolution would never have gone to the length it has.

In New York one must get the visa of the British consulate before the Russian consulate can visa his passport. If the British have any reason to suspect any one, a Russian passport is of no avail — nor an American one either: the suspected person may be taken off at Halifax. The same is true of cargo; although the American government may have granted permits and letters of assurance to export certain articles, the British authorities allow only such freight to pass as they please. At the beginning of the war I remember the indignant protests of captains, owners and passengers at being held up and searched by the British; but now the neutral world has grown used to British domination of the sea, and it is considered perfectly natural that we should sail first to Halifax, and stay there as long as London wishes, without any explanation.

Is there any corner of the world where the Russian revolution has not been felt? Certainly not on the ships of this line, by which the first exiles returned to their beloved home, by which the first refugees, the first eye-witnesses of the tremendous event crossed to America. There is on board an American youth who was in Petrograd the whole wonderful "eight days," but all he saw of it all was the spectacle of three mounted Cossacks firing on the police with revolvers in front of the Gare du Nord, several crowds of singing workmen marching up the Nevski, the police station on fire, and the ruins of the Finland station. His main preoccupation was getting something to eat and trying to leave the city.

There is also a spry old gentleman, originally from Riga, who has lived in New York some thirty years and is now returning to see what the new Russia looks like. And a Russian diplomat, formerly attached to the Tsar's government, but now working for the new regime — whatever that may be by the time he gets home.

All these persons have widely divergent views of what the revolution means, how it occurred, and why, what future developments will be, and who is now in control. All the information they have had has come through the new Russian mission and embassy now in Washington, which everyone agrees does not in the slightest represent revolutionary Russia; through the American press, which is a good deal of a joke to Russians; and through the Root mission, which is spoken of politely but without enthusiasm.

We sit in the smoking-room evenings listening to the diplomat — whom I shall call Tamberley — talk of his fascinating country. He has a smooth-shaven, youngish face, with a tilted nose, which gives him a singular look of mild wonder. It is only when he gets excited — and he does that, like all Russians, when he warms to his subject — that his eyes narrow to cruel slits, and his cheekbones come out strongly, and he looks like Ghenghis Kahn in white flannels.

"Ah, it was a marvelous life, the Russian life," he said smoothly, smiling like a snake. "At five one began to dine; the zakouska, the vodka setting fire to the head, beautiful woman, wonderful food, talk ... Then at ten the ballet, or the opera — often one could not get seats to the ballet from one year's end to the other, and I have paid one hundred and fifty roubles for a stall at the Marinski — and after, at one, two, three in the morning, in a troika over the white snow, singing, out to see the gypsies ... And back again home in the morning ... "

"Yes," the old Russian shook his head. "But think of the other side. You spending in one night thousands of roubles, and in the miserable cellars of Petrograd the frightful poor moaning while the water from the Neva soaked through the walls ... "

I looked at the aristocrat. His eyes were filled with tears. He said nothing.

"What do you really think of this revolution, anyway?" I asked him curiously.

"It was worthy of Russia," he answered, seriously. "If it had been done in another way I should be ashamed. I am not Socialist, I despise all those swarming, methodical democracies, like your country, where the mediocre comes to the top and beauty is always destroyed. But the Russian people, they have the art instinct. They have done it grandly, magnificently. They have made what the French call the *grand geste* — the grand gesture. It is all I care for in life. The ballet, the opera, the grand extravagances of the rich — what are these beside this epic? I am no proletarian — my family is one of the most ancient in Russia, but I am prouder now to be alive, to be Russian, than to be Tamberley ... "

As I write this the Russian Jews down on the third-class deck, those Russian Jews who looked, as they came over the side, like an excursion from Henry Street, are gathered in an excited little close-packed group, there on the deck, below a man who is kneeling on the hatchway above them and holding out his arms. He waves his hands, and men and women begin to sing Russian songs — the old songs of harvest, of the boatmen on the Volga, the great, surging, hymnlike songs with upsweeping, strong chords that lift the heart. At once they cease to be Jews, to be persecuted, petty and ugly — that grand music transforms them, makes them grow and broaden, until they seem great, gentle, bearded moujiks, standing side by side with those who overthrew an empire — and perhaps a world.

Notes

1. This collection includes twenty-seven of Reed's signed articles and one play, "Moondown." I have omitted three of Reed's articles because their quality is noticeably poorer than that of the others. Also not included here are two poems, two book reviews, two unsigned articles, and fourteen notes (all very short) that Reed wrote for *The Masses*.

2. As quoted in Ronald Steel, *Walter Lippmann and the American Century* (Boston: Little, Brown, 1980), p. 81.

3. As quoted in Steel, p. 82.

4. As quoted in Robert A. Rosenstone, *Romantic Revolutionary, A Biography of John Reed* (New York: Random House, 1975), p. 166.

5. Max Eastman, *Enjoyment of Living* (New York: Harper and Brothers, 1948), p. 406.

6. Eastman, p. 406.

7. Eastman, p. 394.

8. The August 1917 issue of *The Masses* was declared "unmailable" by the postmaster of the city of New York under the terms of the Espionage Act. *The Masses* won the ensuing court decision, but by that time the September issue was ready to be mailed and, acting on a Catch-22 logic, the United States government revoked the magazine's mailing privileges because, since it was now considered irregular in publication, it was no longer regarded as a newspaper or periodical within the meaning of the law. The editors managed to publish an October and a November–December issue, which were sold privately and on newsstands. However, without mailing rights, *The Masses* was no longer viable. Eastman allowed the magazine to die a quiet death and, within three months, began a new magazine called the *Liberator*.

9. Daniel Aaron, *Writers on the Left* (Oxford: Oxford University Press, 1961), p. 39.

10. Rosenstone, p. 118.

11. Rosenstone, p. 146.

12. Actually Reed anticipated the fall of Torreón, for the last Federalist troops were not driven out of the city until April 2.

13. Renato Leduc, Preface to *Insurgent Mexico* by John Reed (New York: International Publishers, 1982), p. 25.

14. Rosenstone, p. 167.

15. Rosenstone, p. 181.

16. Rosenstone, p. 199.

17. As quoted in Rosenstone, p. 220.

18. Rosenstone, p. 265.

19. Rosenstone, p. 277.

JULY, 1916

10 CENTS

The MASSES

PREPAREDNESS NUMBER

"AT THE THROAT OF THE REPUBLIC"
John Reed Exposes the Whole Preparedness Plot

Jim Larkin on the Irish Rebellion
Lincoln Steffens on Mexico
Max Eastman at the White House
Dante Barton Describes the Pittsburg Strike

Pictures By

BOARDMAN ROBINSON   *MAURIC̶E̶ ̶B̶E̶R̶*

ROBERT MINOR   *K. R̶. ̶C̶H̶A̶M̶B̶E̶R̶LAIN*

GEORGE BELLOWS   *ART Y̶O̶U̶N̶G̶*

CORNELIA BARNS   *KARL PEARSON*

JO DAVIDSON

After Biost.

Index